SKOKIE PUBLIC LIBRARY

W9-APS-195

DEC 2011

DOCTOR
GOEBBELS

"Our broadcasts in English are, after all, very effective. However, an aggressive, superior, and insulting tone gets us nowhere. I have often said so to our various departments. You can only get anywhere with the English by talking to them in a friendly and modest way. The English speaker, Lord Haw-Haw, is especially good at biting criticism, but in my mind the time for spicy debate is past . . . during the third year of a war one must wage it quite differently from the first year . . . today they want nothing but facts. The more cleverly, therefore, the facts are put together, and the more psychologically and sensitively they are brought before the listening public, the stronger is the effect."

Dr Joseph Goebbels

"The 'little doctor' was probably the most intelligent, from a purely brain point of view, of all the Nazi leaders. He never speechified; he always saw and stuck to the point; he was an able debater, and, in private conversation astonishingly fair-minded and reasonable."

Sir Neville Henderson
British Ambassador to Germany, 1937–1939

Dr Joseph Goebbels, 1933

DOCTOR GOEBBELS

HIS LIFE AND DEATH

ROGER MANVELL AND HEINRICH FRAENKEL

Frontline Books, London

Skyhorse Publishing, New York

SKOKIE PUBLIC LIBRARY

North America edition copyright © 2010 by Skyhorse Publishing, Inc.
United Kingdom edition © Pen & Sword Books Ltd, 2010

All Rights Reserved. No part of this book may be reproduced in any manner without the express written consent of the publisher, except in the case of brief excerpts in critical reviews or articles. All inquiries should be addressed to Skyhorse Publishing, 555 Eighth Avenue, Suite 903, New York, NY 10018.

Skyhorse Publishing books may be purchased in bulk at special discounts for sales promotion, corporate gifts, fund-raising, or educational purposes. Special editions can also be created to specifications. For details, contact the Special Sales Department, Skyhorse Publishing, 555 Eighth Avenue, Suite 903, New York, NY 10018 or info@skyhorsepublishing.com.

www.skyhorsepublishing.com

This edition published in 2010 by Frontline Books, an imprint of Pen & Sword Books Limited, 47 Church Street, Barnsley, S. Yorkshire, S70 2AS. For more information on Frontline books, please visit www.frontline-books.com, email info@frontline-books.com, or write to us at the above address.

Skyhorse edition: ISBN 978-1-61608-029-7
Frontline edition: ISBN 978-1-84832-588-3

10 9 8 7 6 5 4 3 2 1

Library of Congress Cataloging-in-Publication Data

Manvell, Roger, 1909-1987.
  Doctor Goebbels : his life and death / Roger Manvell and Heinrich
Fraenkel.
    p. cm.
  Originally published: London, Heinemann, 1960.
  Includes bibliographical references and index.
  ISBN 978-1-61608-029-7 (pbk. : alk. paper)
  1. Goebbels, Joseph, 1897-1945. 2. Nazis--Biography. 3. Propaganda,
German--History--20th century. 4. Germany--Politics and
government--1918-1933. 5. Germany--Politics and government--1933-1945.
6. Germany. Reichsministerium für Volksaufklärung und Propaganda. I.
Fraenkel, Heinrich, 1897-1986. II. Title. III. Title: Dr. Goebbels.
  DD247.G6M33 2010
  943.085092--dc22
  [B]
                          2010001788

A CIP data record for this title is available from the British Library.

Printed in Canada

Contents

Acknowledgments

OUR THANKS are due to the Wiener Library in London and to the Institut für Zeitgeschichte in Munich for their unfailing and courteous assistance. We would also like to acknowledge the help we have received from the Verlag Ullstein Bilderdienst in Berlin, the Hulton Picture Library and the National Film Archive in London during the period we were compiling the illustrations that appear in this volume.

We also wish to acknowledge permission to quote from the following published works: *In the Shelter with Hitler*, by Gerhard Boldt, by permission of Messrs. Gerald Duckworth and Co. Ltd.; *Failure of a Mission*, by Sir Nevile Henderson, by permission of Mr. Raymond Savage, Literary Executor for the late Sir Nevile Henderson; *The Goebbels' Diaries*, translated by Louis P. Lochner, by permission of Hamish Hamilton Ltd; *My Part in Germany's Fight*, by Joseph Goebbels (1935), by permission of Hurst and Blackett; *The Hitler I Knew*, by Otto Dietrich, published by Methuen; *Hitler's Table Talk*, published by Weidenfeld and Nicolson; *Radio goes to War*, by Charles J. Rollo, published by Faber and Faber. Acknowledgment should also be made to Dr. Rudolf Semmler for permission to quote from his book, *Goebbels the Man next to Hitler*, to Professor H. R. Trevor-Roper and Messrs. Macmillan and Co. for their courtesy in permitting us to reproduce the sketch-plan of the Bunker from *The Last Days of Hitler*, and to M. Francois Genoud for permission to quote from Goebbels' private letters, from his 1925–26 Diary, from his *Michael* and *Kampf um Berlin*, from his Last Testament and from miscellaneous broadcasts, speeches and articles by Goebbels.

ROGER MANVELL
HEINRICH FRAENKEL

Illustrations

The Search for the Facts

JOSEPH GOEBBELS has many claims to be considered the most interesting member of the Nazi leadership apart from Hitler himself. But his place in the earlier history of the Nazi movement is frequently obscured by legends that he was himself responsible either for inventing or fostering, mainly for the purpose of making it appear that he joined the movement much earlier than in fact he did.

Neither Heinrich Fraenkel nor I fully realised the extraordinary character we should discover when we began the research that lies behind this story of Goebbels' personal character and his unique career as a professional agitator and propagandist. The self-portrait that Goebbels was in a most favourable position to create once he came to power has very largely come to be accepted by those who have written about him either in the form of individual studies or in studies of the Nazi movement as a whole.

Long before we planned to write this book together Heinrich Fraenkel had already collected sufficient facts, stories and unpublished testimonies to make him realise that Goebbels' life and character would repay much more detailed investigation. He himself escaped from Germany just in time to avoid being arrested on the night of the Reichstag fire, and he subsequently took part in the foundation of the Free German movement in Britain. He also assisted at the independent legal investigations into the causes of the fire which were conducted in Britain by Sir Stafford Cripps and other world-famous lawyers, and he has written a number of books and pamphlets on Germany under the Nazis.

After the war was over Heinrich Fraenkel visited the Nuremberg Trials, and was able to obtain first-hand information from many of those who had been directly associated with Hitler and Goebbels, including von Papen, Otto Strasser, Hans Fritzsche, Max Winckler, Hjalmar Schacht, Walther Funk and Karl Kaufmann. He was also familiar professionally with the German film world, and he has made a special study of the effect the Nazi régime had on the film industry and on those who remained in Germany and worked in film production under Goebbels' supervision.

Nevertheless a great deal remained to be explained about the character and career of Goebbels. It is true that he had been the subject of much popular journalism, of diaries and biographies written mainly under Nazi influence, and of incidental comment in innumerable books devoted to the history of the Third Reich and the enigmatic character of the Führer. In all this writing, good or bad, Goebbels seemed to be accepted mainly at face value, as a man interesting largely because of his proximity to Hitler. Only one biographer, Curt Riess, began in a book published ten years ago the fascinating task of uncovering what is the most important phase of Goebbels' life if one is to understand his nature and his actions once he rose to power. This phase is the difficult period of his youth up to the age of twenty-seven before he discovered the Nazis and they discovered him.

Here we were very fortunate. Heinrich Fraenkel went to Germany and with the help of Goebbels' sister, Maria Kimmich, obtained the necessary introductions which eventually enabled him to meet a number of people who had known Goebbels both as a boy and as a young man in Rheydt, his native town. There, among many others, he found one of Goebbels' school-teachers, Prelate Mollen, his closest school-friend, Fritz Prang (who subsequently introduced him to the Nazi Party) and Alma, who as a young school-teacher had known Goebbels well and had introduced him to Else, the girl to whom he was engaged for a number of years during the crucial period of his youth, 1922-26. Through Alma, Heinrich Fraenkel was introduced to Else herself, now a happily married woman living in Berlin. From all of these intimate friends and observers of Goebbels he obtained detailed information of him as a schoolboy, a student, a would-be writer and, finally, as an apprentice in political agitation. They have generously given us permission to quote from many of Goebbels' letters which throw a unique light on his mind and character at this time. In addition, the Albertus Magnus Society, the Catholic charitable organisation in Cologne which assisted him with his university education, opened its archives to us. These contained many important letters and reports written by Goebbels while he was a university student. All this information has been supplemented by Goebbels' sister, Maria.

We have also had the advantage of being able to study in detail the unpublished, hand-written diary kept by Goebbels during the years 1925 and 1926—the period of his service as a Nazi agent in the Rhineland-Westphalia district and of his decision finally to work for Hitler's faction in the movement rather than for the Strassers, who were his first employers. This diary has never before been analysed in any detail, and we owe a great debt to the Hoover Institution on War, Revolution and Peace at Stanford University, California, from which we obtained the loan of a microfilm of the diary.

Once Goebbels came to power alongside Hitler, his personal story is closely bound up with the history of the Third Reich to which he devoted every hour of his working life. It is not, of course, our intention to re-tell the long and complex story of Hitler's rise to power and of Germany under his rule. That has been most ably done by others, notably by Dr. Alan Bullock in his detailed and scholarly life of Hitler. Our book is the portrait of one man only, Joseph Goebbels, who took a leading part in this most significant phase of our contemporary history, and of the propaganda methods he devised to assist Hitler achieve and maintain his power. Such account as we give of the history of the Nazi movement is sufficient only to make clear the reasons for Goebbels' opinions and actions.

In our study of Goebbels as Reichsminister we have also been fortunate in having the help of Karl Kaufmann, who became Nazi Gauleiter of Hamburg, and Werner Naumann, who became Goebbels' Under-Secretary of State at the Propaganda Ministry, and was with him in the Führerbunker at the time of his death. The personal accounts given us by these men and many others who worked with Goebbels in either senior or junior capacities have supplemented such important published evidence as can be found in the little-known diaries of his

aides, Wilfred von Oven and Rudolf Semmler. The latter has also
been of great assistance by adding his personal comments to what has
been published. We are also deeply grateful to Frau Lida Baarova for
her assistance in making it possible for the authentic story of her
association with Goebbels to be published for the first time. The
important research work done by Karl Lochner in editing certain
other surviving fragments of Goebbels' later diaries puts every
student of the man and the period in his debt. Goebbels never
ceased throughout his whole career to comment almost daily on
his experiences and to commit to paper at formidable length his views
on contemporary events and persons, including the other Nazi leaders,
most of whom he detested. There is evidence that the microfilmed
record of these diaries which he ordered to be photographed during
the last months of the war is now in Russian hands, but, apart from
the fragments of typescript and manuscript held at Stanford, they
remain unpublished. It is to be hoped these millions of words will one
day be made available for study. Our efforts to obtain information
concerning the survival of these documents in the Soviet Union have
not yet been successful.

The full story of Goebbels as a man and a propagandist of genius is
of the greatest psychological interest; both his public and his private
life were beset with difficulties mainly of his own making through his
pathological vanity. Goebbels has often been thought an unlikely
person to be found among the strong-armed Nazi leadership, yet he
was second only to Hitler in understanding the exploitation of power.
Without him the movement might never have gained its ascendancy
in Germany during the crucial years of 1932 and 1933. It could be
argued that only Hitler and Goebbels prove to have had both the
intuitive and the practical knowledge of how to establish this ascendancy in Germany. Goebbels had a fanatical capacity for hard
work, for constant public speaking and agitation through the press
and radio, and for attending to the details of organisation and administration. When the crisis came in 1944-45, he alone among the original
group of Nazi leaders stood loyally by Hitler and the myth of racial
power they had created. They died together in order to preserve this
myth in the minds of the disintegrating German people whom they

had mercilessly sacrificed in the fatal pursuit of total war. When Hitler was dead Goebbels himself became for the few hours of life left to him Reich Chancellor, head of a State contracted now to a few crumbling streets. Then he placed himself on the Nazi funeral pyre, taking his wife and their six children with him.

Goebbels' career is without any parallel in history. It would, in fact, have been an impossibility without the instruments of modern power-propaganda—the popular press, the radio, the film, the loud-speaker and all the complex machinery that lay behind the organisation, regimentation and the recording of mass demonstrations. If we are wiser now, which is doubtful, it is because Goebbels showed how it could be done by a master in the technique of such forms of propaganda. Both the radio and the sound film were in their infancy when he adopted them to help make people in Germany deluded enough or hysterical enough to give Hitler's régime the degree of power necessary to take the ultimate step and subject the German State to their will, and finally to lead them into the most destructive war the world has known. To understand how this was achieved in so few years it is necessary to understand not only Hitler himself but the curious, repellent, dangerous and yet fascinating character of Joseph Goebbels.

ROGER MANVELL

CHAPTER ONE

The First Years

A HOUSE in the small textile manufacturing town of Rheydt is among those that managed to survive the relentless bombing of the industrial Rhineland during the Second World War. It is Number 156 on the Dahlener Strasse. The front door, which opens directly on to the street, is set squarely beside the two gaunt windows of the ground floor curtained against the passers-by. It is a severe but solid structure, and the first-floor windows look across the street directly down on to a mason's yard stacked with neat piles of stone crosses to commemorate the dead. Cut into the tiles of the steeply sloping roof are two skylight windows which, unless you stand with your nose pressed to the small squares of glass, only give a view of the sun, clouds and rain.

It was in this house that Joseph Goebbels spent his youth. He was born on 29th October 1897, in the Odenkirchener Strasse, but the family moved to the Dahlener Strasse during his infancy. Like most families in the Ruhr, the Goebbels were Catholics. His father, Friedrich Goebbels, was the son of a manual worker who spent his life in a firm of gas-mantle manufacturers, W. H. Lennartz of Rheydt. He had begun as an office boy and rose during the childhood and adolescence of his children through various clerkships in the business until he was eventually rewarded with the minor directorial position of Prokurist. He was, indeed, a petty bourgeois, struggling to keep his cuffs clean in the dirty atmosphere of the factory where he was employed, but earning no more than the working men who had none of his lower-middle class pretensions. His income was around 2,400 marks a year when his sons were children; at that period this sum was worth about £120 a year. The Goebbels, like their neighbours, were always concerned to keep up appearances.

One day, when Joseph was aged four, he was sitting on the sofa in the *gute Stube*, the parlour on the first floor of the house. Suddenly he began to cry so unaccountably that the doctor was eventually brought in to examine him. He ordered an immediate operation. Joseph had got infantile paralysis.

Herr Goebbels was a stern and devout man whose austere manner was to some extent mitigated by a rather deliberate sense of humour. He looked to his sons to raise the fortunes of the family towards the ideal status of the prosperous middle class. He was saddened at the sight of the shrunken frame and stooping shoulders of Joseph, whose growth was retarded by the paralysis that permanently affected his foot after the operation had made him a cripple.

Joseph was not the only child in the house. He had two older brothers, Hans and Konrad, and an elder sister, Elizabeth, who died in childhood. His younger sister Maria, to whom he was later to become attached, was not born until Joseph was twelve.

Frau Katherina Goebbels was a simple woman of little education; she was of Dutch origin and became a naturalised German citizen before her marriage, though Goebbels subsequently always concealed this fact.[1] She spoke German with a very pronounced Rhenish accent. Before her marriage she had been Katherina Maria Odenhausen, daughter of a blacksmith. She was a woman of great strength of character. When her son had become Reichsminister he liked it to be thought that he still held her in great respect. She represented, he said in his published diaries, "the voice of the people", with whom he wished always to keep in contact. He was fond of telling a story (which he may have invented) of how she had once assembled her children round their father's bedside when he was very ill with pneumonia and had made them hold hands and sing and pray, and how almost miraculously their father had recovered. Though her husband, who in later years quarrelled bitterly with Joseph, died in 1929, she was herself to survive her son.

Now, however, in his childhood, there seemed nothing she could do for him but pray. Leading him by the hand, she took him to church constantly and, kneeling beside him, she implored the Heavenly Father to give him strength to endure the burden of his physical weakness and his undeveloped body.

So Joseph's earliest recollections were of unhappiness and abnormality. It was obvious to him that his condition was a worry to his parents, and from his early childhood a seam of self-doubt was deposited deep in his nature. He shut himself away in his little attic room with its sloping ceiling and its single window looking up into the clouds, or if he stood beside it, down into a cramped and gloomy courtyard at the back of the house. It was a bad start in life, particularly for a man who was to become so powerful.

Like other children who for one reason or another cannot follow the rough, gregarious life of boys of their own age, he took to reading very early on. Here he was independent. No one cared what he read, and out of sight was out of mind as far as the rest of the family were concerned. A new energy was born in him, the energy to read voraciously, precociously. Neither his parents nor his teachers offered him much guidance. As soon as school was over and the journey home completed, he shut himself away in his room and read. Among his books was a cheap and already out-dated family encyclopædia, Meyer's *Konversationslexikon*, an abridged edition of a larger work popular at the time. This book became his main source of information about the world and gave him his first sense of the power that knowledge and intellect can achieve.

For as Joseph became older his self-assurance began to develop with him. His large head became less odd-looking as his shoulders matured, and his feats of knowledge and memory, due to his years of reading, began to impress even his father. Joseph's predilection for books seemed to offer some solution to the problem of what to do with him. Was he worth giving the higher education offered by the Gymnasium? Could the meagre family budget stand the strain of pinching and saving in order to send him to a school where he would be expected to stay until he was eighteen years of age? And then perhaps could he win a scholarship to a university? Herr Goebbels must have thought with pride of the chance that one day he could refer to his son as Herr Doktor. And there was no denying that the social status he most desired for his sons went with such a title.

So the decision was taken, and Joseph entered the Gymnasium in Rheydt.

The Gymnasium, the equivalent in Germany of an English grammar school, offered an education which had been little altered for over a century, preparing boys for the final hurdle of the Abiturium or Matura—the examination which entitled those who passed to proceed to the university. Boys were usually eighteen years of age and members of the Ober-Prima (or Upper Sixth) when they took this examination.

Joseph was not popular at school. Already he had learnt to compensate for his lack of normal animal boyishness by showing off his knowledge. He was a good scholar and often top of the form, but few liked him, not even the men whose job it was to teach him. The earliest recollection of his boyhood friend, Fritz Prang, who was also a scholar at the Gymnasium, is that Joseph was always over-anxious to impress his teachers, and that at times he was prepared to be a tell-tale. Prang remembers one particular occasion when Joseph revealed to Father Mollen, the scripture master, that one of his friends was playing truant. Had Joseph not been a cripple, Prang confessed, he would have joined with the other boys to beat the stuffing out of him. They nicknamed him Ulex after Ulysses, the sly one. Goebbels evidently liked this nickname, which stayed with him during his adolescence.

Goebbels was to develop another taste beside reading early in his life—the enjoyment of music. His father took due note of this. Over thirty years later Goebbels recalled in conversation with his aide von Oven how, when he was about fourteen years old, his father summoned him one day:

He had decided to buy me a piano. We were so little used to having presents, that I couldn't grasp it at first. But we went to look at it; it was to cost 300 marks. Obviously it was second-hand . . . It fitted very well among all the knick-knacks of the drawing-room, and I was allowed to go in every day to practise. . . It was meant to be a stage in the plan of life mapped out for me.[2]

Goebbels sat through the winter in the unheated *gute Stube* wearing his overcoat, and sometimes he played for the assembled family. The money for this piano had been saved over many years—pfennig by pfennig.

When Goebbels became Reichsminister his official biographers, such as Bade and Krause, were given material to publish which Goebbels believed would be favourable to him. He claimed to be of peasant stock, because his paternal grandfather, a carpenter, had married the daughter of a farmer who lived near Düsseldorf. These half-truths and legends about himself in his youth and in the earlier phases of his career are in some cases difficult now either to prove or to disprove, and they have come to be accepted through constant repetition even by those who have written quite independently about him. There seems, however, to be little doubt that he was deeply upset at being rejected for Army service on the grounds of his physical inferiority.

When in 1914 war began, Joseph was approaching seventeen years of age and was a member of the sixth form at his school. The excitement was intense, and the boys (already all but young men in their own view) challenged each other to enlist for the Army. Among those who queued as volunteers was Joseph, hoping his spirited response to the emergency would be admired. No doubt the others laughed at the idea. In fact, the Army doctor merely glanced at the diminutive and stooping body in front of him and rejected Joseph outright for military service without even bothering to examine him. The boy returned home and locked himself in his room. For a whole day and night he sobbed like a small child. His mother could do nothing with him. For two days he would speak to no one. Perhaps he was showing off, for it is inconceivable that a boy of his intelligence could have dreamed that the Army would accept him.

Once more, then, Joseph was thrust back on his intellect, and his family had to consider seriously the essential problem of the future. It was plain that he would never be called upon to fight and that he should if at all possible be given the chance of a university education. The war situation, indeed, might give him distinct advantages when the majority of young men were being forced to leave their education incomplete. Both of his brothers eventually served in the Army, while he stayed on at school until he was eighteen. Later, both as political agitator and Nazi official, he was often to show exemplary physical courage as if he wanted to dare the thugs who surrounded him to think him a coward. As Reichsminister he was always ready to criticise the Army and its generals.

There was now no doubt at all in the minds of his father and mother that Joseph should become a priest in the Catholic Church. Prelate Mollen remembers his pupil seemed at this early age to be very keen on religion. His parents had done everything they could for their odd and seemingly clever son by enabling him to stay at school until he was nineteen. There Goebbels managed to establish a better relationship as soon as he reached the dignity of the sixth form. It was less necessary for him to assert himself in order to compensate for his physical inferiority. He could shine intellectually without affronting the other boys; his sharp tongue found plenty to do in the school and his voice began to find its fluency when he became a class orator on speech days. He also distinguished himself as an amateur actor in the school plays. When he finally matriculated in 1917 his examination results were the best, and he was invited by the headmaster to give the end-of-term farewell speech on behalf of the school-leavers. Prang remembers this speech to have been very stilted and pompous, and the headmaster, who did not like Goebbels because of his supercilious manner at school, remarked afterwards that one thing at least was certain: Joseph Goebbels would never make an orator!

Goebbels himself seemed at first to have no particular aversion to the idea of entering the priesthood. Indeed, it probably appeared to him to offer the most immediate opportunity of achieving the thing he really wanted—a position in the world. His young and impressionable mind could hardly have been unaware of the importance of even the humblest priest in the devout Catholic community where he had been raised, and he was no doubt already beginning to respond to visions of the power the priest could wield over his fellowmen.

In spite of his poverty, Goebbels managed in 1917 to enrol for a single term at Bonn University, the first of several universities that he was to attend before he gained his Doctor of Philosophy degree at Heidelberg in 1921 at the age of twenty-four. After his initial term at Bonn, his further education became dependent on receiving a university scholarship from the important Catholic charitable institution, the Albertus Magnus Society. It is in connection with this institution that one of the earliest and most interesting of the Goebbels legends is associated.

Knowing that he was to present himself before a priest at the interview, it is said that Joseph did what he could to make himself impressive. The priest saw the boy was poised ready to assert his knowledge and so he turned the interview into a disarming discussion of the ordinary affairs of the world. What he discovered during this conversation impressed him, but not in the way either Joseph or his parents had foreseen.

"Young man," the priest is alleged to have said, "you don't believe in God. You must on no account take Holy Orders."

It seems a pity that there is no truth whatsoever in this much-repeated story with its Faust-like touch of drama. The first approach to the Albertus Magnus Society was not in fact made until September 1917 when Goebbels was almost twenty years of age. He himself approached the institution directly, not through his parents acting on his behalf. The correspondence survives in the Society's archives, written in Goebbels' neat and scholarly hand that was only too soon to deteriorate into an angular, spidery scrawl which retained the neatness of appearance but was notoriously illegible. The letters reveal he had already begun his university studies but that he and his parents had found the cost prohibitive. The first letter is dated 5th September:

I herewith most humbly beg (*untertänigst*) to appeal to the Diocesan Committee of the Albertus Magnus Society for some financial support for the winter term 1917-18. I passed my matriculation at Easter in the Rheydt Gymnasium (I attach the report) and I then went to Bonn University so as to study Philology (German and Latin) and History. During this one term I managed to make do with some savings which I was fortunate enough to make while a schoolboy by tutoring smaller children. However, I had to break off my studies prematurely since my means were so little and so soon exhausted.

My father works as a clerk, and what small balance may be left from his salary in view of the increased cost of living must be used to support my two brothers, of whom the elder is at the Western Front, while the other is a prisoner-of-war in France.

Unfortunately the holidays did not give me much opportunity for earning money, and all my efforts to obtain some short-term employment were in vain. On account of my handicapped leg, I am exempt from military service and I would dearly like to continue my studies during the next term. This, however, entirely depends on the charity of my Catholic fellow-believers.

I would most humbly ask you to listen to my sincere request, and I earnestly look forward to your early reply.

I am confident that my former religious teacher, Herr Oberlehrer Johannes Mollen, will confirm my statements to be correct.

In deep devotion, with deep respect,

Josef Goebbels (Stud. Phil.)[3]

A second letter followed on 14th September, and was even more formal in its appeal:

As I begged to inform you in my last letter, I was not able, owing to financial difficulties, to complete the last term. Moreover, at the end of June, I was conscripted for military office work, but I am now quite free of that. In the circumstances, I am not in a position to provide a testimonial of diligence with regard to my first term. Would you very kindly let me know whether, in the circumstances, I can do without it, the more so since without your kind and gracious help I would be greatly distressed to have to give up further studies.

I attach the questionnaire, and as soon as I have your kind answer, I will send in the other papers.

In a further letter dated 18th September he is more explicit. The style is still very formal, and he refers to himself in the third person:

The father of the under-signed applicant is a clerk employed by the firm W. H. Lennartz in Rheydt. His income amounts to between 3,800 and 4,000 marks per annum. There are no appreciable savings or funds. The applicant's mother is also still alive. Of the three sons, the applicant is the youngest. His eldest brother (24) is a gunner on the Western Front. The other brother (22) is a P.O.W. in France. The only surviving sister is eight years old.

In view of the increased cost of living and the need for supporting the other two sons (their priority is due to their being soldiers), the parents are not in a position to give financial support to the applicant's studies.

On the same sheet of paper there is a notable commendation of Goebbels written by Prelate Mollen:

Herr Goebbels comes from decent Catholic parents and can be recommended on account of his religious attitude and his general moral demeanour.

Two other officials added their recommendations of the candidate. Goebbels' application to the Society for assistance was accompanied by a school report on his progress in studies, his conduct and his character. It represents him as an outstanding pupil. His behaviour, attendance, neatness, diligence and handwriting are all marked in the highest grade, 'very good'; in his studies Religion, German, Latin are also marked 'very good', and his Greek, French, History, Geography, Mathematics and Physics are marked 'good'. Goebbels' appeal was successful. The Society decided to make him a grant in the form of a series of interest-free loans. After a third appeal, dated 8th October, in which he very respectfully asks for immediate payment to help him with the cost of books and fees, he received his first loan of 185 marks*. In all between 1917 and 1920 the Albertus Magnus Society lent Goebbels a total of just 964 marks. Had they known the difficulty they were eventually to experience in getting the repayments out of him, they would undoubtedly never have lent him a single mark. They had in the end to resort to legal pressure and they did not achieve a final settlement of the debt until 1930, when Goebbels was already a member of the Reichstag and a notorious anti-Catholic. The complete documentation of this long struggle survives in the Society's archives.[4]

*The mark in 1917 was worth about one shilling or twenty-five cents according to the values of the period. By 1920, however, it was beginning to decline prior to the catastrophic inflation of the years 1921–23.

In addition to these loans, his father allowed him fifty marks a month, and at times his mother managed to send him small presents of money.

The German universities at the beginning of the century had only four faculties—Theology, Medicine, Law and Philosophy. Philosophy was something of an academic miscellany incorporating every subject not regarded as part of the first three faculties. It included subjects as diverse as Literature, Mathematics, Politics, Economics and the History of Art. It was the faculty proper to the student who intended to become a fully qualified teacher. Students in the Faculty of Philosophy took a *Staatsexamen*, or final examination which entitled them to become masters in the Gymnasia. Taking a doctorate (or Ph.D.) was not obligatory, but most students did so for the sake of the prestige the title brought them. Most educated people in Germany liked to have the title Herr Doktor. The doctorate required some three years' study at a university, after which the student presented a short thesis or dissertation on a subject chosen by his professor, and followed this by submitting himself to an oral examination.

At Bonn Goebbels was reading History and Literature and specialising at this early stage in his academic career in the study of Goethe's dramatic works. He had joined the Catholic Students' Union known as Unitas, membership of which was considered desirable by the Catholic authorities, and, judging from the records held by the Albertus Magnus Society, he appeared to be a good student. Then begins the unsettling movement from one university centre to another. Although it was customary for students to study in two or three universities, Goebbels' peripatetic career during his four years of study shows abnormal restlessness. For the summer term of 1918 he went to the University of Freiburg, where he was excused payment of any fees and studied the writings of Winckelmann, the eighteenth-century Catholic archæologist and student of classical art, and the influence of Ancient Rome and Greece on the Middle Ages. In the winter he moved on to Würzburg University, where he continued his studies of ancient and modern history.

Some letters survive written in October and November 1918 by Goebbels to his school friend Fritz Prang in Rheydt and to the Prang family. They are particularly revealing of the way his character was developing now that he was fully established as a student and was living in rooms away from his family. They are written from Würzburg. The first of them, dated 2nd October and addressed to Fritz, is an interesting comment on conditions affecting the attendance of students in German universities during the last months and weeks of the war. Goebbels had to attend university in a town where he could find a lodging rather than go to the university of his choice:

My dear Fritz,

Accept my sincere greetings, first of all, as well as my considerable displeasure in having to tell you right away that my long-cherished dream has not come true: for this term, alas, I have to forget about Munich once again. In the whole city there were no rooms to be had and the food situation, also, seems to be pretty bad. No, I *didn't* sit down in front of the station to cry my eyes out. I simply packed my belongings and beat what you might call a strategic retreat. Now here in Würzburg I have been very lucky indeed. A wonderful room right beside the river. Very good food and—well, what more can one expect these days? As for Munich, I hope to have another go during the Christmas break.

He then goes on to describe the beauties of the ancient city of Würzburg in the flowery terms of a guide-book, supported by literary quotations and a reference to himself as "a young son of the Muses":

The University is good. For this term I am concentrating again on the History of Art and recent German literature. I hope this winter to make some good headway *in artibus liberalibus*. And you, my dear fellow? Well, I should hope that in the course of the next few weeks you will find your way to this beautiful seat of the Muses. You will certainly never regret it. What about breaking your present sojourn by a short visit here? It would really delight me. Tonight I mean to read Rabindranath Tagore's 'Gardener', a wonderful collection of love songs which I can commend to you most heartily. Do not forget, please, to send me the small Christmas sketch as soon as possible. And do remember me, please, to your esteemed Frau mother and your Herr father, and accept the most sincere greetings of your ULEX.

By now it was clear that Goebbels fancied himself as a literary man, and was prepared to use his letters to his friends as opportunities for stylistic display. This reached its height when he heard the following month of the death of Fritz's brother Hans in the very last days of the war. He wrote a stiffly formal letter on 13th October to the whole family in which he tried to match correctness of feeling with a suitably heroic style of writing:

I have just heard from Fritz the shocking news of the heroic death of your dear son and brother Hans, and I feel the urge to offer my most sincere condolence in your grief about this too, too sad loss. Considering that for a while I was very close to Hans and that I have spent many a quiet hour with him, you will allow me to devote a few words of reminiscence to the young hero.

Hans was a true and loyal comrade. What drew me to him particularly and will always make me proud to have known him, was his pure and unspotted character, his truly noble attitude, and his unspoiled way of life, even though in his restrained and yet virile way he was not the type to conquer hearts in a flash. He certainly did something rather more precious: he knew how to win the hearts of his friends for ever in hours of quiet communion . . . I think that you, *verehrte* family Prang, will find some solace in such thoughts. If indeed it is the lot of him whom the gods love to die young, you must know that Hans was one of those select few.

About a month later, on 11th November 1918, the Armistice was signed in Marshal Foch's private railway coach, which Goebbels was one day to bring back to Compiègne when Germany was able to celebrate her triumph over France. The complex political situation in Germany which had led up to the Armistice naturally excited the students, as it excited the rest of Germany. The High Command, at first in favour of an Armistice, at the last moment turned against it and so shifted the responsibility for proceeding with the acceptance of peace terms solely on to the shoulders of the civil Government. Ludendorff, who was subsequently to endorse Hitler, had resigned from his post in the High Command at the end of October, and had fled abroad in disgrace; faced with the knowledge that the defeat of Germany was being admitted, soldiers, sailors and workers began to mutiny throughout the country demanding peace, and the first Republican Government was set up in Bavaria on 8th November. The Kaiser was forced to abdicate and fled to Holland as soon as it was realised that neither he nor the High Command could rely further on the loyalty of the Services. On 10th November a Socialist revolution was proclaimed in the big cities and a Republican Government founded.

In a letter dated 13th November, a few days after the revolution, and addressed to Fritz Prang, Goebbels gives his comments as a student on these events. They are in startling contrast to his thinking once he had become a National Socialist, particularly in his complete acceptance of the fact of Germany's defeat:

A few days ago in the Auditorium Maximum here we had a big meeting of almost all the Würzburg students who wished to see how they stood vis-à-vis the burning questions of our new political situation. And in the course of the debate, a word was spoken which I would like to send you in answer to your dear and friendly lines. The question was raised as to how German students should face the new powers-that-be, and one of the older students (wounded in the war) had his say: "I think that for the time being the most decent line for us to take is to watch matters calmly. Just now the blind and raw masses seem to be on top. But maybe the time will come again when they will feel the need for an intelligent lead, and then it will be for us to step in with all our strength."

Don't you also feel that the time will come again when people will yearn for intellectual and spiritual values rather than brutal mass appeal? Let us also wait for that moment, and meanwhile persevere in steeling our brains for the tasks then awaiting us. It is bitter enough to have lived through those dark hours of our Fatherland, but who knows if one day it might not profit us after all. The way I see it, Germany has certainly lost the war, but our Fatherland may well turn out the winner.

After further condolence on the death of Hans, he ends his letter by quoting Horace!

For the summer term of 1919, Goebbels went back to Freiburg. Although he was still let off the payment of fees and was receiving further loans from the Albertus Magnus Society, his devotion to Catholicism had now begun to weaken, for he is no longer recorded as a member of Unitas.

For the winter term of 1919, he transferred to the University at Munich, where he received the last of the loans that he was to get from the Albertus Magnus Society. After this, he failed to keep them informed of his movements or to give them any report of his progress as a student, though he should have done so once a year in view of the support he had received from them during the first two years of his academic career. There can be little doubt that he was by now beginning to sever his connections with the Catholic Church; in any case he was about to come under the stronger influence which was to fire his literary ambitions and persuade him that he could become a professional writer. He was to retain this ambition for the rest of his life, taking the massive fees and royalties he exacted for his published articles, speeches and diaries during the period of his political power as the sign of his literary success.

A letter of the greatest interest written to Goebbels at this time by his father was published shortly after the last war in a Catholic journal.[5] It is dated 7th November, by which time Goebbels was already in Munich. It is plain from this letter, and particularly from the last part of it, that he was developing the tendency to self-dramatisation as 'the prodigal son' which was to be characteristic of him throughout his life. He is not content to lose his faith quietly; he must stir up emotion about it, not only in himself but in those who love him. There is a certain nobility in this letter which speaks well for Herr Goebbels and reveals the depth of his affection and response to the son whose future life was to distress and disappoint him so greatly:

Dear Joseph,

My letter of the day before yesterday should have reached you by now. But I wish to revert briefly to your dear lines of the 31st ult.

They contained much to please me but again much to give me a great deal of pain. I do believe, though, that with some goodwill on both sides our former relationship of complete confidence could quickly be restored. Obviously this could not be done unless you are absolutely candid and truthful to your father.

I have at all times been convinced that you have never shown any lack of diligence and perseverance in your studies, and have thus achieved successes that may have been envied by many another undergraduate. And I am particularly pleased that you seem to have kept your moral standards, and what you say about that was indeed balm to a father's heart.

However, then you continue: "But if I should lose my faith . . ." I take it that I may assume you have not lost it yet, and that you are merely tormented by doubts. In that case it might reassure you to know that no person, particularly no young person, is ever completely spared such doubts; and that, indeed, those who suffer these doubts may be all the better Christians for it. Here, too, there is no victory without a struggle. Hence, to make this a reason for keeping away from the Holy Sacraments is a grievous error; for who would claim at all times to have approached the Table of the Lord with the childlike pure heart of his very first Holy Communion?

I now have to put a few questions to you, for if our relationship is to be restored to its former confidence—and no one could wish that more earnestly than I do—I must have no doubt about your answers to these questions:

(1) Have you written books or do you intend writing anything that would not be compatible with the Catholic religion?

(2) Are you contemplating going in for a profession not suitable for a good Catholic?

Now, if you can answer both questions in the negative, and if your doubts are all of a different nature, I can tell you only one thing: Pray and go on praying, and I, too, shall pray to our Lord to help you work out everything for the best.

If then you should still consider yourself in danger of losing your faith, I should like to take your mind back to the year 1915, when, early in the morning, you knelt next to me at the death-bed of our darling little Elizabeth and when, with me, you prayed for the soul of that little angel, taken away so soon. What then was the one consolation in our grief? It was merely this, that the dear little soul had been properly provided with the last rites of our Holy Church and that we could pray for her *together*.

Whatever you may feel in your heart of hearts, even if it is worse than I can imagine, I am sure that if only you will show some courage you will regain your peace of mind; and if you still feel that you cannot, do come home, my son, and talk it over with us. You can have the fare from me any time you say so. . . .

You write in your letter: "Why don't you tell me that you curse me as the prodigal son who has left his parents and gone into the wilderness?"

And then again you write: "If you think that I can no longer be your son . . ."

Well, being a Catholic father, I do neither the one thing nor the other. I will just go on praying for you as I have prayed for you so often.

You need not hurry in your answer to this letter, but do keep up the correspondence with us at home. I hear that the parcel post is no longer to be restricted, hence one of these days I am going to send you a food parcel.

With very kind regards, also from your mother and from your sister and your brothers, I remain your loving Father.

It is interesting to see in this letter that Goebbels' desire to show off to himself as well as to his father led him to assume the dramatic rôle of the Apostate.

In 1920 Goebbels moved to the University of Heidelberg, where he was to graduate the following year. The influence under which he now came was that of the celebrated Jewish Professor of Literature, Friedrich Gundolf, who was the most famous contemporary literary historian in Germany, and author of what is still the best-known biography of Goethe. Gundolf was not only a highly distinguished man academically, he had about him a certain glamour, of which no young student of literature could remain unconscious, for he was closely associated with Stefan George, the most advanced and esoteric poet of early twentieth-century German literature. Gundolf was an important figure in the literary circle that surrounded the famous man, and to be a student working with Gundolf was to share, not too remotely, a sense of being in at the fountainhead of literary fashion and highbrow good taste. No doubt the young provincial student from Rheydt felt that he had arrived, and was inordinately proud of being a student in the Jewish professor's department at the University. He was now twenty-three years old, and his studies at Heidelberg included History, Philology, Art and Literature.

He now started work on the thesis for his doctorate. His subject was an examination of the work of Wilhelm von Schütz, sub-titled 'A Contribution to the History of the Romantic Drama'. Goebbels was later to withdraw the thesis from the University archives and retitle it 'The Spiritual and Political Undercurrents of the Early Romantics'.[6] That, of course, was when he was Reich Minister and needed to imply that his interests were political during the period of his studies. They were, in fact, largely æsthetic. Politics were still to come.

It is necessary to understand the shaping of Goebbels' extraordinary personality during this important period of his adolescence and early maturity. No one denies his intelligence, but there is evidence in his attitude to the Albertus Magnus Society that he was already developing the selfish opportunism which was to be so significant a part of his nature. Plainly he was already making himself as independent as possible of his family and background. It is difficult now to think of him as a young and poverty-stricken student asking for petty loans and moving every few months during the greater part of his academic career from one place to another. He lived in a succession of hired rooms from which he wrote his numerous requests to the Albertus Magnus Society for money or his reports on his progress—No. 18 Portstrasse, Bonn; the fourth floor of No. 2 Breisacherstrasse, Freiburg; the fourth floor of No. 8 Blumenstrasse, Würzburg; back in Freiburg at No. 8 Goethestrasse; in rooms with a family called Vigier in the Romanstrasse, Munich. Only in Heidelberg, when he was a young man of twenty-three, do we begin to find evidence that he was discovering his ambitions more completely and evolving a self-consciously assured outlook mixed with considerable vanity.

He had many reasons which would make him feel passionately the need to assert himself. His mother and father were, in effect, working-class people of little education, speaking with a strongly-marked local accent, even though they no doubt rated themselves as lower-middle class. As an adolescent boy and as a student he had in three years left his home town and the Rhineland itself to work briefly in universities as far apart as Munich and Heidelberg. In each of his universities he had been in constant contact with cultured people. His own Rhenish accent became clear and cultivated, though he retained the traces of it in his magnificent voice to the end of his life. But during all this time he was poor, supporting himself on the meagre grants from his family (and particularly from his mother), on the money from his scholarships and on such small sums as he could earn as a tutor and part-time secretary. As we have seen, at most of the universities he was excused the payment of fees, but a young man of his pride, not to say vanity, must have felt bitterly the social stigma of poverty.

He had also to learn to deal with his physical infirmity. He was very slight in build and his shoulders sloped steeply. He was little more than five feet tall and his weight was in the region of a hundred pounds. He walked with an unmistakable limp, but had become adept at disguising it. He had little money for either food or clothes, so he had to develop his social assets through the conscious development of his personality. He had two great advantages which he began to exploit very early in his life—his voice, which could be either caressing or powerful as he willed, and a certain magnetism in his looks.

His face was lean and oval, his nose pronounced and long, and his cheek-bones high. He had a wide, volatile mouth, with a charming smile that he used often. He had dark brown eyes that responded readily to emotion, but could be penetrating in their stare. He had beautiful hands, lean, well-veined and mobile, which he also learned to use as part of his self-expression. Coupled with the natural quickness of his intelligence, these assets in his looks were of great importance to him. Later on, as we shall see, many shrewd observers were to attempt to describe his character. In no sense was he either by appearance or mentality the popular conception of an 'Aryan' German. He was more Celtic or Romantic in appearance. He seemed a Latin rather

Friedrich Goebbels   Maria Katherina Goebbels

The house in Rheydt where Goebbels was brought up.

Rheydt Gymnasium, 1916: *left*, acting in *Die Quitzows* by Wildenbruch; *right*, with members of the Sixth Form.

With Else and Alma, who wears a hat.

than a Saxon in both temperament and mentality, as Professor Trevor-Roper has said.[7] Sir Nevile Henderson compared him to an Irish agitator with a Celtic manner.[8]

One of his earliest writings was a short novel called *Michael*, which he wrote in 1921 shortly after his graduation, but which was rejected by such publishers as Ullstein and Mosse to whom it was submitted until in 1929 Eher Verlag, the Nazi publishing house, found it good policy to print it.[9] Later the Eher Verlag let it run through a few small editions. It is an extraordinary novel from the literary point of view, yet without doubt it reveals to a considerable extent the attitude of Goebbels himself during the period he was a student.

When *Michael* was eventually published, Goebbels wrote a florid dedication to his college friend Richard Flisges, who had died six years earlier:

1918
Your wounded arm still in a sling, the grey helmet on your head and your chest covered with medals—that's how you faced those staid citizens to pass matriculation. They failed you because you didn't know some figures or other. They said you weren't mature yet.
OUR ANSWER WAS: REVOLUTION!

1920
We were both about to suffer spiritual breakdown and capitulate. But we helped each other up again and hardly faltered.
MY ANSWER WAS: SPITE!

1923
You challenged fate. Do or die! But the time was not yet and you must needs be victimised.
YOUR ANSWER WAS: DEATH!

1927
I stood at your grave. In gleaming sunlight a quiet green hillock. It spelled Mortality.
MY ANSWER WAS: RESURRECTION!

Flisges is to some extent a mysterious influence in Goebbels' life. He was a sick man who had been badly wounded in the war and decorated for his bravery. Yet he emerged from the struggle an anarchist unable to find a satisfactory way of life for himself. As the dedication to *Michael* shows, he failed his university matriculation in 1918. He turned to Marx and Engels, to Communism, to pacifism, to any form of criticism of the liberal Government of post-war Germany which could act as a conductor for his hatred and frustration. He introduced Goebbels not only to the theoreticians of Communism but to the works of Walther Rathenau, the German statesman and philosopher.[10]

Through Flisges Goebbels discovered Dostoevsky. It is clear that both these young men read and discussed books which seemed to them to offer some kind of analysis or solution to their spiritual and social problems. Their late adolescence was spent in the difficult, destructive atmosphere of post-war Germany, a cruel time for any young intellectuals to try to achieve a balanced view either of society or of their personal conduct. Goebbels was still attracted by certain elements in Christianity, and Dostoevsky's emotional mysticism fed what was left of his religious imagination. Soon, in addition to *Michael*, Goebbels was to write a play in verse called *The Wanderer*.[11] It is about Christ. It was never published.

Goebbels, therefore, in company with his friend passed through a phase of nihilism which left a destructive adolescent element in his nature which he never outgrew. In later life he would frequently act with the petulant cruelty of a very young man determined to avenge himself on a society that seemed to him insufficiently perfect for his taste. He thought of himself as a mature revolutionary. Only too often he seems to be avenging the humiliations of the early days when his numerous articles for the *Berliner Tageblatt* were being rejected by its Jewish editor, Theodor Wolff, and Richard Flisges was pressing him to read the works of the Jewish writers, Marx and Rathenau.

Flisges, still uncertain of his proper place in society, became a labourer and was killed in a mining accident in July 1923. By that time contact between him and Goebbels seems to have been virtually severed. But the young nihilist still remained in Goebbels' thoughts, a martyr to the wickedness of the German social system. Fusing himself and Flisges into a composite romantic figure, a Byronic warrior, Goebbels wrote

his brief novel *Michael* while still a young man under the direct influence
of this friendship.

Michael is barely thirty thousand words in length, and is therefore
in effect a long short-story. Goebbels writes in the first person, and
uses his favourite literary form, the diary. He had kept a personal diary
from the age of twelve, and it is evident from the style of his writing
that in adolescence he grew to be the kind of person who fancied himself on paper, writing in a narcissistic and highfalutin style like a youth
making heroic faces at himself in a mirror or striking handsome
attitudes. To keep a diary which is a record of things done, people
met, places visited or even more intimate experiences is one thing, but
to pour out for one's private reading self-conscious phrases, long chains
of coy exclamations and lush emotionalisms all paragraphed like blank
verse is quite another. Goebbels fingered his literary emotions like a
miser stroking his gold.

Michael is the diary of a hero who combines the occupations of a
soldier, a worker, a poet, a lover, a patriot and a revolutionary. Here
is the opening:

No longer is the stallion neighing under my thighs; no longer am I
hunched over a gun or tramping through the muddy clay of neglected
trenches.

How long it is since I walked the vast Russian plain or the shell-
ridden French countryside!

A thing of the past!

Like a phoenix rising from the ashes of war and destruction. Peace!

The very word is like balm on a wound still trembling and bleeding.
I seem to grasp the blessing of that word with my hands.

When I look out of the window I see German land: towns, villages,
fields, woods . . .

Homeland! Germany!

Michael leaves the death-wishes of war behind him and becomes a
student "anxious to grasp life with every fibre of my being". He is in
rooms; he is his own master. He meets an old school friend who asks
him what he is reading at the University. He reflects:

May 12

What indeed?

All and nothing. I'm too lazy and, may be, too stupid for exact science.

I want to be a man. With a profile of my own.

A personality! On the road to a new Germany!

May 17

I've been wondering a long time what it is that makes me drink life so copiously.

It's because I stand on the hard soil of my homeland with both my feet. The smell of the soil is around me. And in my veins the peasant-blood is welling up healthily.

Armed with the friendship of Flisges, Goebbels could afford these dreams of feudalism and chivalry in the person of Michael. He was now no longer crippled, no longer the son of an urban clerk, no longer rejected for the Army; he was fused with the body and spirit of his friend writing a fictitious diary alongside his own, personal one.

Michael meets a girl at the University called Hertha Holk with whom he becomes intimate. They go for long walks and indulge in deep talk. To her he proclaims his ardent patriotism—"For a young German, these days, there's really only one thing to be done: to stand up for the Fatherland!" Apart from her he grumbles (and he is here surely quoting his own diary) about how short he is of money—"money is muck, but muck isn't money!" With her he claims to enjoy the delights of music and the delights of love:

A thousand insects humming. The grass is indescribably green. I kiss Hertha Holk on her soft yearning mouth. We are both very much ashamed.

Quiet, quiet summer afternoon . . .

In her street we part from one another . . .

I carry my happiness like a sweet, sweet load.

Night! . . .

I walk back to the town and pluck some roses from the garden walls.

More and more red roses.
I stand at Hertha Holk's window . . .
I put a bunch of red roses on her window-sill.
I am happy, happy as I walk home.
Blessed hour!

"Hertha Holk," he says (he always uses the affectation of quoting full names), "gives me joy and strength alternately. I cannot thank her enough." She inspires him to write.

Meanwhile, another figure emerges, a further image from the misted mirror of Goebbels' relationship with Flisges. This is Ivan Wienurovsky, a nebulous Russian student who lends Michael Dostoevsky's novel *The Idiot*. This book affects him deeply:

The spirit of Dostoevsky hovers over that quiet and dreamy land. When Russia awakens the world will witness a nationalistic miracle.

A nationalistic miracle? Yes, that's it! That's what political miracles are like. The International is merely a dogma, but the miracles of a nation are never caused by the intellect, they're a matter of the blood. But they've got the will power of that one man Lenin. Without Lenin no Bolshevism.

Once again, it's men who make history. Even when it happens to be bad.

Talking to Hertha a little later he says:

I think and act as I have to think and act. In us is a demon leading us to our destiny. There's nothing one can do about it.

Out of the Goebbels-image within the character of Michael comes the desire to write, inspired by both Hertha and Ivan and by the spirit of Dostoevsky. He chooses for his subject Jesus Christ:

I talk to Christ. I had thought to have vanquished Him, but I had mistaken Him for His false priests.
Christ is hard and inexorable.

He whips the Jewish money-changers out of His temple.

A declaration of war on Money.

Yet, if one said that today, they would put one into a gaol or madhouse.

We are all sick.

Hypocrisy is the characteristic of a decaying bourgeois epoch.

The ruling class is tired and has no courage for new adventure.

The Intellect has poisoned our people.

Then he adds:

Hertha Holk looks at me and shakes her head.

Like Dostoevsky he becomes possessed, "given to phantasma", suffering in "creative loneliness". Then term is over. Hertha returns to her home, and Michael goes to one of the Frisian islands off the northern coast to write his Messianic play. "I lie on the downs and wait for a word from God's mouth." Here he receives a letter from Hertha which gives us Goebbels' own picture of how he liked to think women would regard him:

. . . sometimes I doubt your love, and then I would cry my eyes out. Forgive me! Sometimes I lie awake all night, homesick for your fierce pride . . . I know you'll find your way, for you are strong. But you should take life as it is. One can't change much anyway. You should save yourself all those detours. I know you'll answer me that the detours may be the best part of the road. But then the straight road will never lead you astray.

Your Hertha Holk

"A genuine woman," he writes, "loves the eagle." Then suddenly comes a violent outburst:

No Jews here at all, and that is truly a blessing. Jews make me physically sick, the mere sight of them does this. I cannot even hate the Jew. I can merely despise him. He has raped our people, soiled our ideals,

24

weakened the strength of the nation, corrupted morals. He is the poisonous eczema on the body of our sick nation. That has nothing to do with religion. Either he destroys us, or we destroy him. . . .

Christ cannot have been a Jew. I do not have to look for any scientific proof of that. It just is so!

Intrusive, violent and indecent as this passage is, one cannot be sure whether it is not a final interpolation when Goebbels was preparing his novel for the press seven or eight years later. Only a sight of the original manuscript could show how much he thought fit to add to his book when he had become a professional agitator for the Nazi party and one of the most violent of their anti-Jewish element. Here the outburst only serves to introduce the assertion that Christ could not have been a Jew.

The men and women of the island inspire him ("I'd like to be a priest on this island, to explain the Sermon on the Mount to these simple people"). He calls them "strong and proud". The women are healthy and beautiful, "the eternal sea reflected in their eyes".

The revolutionary in him is stirred. In his talks with Hertha he had already expressed his hatred of the cowardly, property-loving bourgeoisie, the affront of old age to the wilful freedom of youth. Now he writes:

One class has fulfilled its historic mission and is about to yield to another. The bourgeoisie has to yield to the working class . . . Whatever is about to fall should be pushed. We are all soldiers of the revolution. We want the workers' victory over filthy lucre. That is socialism.

So he is a Socialist, a patriot, the admirer of a mythical master-race, and of a Christ who was anti-Jewish. Ivan writes to him and tells him he must come to Munich, because it is the most interesting town in Germany. Then Hertha writes to say she has rented rooms for him in Schwabing, the Latin quarter of Munich, where they are to spend the winter term.

Meanwhile, his relationship with Hertha becomes deeper and more complicated. His vanity seems to demand that his love should be complex. She is his "torment and delivery". "On my evil days I can hardly do without her . . . I make Hertha Holk suffer a great deal." They spend the Christmas holidays in the mountains together. "I thank her for being my solace and my strength . . . We hurt one another in petty squabbles . . . Oh you mountains! You towering mountains! . . . Our life is a chain of crime and punishment, with an inscrutable fate guiding us." As the New Year is born Hertha says to him: "You are to be a man who will make his mark for the Fatherland."

The remaining winter months are a torment as he works laboriously at his verse-drama. The influence of Ivan is strong. Michael refers to him as his "demon". Hertha hates and distrusts Ivan; she "cannot understand my torment"; indeed she makes it worse. Behind the personal relationships, the talk about revolutionary politics goes on continuously:

Our people have been forced under a yoke. The world's master-race (*Herrenvolk*) is reduced to slave labour, from high up to low down and from low down to high up.

But we won't get there by speeches and resolutions. We need a holy thunderstorm.

Long live the Republic—that's what they are shouting on the street. What's the Republic to us? Long live Germany!

Later he says, rather humourlessly, "I want to be a sign-post. I want to serve the Fatherland."

Again, one cannot be certain how much Goebbels saw fit to insert into his youthful novel in order to make it reflect more exactly his later thoughts at the time of its publication in 1929. Although the whole trend of the book seems to be a mixture of the mystical and the nihilistic together with a foretaste of desire for the Nietzschean hero which anticipates Goebbels' future public attitude to Hitler, the passages of anti-Semitism and those referring to a Messianic speaker to be quoted later read much more decisively and fiercely than the rest. They are, for instance, very different from the vaguely demoniac dialogue Goebbels composed between Michael and Ivan.

26

"Ivan Wienurovsky, you want to rob me of my fatherland. You are making me a beggar."

"Merely growing pains. I want to educate you, to give you courage."

"I despair."

"That's what the world is like."

"You are a devil."

"The devil is merely a fallen angel."

"I hate you!"

"No matter. I shan't let go of you, Michael!"

"So you want me to be your slave?"

"Yes, I do."

I get up and slap his face.

But in March he receives a letter from Hertha in which she says, "I suffer because of you. Why cannot we understand one another? I love you beyond measure. That's why I suffer so much. If you despair I must despair with you and I shall have nothing to hold on to . . ."

When April comes he is back in the mountains, but on his return he finds another letter from Hertha in which she says she is leaving him. In despair he goes to her house, but she has gone and no one knows where she is to be found.

But ten days later comes the great revelation. On 27th April he goes by chance to a political meeting where he hears a speech delivered by an unnamed Speaker of extraordinary magnetism and power:

. . . I sit in a hall I have never been in before. Among utter strangers. Poor and threadbare people most of them. Workers, soldiers, officers, students. I hardly notice how the man up there begins to speak, slowly, hesitatingly at first.

But then all of a sudden, the flow of his speech is unleashed. It's like a light shining above him. I listen. I am captivated. Honour! Work! The flag! Are there still such things in this people from whom God has taken His blessing hand?

The audience is aglow. Hope shines on grey faces. Someone clenches his fist. Someone wipes the sweat off his brow. An old officer sobs like a child.

I am getting hot and cold. I don't know what's happening to me. I seem to hear guns booming. A few soldiers get up and shout "Hurrah", and no one even notices it.

And the man up there speaks on, and whatever was budding in me falls into shape.

A miracle!

Among the ruins is someone who shows us the flag.

Those around me are no longer strangers. They are brothers. I go up to the rostrum and look in the man's face.

No orator he! A prophet!

Sweat is pouring down his face. A pair of eyes glow in the pale face. His fists are clenched.

And like the Last Judgment word after word is thundering on, and phrase after phrase.

I know not what I do. I seem demented.

I shout "Hurrah". And no one seems astonished.

He on the rostrum glances at me for a moment. Those blue eyes sear me like a flame. That is an order!

I feel as if I were newly born.

I know now whither my path leads me. The path of maturity. I seem to be intoxicated.

All I remember is the man's hand clasping mine. A vow for life.

And my eyes meet two great blue stars.

So overcome is he by this transcendent experience that he decides to leave Munich without a word to anyone. He goes to Heidelberg where he is idle, reading books and papers, or sitting doing nothing "for hours, listlessly and aimlessly". That the great unnamed Speaker should have had this particular effect on him is, to say the least of it, strange. It seems as if Goebbels felt that Michael's intellectual nihilism had been knocked out by this initial dynamic contact with the Messiah. However, if it is true that it was in June 1922 that Goebbels first heard Hitler speak (that is, at about the same time that he was writing his novel), it may actually have had this devastating effect upon him. On the other hand this passage and the one describing how he hears the same Speaker for a second time may well have been later interpolations.

Michael, however, is at a loss as to what he should do. He decides:

Life can only be maintained when one is ready to die for it. The working class has a mission in Germany. To save Germany is a mission of world-wide importance. For if Germany perishes the lights go out in the world.

Then the character of Michael takes on its other facet, that of Richard Flisges. He leaves the University to become a miner; he goes to live with a miner's family in a bare room with a bed, a chair and a table. He has only two books with him, the Bible and *Faust*. He lives now by the sweat of his brow. He is proud and lonely. He is still in love with Hertha—"I have loved Hertha Holk, and I will probably love her for ever. But she isn't the comrade to understand one fully." Later he transfers to a mine in Bavaria, where once more he hears the un-named Speaker:

That evening I sit in a big hall with a thousand others and see him again, hear him who awakened me.

Now he stands in the midst of a loyal congregation. He seems to have grown in stature. There is so much strength in him, and a sea of light gleams from those big blue eyes.

I sit among all those others, and it seems as if he were speaking to me quite personally.

About the blessing of work! Whatever I merely felt or guessed, he puts it into words. My confession and my Faith: here they gain shape.

I feel his strength filling my soul. Here is young Germany, and those who work in the smithy of the new Reich. Anvil still, but hammer before long.

Here is my place.

Around me are people I never saw and I feel like a child as tears well up in my eyes.

In October he learns that Ivan, now back in Petersburg, has been the victim of political assassination.

The last entry in Michael's short diary is that for 29th January. His landlady implores him not to go down the mine the next day. She had dreamed he had been killed by a stone. He laughs it off. But like Flisges, he is killed in an accident and the book concludes with a letter written by a miner to Hertha Holk telling her that Michael died with a smile and that in his copy of Nietzsche's *Zarathustra* he had marked the passage: "Many die too late and some too early. Strangely still sounds the lesson: Die at the right time!"

Michael was first published in 1929, some seven years after it was first written. Goebbels was then Gauleiter of Berlin, a Deputy of the Reichstag and Head of Propaganda for the Nazi Party. He would therefore have had every inducement to add sections to his early novel to imply that he had seen the light in his youth and proclaimed the coming of his Messiah. As we shall see, it was Hitler's blue eyes that impressed him when he first met his future Leader, as it was the blue eyes of the great Speaker that impressed Michael in the novel.

It is well-known that morality in Germany during the years following the defeat in 1918 declined in the direction of anarchy. Young girls even of good and respectable families felt it unfashionable to remain virgin, and sexual licence spread throughout the capital and the larger cities and freed itself from the control of the Catholic and Protestant churches and of the stricter traditions of the bourgeois German families. Though there was some attempt by the middle nineteen-twenties to re-establish the previous codes of respectable behaviour among the middle classes in Germany, the period during which Joseph Goebbels grew to manhood was the period of the greatest moral licence as well as of the greatest economic instability—for the mark which was still nominally worth a shilling in 1918 had utterly collapsed by 1923. If we are to believe the evidence in his diaries of 1925-26 Goebbels was as proud by then of his prowess as a lover as he was obsessed by his poverty.

The first record there is of a serious love-affair in Goebbels' life is his association with the girl called Anka Stahlhern.[12] It was not a happy love affair, and it seems to be reflected fairly faithfully in the account of the relations between Michael and Hertha given in Goebbels' novel. The love affair may well have lasted from about 1918 to as late as 1922. Prang recollects her to have been blonde, vivacious and good-looking; she was of good family and taller in stature than Goebbels. Anka's family was opposed to this infatuation and eventually succeeded in breaking it off, though it is evident from a certain number of letters that survive in a collection of private family papers that Goebbels and Anka made each other very unhappy.[13] This particular group of surviving letters (from the period 1918-20) also show Goebbels' gradual disillusionment with the Catholic Church. There is also a letter among the family papers in which one of Anka's aunts complains bitterly of Goebbels' behaviour to her niece, who has been seen leaving his rooms in the small hours. She is indignant that such a relationship should exist between her niece and a poor undergraduate quite unable to support a wife.

There is further evidence of a certain crisis at this time resulting from Goebbels' adolescent emotionalism in the survival of a 'Last Will and Testament' dated 1st October 1920.[14] It was written at a time when he had quarrelled with Anka and "wanted to leave this life which had become Hell for him", and it appointed his brother Hans "the administrator of his literary estate" (*literarischer Nachlassverwalter*) following his suicide. This grand term, suitable perhaps for an established writer whose works are valuable properties, was chosen by Goebbels to describe his mass of unpublished drafts of plays, poems and other miscellaneous writing, of which, although it had been rejected, he was inordinately proud. The survival of this document in the family papers would have been no more than a curiosity had it not become the basis for a prolonged legal dispute over Goebbels' copyrights. Hans on his death-bed was prevailed upon by his nurse to let her keep the papers intact after Goebbels had ordered his brother to destroy them during the last weeks of the war.

Anka was to reappear later in Goebbels' career; she came to him for a job during his first year as Minister. Goebbels helped her by getting her work on the editorial staff of *Die Dame*, but he was angry when he heard that she was in the habit of producing a copy of the Jewish poet Heine's love poems that he had once given her and boasting about the florid inscription that the Minister had written in his youth! He was, of course, much more embarrassed by that time to be revealed as a former admirer of Heine, whose work he had been instrumental in suppressing and burning, than as an admirer of a pretty girl. Anka died a few years after the war.

After the failure of his love-affair with Anka, Goebbels lost no time in forming a close friendship with another girl, Else. Fritz Prang, who claims that Goebbels' pose as a young philanderer was largely due to his desire to assert himself and show off, was himself friendly with a young school-teacher in Rheydt called Alma, and it was through her that Goebbels first met Else. He was back now living in Rheydt. His formal education was finished and the need for congenial work was uppermost in his mind in order that he might keep himself while he tried out all his vague plans for becoming a man of letters or a man of the theatre. Else, like Alma, was a school-teacher in Rheydt, though her family lived in Duisburg. She taught little Maria needlework and physical training. She became a friend of the Goebbels family and was therefore a constant visitor to their house where she came to know Joseph extremely well. She gradually fell in love with the brilliant, energetic, rootless young man; she recollects that the first thing that struck her about him was his very beautiful and expressive eyes; he was "all eyes", she says. Fritz, Alma, Joseph and Else formed for a period a happy group of young people, always going about together, sailing, walking (for Goebbels made light now of his limp), sitting in the cafés flirting and philosophising or enjoying the luxury of visiting the Prangs' wealthy home. Prang was becoming interested in politics; he joined the Nazi Party as early as 1922. But at this stage Goebbels had no thought other than for literature and journalism. One thing he impressed upon Else—his absolute belief in his own genius as a writer. Flisges, too, was a member of this group, adding his own politic nihilism and love of Dostoevsky to the discussions. Else recollects him to have been very handsome with the temperament of an idealist and a dreamer.

Goebbels was determined never to become a teacher. Everyone tried to persuade him to take up what seemed an obvious profession for so highly qualified a young man living penniless at home. He did not in fact mind how many occasional jobs he undertook for money, but he refused to bind himself to a fixed career by becoming a schoolmaster. His ambitions were larger and loftier, and he kept both Alma and Else busy copying out the manuscripts of his verse-plays, poems, novels and articles, because his handwriting, neat and meticulous though it always appeared at first glance, was notoriously illegible. But he had no success with this work. Everything he wrote was rejected by publishers and editors, including his story *Michael*. He lived at home and helped towards keeping himself by accepting such small opportunities for tutoring and book-keeping as came his way. Meanwhile he continued to write furiously.

It was Else who eventually secured him what appeared to be a more settled job when she found him to be on the point of suicide. Her family knew one of the deputy managers at the Cologne branch of the Dresdener Bank, and through him Goebbels was offered a minor clerical job. This he disliked heartily, and he gave little satisfaction to his employers. Nevertheless he stayed at the bank eight or nine months. Then it was Prang who came to the rescue; he found Goebbels a job calling out the position of shares at the Cologne Stock Exchange. The first professional use to which Goebbels put his beautiful voice was not making idealistic political speeches, as he would subsequently have had us believe, but shouting out the latest price for I. G. Farben, Krupp and the Vereinigte Stahlwerke. He had no contact whatsoever with the Ruhr Resistance movement against the French occupying forces, and it was his friend Prang, not himself, who secured the low Party number from the Nazis in the days when it was easy enough to get one. Later when a three- or four-figure number became proof of one's early allegiance to the Party, these numbers were only obtainable on the black market. Goebbels subsequently liked it to be thought that he was already a member of the Nazi Party in 1922, after having heard Hitler in Munich (like Michael in the novel) and having immediately signed up, receiving the party badge with the number 8762. However, it seems unlikely that he ever heard Hitler speak in 1922; it can be taken as certain he never sent the legendary letter to Hitler when he was imprisoned in Landsberg gaol, and he certainly undertook no propaganda work at all during 1923 when he was working in the bank and on the Stock Exchange. He did not in fact meet Hitler until late in 1925.

It was now that the seeds of Goebbels' radicalism and violent anti-

Semitism were being sown. Up to this time there had been little or no anti-Jewish feeling in him. His favourite professor had been a Jew; the family lawyer, Dr. Joseph, was a Jew of some cultural inclinations, and Goebbels liked talking with him; furthermore, Else herself was the daughter of a Jewess. As manuscript after manuscript came back from the publishing houses Goebbels became convinced that unless you were a Jew, "one of the boys" as he put it to Else, you could get nowhere in literature, the theatre, films or journalism. Else watched his anti-Semitism grow. The Jews, he felt, controlled the culture of Germany, and so rejected his magnificent writing out of hand. The celebrated Ullstein house was among the publishers that had rejected *Michael*.

In December 1922 Goebbels wrote Else a Christmas letter in which he laments in the purplest prose, reminiscent of *Michael*, the ruins of his young life and the hopeless position of being a rejected genius in a materialistic world. By this time the mark had so fallen in value that no one knew from day to day whether the millions of marks in their possession would in fact carry them through the week:

About to write you a few lines for Christmas. I know well enough that I can give you no lesson in Scripture nor any glad tidings . . .

The world has turned itself into a mad-house, and even some of the best are prepared to join the obscene dance round the golden calf. Worst of all, they will not admit it; they just try to explain it. New times, so they say, demand new men, and one should adjust oneself to new circumstances . . .

I cannot join them. I can see no peace, either in this world or in my own soul . . . Wherever spiritual values used to reign and Love was triumphant, now there is a deal of common worldliness. People call it keeping up with the times. Great Fate, how can I stand up to thee? I can no longer be thy faithful servant. They have all left thee, they have forsaken thy banner and have gone out into the world. And now it is my turn. I too must go. How then can I speak of peace at such a time? I must forsake my home and flee into the world.

> *Ein Tor zu tausend Wüsten, stumm und kalt—*
> *Wer verlor, was Du verlorst, macht nirgends halt.*

Flieg, Vogel, schnarr Dein Lied im Wüstenvogelton,
Versteck, Du Narr, Dein blutend Herz in Eis und Hohn.
Die Krähen schrein und ziehen schwirren Flugs zur Stadt.
Bald wird es schnein; weh dem, der keine Heimat hat.★

My dear, is this poem of desperate loneliness to be my only "message of cheer" for you this year? Is there no solace in this world of chaos and madness? Why then do I suffer so? Because I expected too much of this world?

What is it that makes me suffer so immeasurably? It is not that I have to go into the other world. It is because my own world has come to an end, and I myself have had to smash it.

But why did I do this? Was I forced to do so? Yes, I had to smash it, for however beautiful and heavenly it was, it was only a mere sham in the shallow lowlands of Olympus. It is only up there in the uplands that we can find the realm of the spirit, the realm of peace, the realm of love. Down here it all makes so little sense. . . .

And even if out there in the world the money-changers sneer and mock at real love, should not our love, my dearest girl, should not our great and abiding love still adorn our lives?

That is my only hope, and it is that hope that gives me even now the strength to walk out into the world with courage and with resolution.

I beg you solemnly, my dear, to help me keep and cherish this love of ours—a love so great that I would willingly sacrifice everything to it, if only for the reward of cherishing it with you in these blessed hours of the spirit and of peace and love.

Else watched Goebbels become moody and cynical. He began to talk again of suicide. These bouts of extreme depression alternated with the gaiety inspired by the company of his close friends. Alma says that she had never met anyone who laughed so heartily at the slightest

★ A gate to a thousand deserts mute and cold—
Whoever lost what Thou hast lost can nowhere rest.
Fly away, bird, and croak your song, your desert song,
Hide, oh fool, thy bleeding heart in ice and mockery.
The crows are croaking as they wildly wing their way to the town.
Soon it will snow. Woe to him who has no home!

provocation. Like so much in Goebbels' character it is difficult to say where moodiness ended and conscious posing began.

Else spent an increasing amount of time with Goebbels. She was quick, amusing, intelligent, feminine and very good-looking. Like the rest of his friends she called Goebbels Ulex, but she also had her own special name for him—Stropp. They would see each other home, going backwards and forwards through the night, walking and talking and making love, passing from his house to hers and then back again. When Goebbels was working in Cologne, only thirty miles from Rheydt, they wrote each other interminably long love-letters even though they were seeing each other at least once or twice a week. She confesses that she considered herself engaged to her lover from about 1922, that is before Goebbels left Rheydt to work in Cologne. When they went away together for short holidays to the sea, it was normally Else who had to pay the bills. Goebbels had no money whereas she had her teacher's salary and her family was comfortably off. They were to remain on terms of close friendship for almost five years.

Else considered that one day she would marry this bright, uncertain, moody man with the fine eyes, hands and voice. She even recalls discussing with Alma whether a man with a deformed foot would be a proper father for her future children; they decided this disability would not be congenital, since it was largely due to an operation sustained in childhood. His body was so slender that when she saw him from behind she thought he looked like a boy of twelve.

In spite of her extreme love for him, Else was always aware of the difficulties of the situation. Goebbels was all pride and no money. Sometimes he borrowed money from her. She had also to endure his moods. At one moment he was carefree and exuberant, a charming and witty companion. Then as suddenly he would change and become possessed by his suicidal depression. It was at these periods that they quarrelled. The engagement was broken and reassembled countless times with agonised protestations and reams of letters. Goebbels' mannered attitude to love and his innate vanity emerge in this letter to Else dated 5th June 1923, and written during the period he was working in Cologne:

My dear child,

You mustn't be angry about my not writing in ink; during my holidays my ink-pot has dried out and I think you will prefer having this sort of letter to having none at all . . .

Now I have moved in again with all my belongings, and being within my own four walls, I feel quite well. Your roses have found a spot right in front of your picture, and they smell beautiful, one even nicer than the other. At the bank nothing seems to have changed, and the only thing I was really interested in didn't happen. There will be no money before the 15th. That means you will have to wait another week.

Today, after office hours, I took a stroll through the town and I saw quite a few pretty things. What a pity that the damn trains aren't working and that we can't look at it all together. And as for the money? Well, we'll get it somehow. (Have you got any? No?? Me neither!)

It is high time for the two of us to be joined together. Whenever I am away from you I yearn for you and can find no rest either in work or at play. It seems to me as if we hadn't met for weeks and weeks, and yet I can count the hours with the fingers of my hands since we had to part. Why have we two, so much in love with one another, been born into so wretched a time? . . . Often I feel ashamed of being so distraught and depressed . . .

Cannot and should not a person these days be excused for occasional weakness and indecision? . . . Why must so many give me up as hopeless and consider me as lazy and unreasonable and un-modern? And yet I feel my laziness and unreasonableness and my being old-fashioned is the best thing about me . . .

I am firmly convinced that the time will come for me to use my real strength. I just want to preserve it and my heart and my conscience for a better cause. It isn't the industrial tycoons or the bank managers who will bring about the new millennium. It will be done by the few who have remained loyal to themselves and who haven't soiled their life with the so-called treasure of the world that has lost its gods. I am waiting for a new epoch to do what I cannot do today. And should that new epoch come too late for me, very well, it is quite commendable to be a mere pathfinder of a new and great epoch . . .

Good gracious, the clock is striking twelve and I have promised you to go to bed early, haven't I? If I could stay up longer I could fill another ten pages. But then, you want it this way. Hence—goodnight. Your ULEX.

If it was Flisges who first gave a nihilistic twist to Goebbels' early idealism, it was Prang who first introduced him to serious politics. His views, broadly speaking, were left-wing, and when his job at the bank terminated, he began the long search for permanent employment which eventually brought him into politics.

On 23rd January 1924 he sent a letter of application for work to the *Berliner Tageblatt*, enclosing a lengthy note on his career so far as it had gone. He claimed to have been working in his brother's business, which did not in fact exist. He asked for a salary of 250 marks a month, and a job on the editorial staff. He was unsuccessful. He also had ambitions in the theatre. Joachim von Ostau[16] recollects how a friend of his, a stage producer in the Rhineland, told him much later when Goebbels was famous that at this early period a young man had come to see him in his office, neatly but shabbily dressed, with burning eyes and a hollow face, and limping as if he had a club-foot, to ask for a job as assistant producer, or, indeed, for any job connected with the stage. He said that he was trying to write plays himself and that he was eager to become a producer, or at least help in stage production, that his name was Goebbels and that he had had no previous stage experience. What a chance lost, admitted the producer to Ostau. Here would have been the very man to produce crowd scenes with genius! Once again, Goebbels was deflected from his obvious ambitions and left free to give his talents to political agitation. Else recollects the bitterness of his disappointment when he failed to gain any foothold in the theatre.

It was during 1924 that Goebbels began his political career. Prang, as we have seen, had been an early convert to Nazism. Although his family was wealthy and utterly opposed to their son becoming involved in this kind of violent political activity, Prang persisted. He visited Munich to hear Hitler speak; he brought home copies of the Nazi pamphlets and journals and gave them to Goebbels who read them with growing excitement. Then one day he took him with some other friends to a meeting organised by a Socialist group; Prang and the rest dared Goebbels to get up on the platform and speak in the debate. He did so, Prang remembers, looking slight and shabby in a jacket too big for him. The audience booed him. When order was a little restored he began to speak.

"*Meine lieben Deutschen Volksgenossen*," he said.

This was right-wing with a vengeance; there were shouts and sneers and laughter. Goebbels stood there plainly unable to do anything. Someone shouted at him, "You capitalist exploiter!" Then his anger was roused. What had he got in his pocket to justify such an insult? Suddenly an instinct asserted itself. Somehow he seemed to know what it was he must do to defeat a cheap heckler. He shouted back at the audience.

"Will the man who has just called me a capitalist exploiter come up on this platform and empty his purse. I'll do the same, just to show which of us has the most money."

He poured his few coins out on the table. He won over his audience by this instinctive gesture; it was a political agitator's baptism of fire. He had taken his first, infant's step.

As his interest in politics grew during the winter of 1923-24, he attended more meetings with Prang, and on one occasion went with his friend to a congress at Weimar where the nationalistic speeches he heard so stirred his blood that he could not stop talking politics when the meetings were over and there was a chance to wine and dine at Prang's expense with a beautiful girl—the daughter of a rich landowner visiting the conference. She was far more interested in the social possibilities of the evening than in Goebbels' political enthusiasm. Prang eventually got rid of him and pushed politics aside in order to attend more fully to the opportunities the girl offered.

Among the odd jobs Goebbels was always ready to do there occurred one at this time that brought him directly into politics. He became secretary at one hundred marks a month to Franz von Wiegershaus, Reichstag Deputy of the Völkische Freiheitspartei, one of several small right-wing groups that shared substantially similar nationalistic views to those being so loudly advocated by the Nazis in Munich. Wiegershaus lived in Elberfeld and edited there the paper belonging to his minority, the *Völkische Freiheit* (*People's Freedom*). Goebbels' duties included helping to edit this journal, and soon he found that he was also expected to speak at public meetings. It was at these local meetings of the Freiheitspartei that he came into close contact with members of the Nazi movement, to which he seemed at first to have been strongly opposed. Towards the end of the year, however, he approached Karl Kaufmann, who was at that time Gauleiter of the Nazi Party for the Rhine-Ruhr District, and offered him his services. Kaufmann discussed the matter with Gregor Strasser, who was the leading figure in the movement in the north of Germany and who was considering at the turn of the year producing a small weekly journal to be what the Strassers rather bombastically called the Party's *geistiges Führungsorgan* (organ of spiritual leadership). Gregor was to be the publisher and Otto the editor, and they needed an editorial assistant. Hearing of Goebbels through Kaufmann, they wondered if he might be suitable for the position at a salary of two hundred marks a month, double what he was getting from Wiegershaus.

Otto Strasser arranged with Kaufmann to interview Goebbels. Kaufmann characterised the young man as "*sehr gescheit aber sehr wendig*" ("very intelligent but very unreliable").

Both Kaufmann and Otto Strasser confirm this account of Goebbels' introduction to the Nazi movement. Otto Strasser said how surprised he was by Goebbels' personal appearance at the first meeting. He felt that any political opponent could have pushed him over with one hand. He wore a grey suit, threadbare but tidy, and, in spite of it being late in the autumn, no overcoat. Although the chance of work with so important a man as Strasser must have meant a great deal to Goebbels, he showed no subservience. He seemed, in fact, almost haughty as he looked at Strasser, who remembers to this day the effect of his large and very penetrating brown eyes. He spoke very slowly and very pointedly in a voice of great beauty. He said that he thought the Völkische Freiheitspartei had no future.

"The leaders know nothing about the people," Strasser remembers him saying. "They are afraid of socialism, but I am convinced that only a kind of socialism and nationalism can save Germany. I don't mind admitting that it was your brother Gregor who helped me to understand these ideas. He is a genuine socialist, and it is his synthesis of socialist ideas and nationalist emotions that must be observed without any equivocation by us National Socialists."

Strasser noted the way he said 'us' as if he were already one of the Party's staff. Goebbels continued talking—"We are going to win the German working man for National Socialism. We are going to destroy Marxism!"

His eyes shone as he spoke. Then he raised his beautiful hands in a passionate gesture as he concluded his eloquent attempt to convince Strasser he was the man for the job. "As for the bourgeois refuse," he said, "we shall sweep that away into the dustbin!"

Strasser was impressed. More particularly he noted the young man's voice, which he handled as a violinist handles his instrument.

They decided to engage him on secretarial work for the Northern Party organisation and as editorial assistant for the future journal. Goebbels in fact stepped into the place vacated by another young man, Heinrich Himmler, whom the Strassers had dismissed for inefficiency. Himmler went back to his original occupation of poultry-keeping. His time was yet to come.

CHAPTER TWO

"History's Children"

DURING the next two years Goebbels was to establish himself with the National Socialist Party. By the time he entered the employment of the Strassers in 1925, the National Socialists were already reorganised after the unsuccessful putsch of 1923 and had begun the task of spreading their influence over Germany. Their two main centres were Berlin in the north, where Gregor Strasser (a pharmacist who was comfortably off and had great political aspirations) was in the ascendant, and Munich in the south, where Adolf Hitler had taken charge once more. Both men were ambitious for power, but the personal struggle between them was not yet joined.

Germany herself was in a state of unrest following the period of inflation and of passive resistance against the French and the Belgians. Independently of the rest of the Allies, France and Belgium had occupied the Ruhr in January 1923 and systematically begun to confiscate its coal. The Government of Stresemann had stabilised the currency at the expense of the working and middle classes, and in many parts of Germany there was open strife between the combined forces of the Army and Police and the workers, who were in a state of revolt in the main German cities. Blood flowed in the streets, and there were many killed in these savage riots. The State Governments of Saxony and Thuringia, which contained strong Socialist and Communist elements, were suppressed by force at the instigation of the Reich Government.

It was in this atmosphere of social and political tensions that the National Socialist Party began to flourish. The Party had originated as the Deutsche Arbeiter-Partei—the German Workers' Party—when Hitler discovered it in Munich in 1919 and became its seventh member.

Its funds at the time were 7.50 marks. It was violently revolutionary and anti-Semitic. In April 1920 Hitler left the Army to give the whole of his time to politics. He and Feder drew up for the Party a twenty-five point programme which even so early as this demanded, among many reforms, the self-determination of Germany, the abolition of the Treaty of Versailles, the exclusion of Jews from German citizenship, the abolition of unemployment, a widened application of the death penalty to those whom the Party regarded as anti-social, the formation of a National Army and the tight control of the press in the national interest.

Hitler himself, before he had enlisted in 1914, had spent many years destitute in Vienna. He was born in 1889, and was therefore eight years older than Goebbels. His native town was Braunau, on the Austro-German border. His father, who was illegitimate, was the son of Maria Anna Schicklgruber, but his name had been legalised to that of his father, Hitler, some twelve years before Adolf, his third child by his third wife, a cousin, had been born. He was a Customs officer, a difficult man given to marrying only when children had already been born or conceived by the women with whom he was associated. But like Goebbels' father, who belonged to the same class as Hitler's, he was ambitious for his son's education. Adolf was sent to a secondary school where he did reasonably well as a scholar. But at the age of eleven he was already determined to be an artist, a career to which his father (a man of sixty) was stubbornly opposed. Hitler met this opposition by refusing to work at school, and his education suffered accordingly. By the time he left school his father had died, and his indulgent mother let him study art in Munich. He failed in his ambition to enter the Vienna Academy of Fine Arts. When Goebbels met Hitler it was a case of the man who had failed as a writer meeting the man who had failed as a painter; a great deal of this early frustration stayed alive in them both to exacerbate their political temperaments. But, like Goebbels, Hitler when young learnt to love music, particularly the operas of Wagner, and to identify himself with romantic and nationalistic imagery. When his mother died in 1908 he was left, while still short of twenty, without any means of support. He went to Vienna where he was only too soon to adopt the life of a vagrant, sleeping in the open or lodging in a doss-house, his only friend a tramp called Hanisch with whom he eventually had a legal dispute over the money they earned together. Hitler and Hanisch formed a labouring team to do odd jobs. At times they sold the postcards which Hitler painted. For four years Hitler earned what money he could drawing architectural pictures, posters and advertisements. His passion was politics. He preferred talk to manual work, and he read a great deal on every subject from history to the occult. He was already violently anti-Semitic, anti-radical and anti-democratic, and even in the doss-house he was resentful to the point of hysteria of any opposition to his views. He loathed Vienna, and eventually moved on to Munich, where he led the same kind of lonely, vituperative, self-destructive life that had made him socially impossible in Vienna. On 1st August 1914 he stood in the great crowd that had assembled in the Odeonsplatz to greet the declaration of war. Heinrich Hoffmann, who was later to become Hitler's personal photographer, happened to be present and photographed the scene. Years later they examined the print and eventually found the Führer's ardent and excited face peering upwards in anticipation of the new life before him in the Army.

This was the man to whom Goebbels was to dedicate his life. Meanwhile, during 1925-26, he was to come to Hitler's notice and win his favour. They were to discover each other.

In 1920 Hitler had changed the name of his Party to the National-sozialistische Deutsche Arbeiter-Partei (N.S.D.A.P.). He designed the swastika banner, incorporating this ancient symbol of the sun which was used by early civilisations in many parts of the world. In 1921 he became Chairman of the Party and in the same year he formed the semi-military Sturm-Abteilungen (the S.A., or Storm Troopers) under the guise of a sports and athletic association. One of those associated with this movement was Rudolf Hess. By 1923 Bavaria had become a hotbed of nationalistic feeling and militarism, and one of the Party men entrusted with the work of organising this nationalist movement was a former officer of the Imperial German Army, Captain Röhm. At the same time Flight-Captain Hermann Göring was put in charge of the Storm Troopers.

Bavaria itself was politically in a state of revolt against the Reich Government in Berlin, and in the famous putsch of November 1923

Hitler and the National Socialists, in association with General Ludendorff, made their first abortive bid for power. The putsch failed, and in February 1924 Hitler was formally sentenced to imprisonment in Landsberg fortress, where he had been detained since his arrest in November and was living at ease with Rudolf Hess composing his political testament *Mein Kampf*. He was to be released the following December. The National Socialist movement may have seemed crushed, but all the elements which were to come together to revive it in 1925 after Hitler's release continued to ferment. Among those were Gregor and Otto Strasser; Gregor, who had joined the Party in 1921 and had taken part in the putsch, was in 1924 a Deputy in the Bavarian Diet and the founder of the *Berliner Arheiterzeitung* of which Otto was the editor. The paper became the mouthpiece of the Strassers' own version of National Socialism.

One of the main targets of National Socialist propaganda was Stresemann who, as the author of Germany's more conciliatory foreign policy, was concerned to secure the evacuation of the Ruhr and the Rhineland, to settle the problem of reparations and to build up Germany's economy through arranging foreign credits. To the National Socialists Stresemann's methods of achieving his aims simply represented appeasement of the Allies. When the Dawes Plan for reparations came into operation in 1924, foreign credit poured into Germany, and the Ruhr was gradually evacuated during 1924-25. (The Rhineland was not to be finally rid of Allied soldiers until 1930, leaving Germany free to rearm unmolested.) In 1925 the Locarno Treaty was signed guaranteeing Germany's frontiers with France and Belgium and obliging her to keep a specified area of the Rhineland demilitarised. Also in 1925 Hindenburg was appointed President at the advanced age of seventy-seven. He was to live long enough to make Hitler Chancellor.

In 1926 two other events roused the National Socialists. The first was the vexed question of the expropriation of the estates of former German reigning families, and the second the country's admission to the League of Nations. The first problem involved compensation, the princes on the one hand demanding exorbitant sums while the Socialists and Communists were calling for expropriation without any compensation at all. This question was to divide Strasser, Goebbels and Hitler. As for the League of Nations, Goebbels was within only seven years to pay a brief visit to Geneva as Hitler's personal representative at the League; on his return Germany withdrew from the League after a matter of days.

Goebbels was soon employed not merely as Gregor Strasser's secretary but also as a Party speaker and representative in Rhineland-Westphalia. He continued to be based at Elberfeld in the Rhineland-Nord *Gau*, or district, of the Party. His salary was 200 marks a month, and he worked in association with Karl Kaufmann, who was Gauleiter or Party Leader for the Rhineland-Westphalia district, and was in charge of the office in Elberfeld. By a stroke of good fortune, one of the rare links in the chain of Goebbels' diaries survives from this period and is preserved in the Hoover Institution at Stanford University in California. This diary, which is in manuscript and covers over two hundred pages in a series of notebooks, belongs to the period 3rd August 1925 to 16th October 1926. It is of the greatest importance in the history of Goebbels' career, because it was during this period that he came into direct contact with Hitler for the first time and finally decided to throw in his lot with him rather than remain with the Strassers. Only ten days after the last surviving page of the diary ends, on 26th October 1926, Hitler appointed him Gauleiter for the Party in Berlin.

The diary is written in the same strained, highfalutin style as the novel *Michael*, even though Goebbels was twenty-eight years old when he wrote the greater part of it. It is the only strictly private document of any length and importance written by Goebbels that is known to survive, a record of his life meant only for his own eyes. It is composed in the form of notes, and it contains a strange and revealing mixture of slang, obscenity and childish vituperation against any people or events he dislikes. Also there is the same literary posing that distinguishes the style of *Michael*, even though in this case he is writing only for himself. Mixed with occasional quotation—which ranges from 'Laugh, clown, laugh' to lines from Goethe's *Faust*—are gauche attempts in poetic prose to describe his private reactions, more especially to Hitler and to Else, the girl with whom he was in love.

For his relations with Else haunted him. Duisburg, where her family lived, Rheydt, where she worked, and Elberfeld were only thirty miles apart, but the demands of his new political work constantly took Goebbels round the whole of the Rhineland-Westphalia district to which he was attached. He lived in rooms which Else describes as commonplace, but as often as he could he went back to Rheydt to his parents' home, where Else was accepted as if she were already one of the family.

But Goebbels' temperament demanded difficulties. His vanity, his irregular mode of life, his prolonged adolescence and lack of emotional self-discipline, made him in many respects an impossible lover. As the result of his growing success as an agitator and his theatrical love of experiencing power over an audience, he was frequently out of hand, saying any vainglorious thing that came into his head. Still deeply disappointed at his lack of immediate success as a writer (he was convinced of his outstanding talent, even genius, and ceaselessly pointed this out to Else), he turned the venom of his frustration into public speaking. His anti-Semitism—which Else agrees was due initially to his rejection by the Jewish press, and in particular by the Ullsteins—became savagely over-developed, and his destructive radicalism fitted in with the Strasser line in National Socialism, which diverged from that of Hitler precisely in this matter.

With Else he blew hot and cold throughout the whole of this eighteen-month period, which was to be the last phase of their stormy love. In August he says: "She's got a crush on me like a flapper. She's so happy about it, I wouldn't grudge it her, and I love her with all my heart." In September she is "dear and full of goodness . . . grey, grey leavetaking . . . I have a great need for Else, thou sweet, sweet woman . . . Else writes in sweet blood"; in October "Else is coming. Joy on joy! Life is so beautiful! Laugh, clown, laugh . . . She is giving me a beautiful pullover. A sweet night; she is so dear and sweet and good to me. And sometimes I have to hurt her so much." However, there is also the warning note: "We've spent some hours full of happiness and pain. . . . Why, oh why must I hurt Else so? . . . How gruesomely beautiful life is." In November he writes, "With Else both bliss and trouble," while in December, following an occasion when she failed to meet him and offered no explanation, she sent him "a desperate farewell letter . . . How it hurts me to think that she is now so terribly lonesome", he goes on, and underlines the words. So he wrote and suggested a meeting in Düsseldorf, and adds in the diary, again under-lining the words to satisfy his need to talk to himself on paper, "If she doesn't turn up it's all over! Then we'll just have the bust-up which, one day, must come anyway."

They met in Düsseldorf, determined, according to Goebbels, to break it all off. But, still according to Goebbels, "she sobs and pleads. Hours full of torment. Until once again we found one another. It's the old story. But what *am* I to do about it? I must have a person to love. She is happy at times. And me? I don't want to talk about me. Maybe I can't have it otherwise. Maybe there's a curse on all my dealings with women. It's so tormenting a thought. It could make one despair."

And so the gushing words are resumed in the style of a teen-age boy. Yet, it must be remembered, Goebbels now was twenty-eight years old. Else's explanation gives another point of view. She remembers him now to have been boyishly energetic and as moodily tempera-mental as an adolescent. In spite of the way he writes in his diary, she claims it was always he who pursued her, and not the reverse. She was fond of him and gave way to him, but as time passed and he did not change she wanted more and more to break their engagement off. But at Düsseldorf he prevailed once more, pleading himself as he claims she pleaded with him.

So relations were resumed again. In January it is "lovely hours. . . . Walked along the Rhine arm-in-arm. No money for lunch. And yet so happy, so contented . . . farewell, you sweet woman." On 31st January he writes succinctly: "Sent Else a nasty letter"; no more. In February he could afford to be patronising: "She had tears in her eyes when she left. How small and touching are her little troubles! It is pouring with rain." In April he awaits her with passion. "There is so much yearning in me," he cries.

By early summer Goebbels, as we shall see, was suffering from in-ordinate vanity because of the special attentions paid to him by Hitler. In June the diary begins to refer to renewed differences between the lovers, and in the middle of the month he writes: "Else sends me a brief and frightfully matter-of-fact letter breaking it all off. What am I to do? She is, of course, completely right. We can no longer be even comrades to one another. Between us there is a whole world."

Fundamental to these differences now was the fact that Else had Jewish blood in her veins and belonged by temperament and upbringing to the comfortable middle class of the Rhineland. But by the end of July she was back again. "Letter from Else. Forget the past. That is Else all over! I sometimes can't understand at all why she loves me so. In a way she is really a little petty bourgeoise." Nevertheless he accepted her return with some display of ardour. "Am I a woman-eater?" he asks himself after they had met by chance when she joined the train at Duisburg just as he was hoping to establish satisfactory relations with a pretty woman he had found on the journey! But you cannot eat your cake and have it. In September it was all over. "Else wrote me a farewell letter. So be it. *In Gottes Namen!*" They met to say good-bye. "Oh how it hurts. She goes, never to come back." Within a few weeks he was in Berlin for good, and the tortuous, tormenting love affair was finally over.

It is not without interest that Else's friend Alma was at any rate for a while in his thoughts even when he was ostensibly engaged to Else. He writes as if he had a brief affair with her possibly when Else was on holiday in Switzerland during August 1925. There are slight references to other girls which suggest casual love affairs. And Goebbels' sense of the dramatic could not be satisfied unless he was able to toy with his memories from the past. The troubled relation with Anka had lasted almost as long as the affair with Else, and he likes to recall it now and then. "These days I think so much of Anka, *dieses prächtige Frauen-zimmer*. . . . Anka, I'll never, never forget you . . . She certainly doesn't think of me . . . Why did Anka have to leave me alone? Was it a breach of promise? And if so, was it on her part or mine? I mustn't think about these things. Only work can relieve me of my anguish."

People who are uncertain in their understanding of human relationships frequently seek an emotional substitute in pets. The Goebbels family had a pet Alsatian called Benno, and throughout the period of his work in Elberfeld Goebbels was always trying to get hold of Benno.

in spite of the unsuitability of his mode of life for looking after an animal, particularly one of Benno's size. But Benno was another outlet for Goebbels' ill-spent emotions, and he frequently appears in the diary. "Benno's such a clever animal," he remarks after taking him for a walk in Rheydt. "Dogs so often put us humans to shame by their loyalty and their kindness." In June 1926 he was making one of his efforts to get the family to send Benno to Elberfeld. "I look forward to getting this good friend to live with me again. Maybe he will be my only real friend." Later, when Benno had arrived, he notes: "Benno lying under the bed and snoring away. He is like me, alternating between complete inertia and wild bouts of chasing. In a way, that is what I really want. A bit of fighting for me is as important as water for a fish."

The struggle that he made out of his work and the worry that this gave him he relieved by ceaseless intrigue to better his junior position in the *Gau* office. For it is now, so late in his life, that his prolonged adolescence seems to have passed and his character as a mature man began to take its shape. He still, however, had a boyish yearning for his week-ends at home with the family, though his relations with his father were by no means happy. To both himself and to them he played the part of the over-worked enthusiast who always had a mountain of administrative labour waiting for him whenever he returned from the crowded halls where he had rushed to address audiences that hung gripped and tense on his two-hour orations before relaxing into prolonged applause. He is coyness itself about his need for sleep, even though he is, after all, only addressing his own image on paper. "Work galore . . . I'm fagged out. I ought to sleep for a year. . . . Lots of post and work. I'm so tired, so tired. . . . I look forward to Christmas! That means quiet, quiet! . . . Good night!" he says, peeping at himself from his notebook. "So tired, so tired" recurs on page after page.

The theme became an obsession with him. "I am desperate. I am up to my eyes in work. I don't know where to turn. I've bitten off more than I can chew. . . . And I must do everything alone. Horrible slave-driving. . . . Mother, help me. I can't go on. I barely weigh a hundred pounds. They are exploiting me with far too much work."

In May 1926 he wrote: "I shouldn't like any more to have so much talking to do. Much rather devote myself to the paper and administration. Though even there I would have more work than is good for my health." On 29th October 1925, his twenty-eighth birthday, he says: "I'm getting old. It makes me shudder to notice it. My hair is beginning to fall out. On the way to getting bald. But in my heart I want to remain young for ever and ever." Three months later he writes: "I look completely emaciated. Horrible!" Even the suspicion he might be ill excites him. In September he feared for his nerves: "I shall have a nervous breakdown. I am absolutely a nervous wreck." In December he suffers a typical attack of depression: "Terribly depressed once again. . . . At such times I suffer the most horrible hours of my life. Particularly when quite alone in a slow train home. Sometimes I *yearn* for a *family* and *peace*. Stay still, my heart!!" He hated the trains and the long hours away. "Once again homelessly *drifting* for a *whole week*. Oh, what an *awful, merciless* world! . . . Woe to him who hasn't a home!" He even feared he had tuberculosis when he had a pain in his back. However, he may well have rather fancied these depressions as a necessary element in his complex and interesting character. In September 1925 he says the opposite: "Off again soon. Back to the gypsy life. But I love that sort of life very much," and again later on: "Now the travelling starts again. . . . There's a relief in the energy of moving about." With another burst of coyness he calls himself "you old restless". He rather fancied his peripatetic nature.

Goebbels' diminutive salary of 200 marks a month (£10 according to the value of the time) was a constant worry to him. Virtually the first entry of the diary is: "No money." On 14th August he cries out to himself: "Money. Money. Money. I am completely broke. It's enough to make one sick." The following day he had to telegraph home for assistance, and there are many later references to the inadequacy of his salary to make ends meet. In January 1926 he complains that his debts are weighing on him.

Usually it was to the family that he turned to get him out of financial trouble. But life at home was not always easy, mainly because of his father. "Father is always the same, a good, well-meaning bourgeois."

"Two days in Rheydt. Much joy, but also a good deal of trouble and annoyance." The main cause of the trouble between father and son was Goebbels' apostasy. "From home not a word for quite some time now. The family is angry with me. I am an apostate." "I have got into a hell of a lot of trouble so that I wouldn't mind leaving again right away. But I don't, because I don't want to hurt mother." But generally his visits home were happy ones. "They spoil me with all their blessings and their kindness and love." "Tomorrow I will stay home. That is what I look forward to with all my heart. I suppose that at home, after all, they are really my best friends. How much have I lost? And what have I got in exchange for it?" This last remark was written in August 1926 when he had already secured the attention of Hitler.

His relations with the Party were as deliberately complex and passionate as his relations with women. In August 1925, when the diary begins, he had worked for only a few months and was in a very junior position. Nevertheless his vanity was roused because of his success as a speaker, and he set himself out to charm his immediate superior in the *Gau* office at Elberfeld, Karl Kaufmann, and his ultimate superiors, the men who had engaged him, Gregor and Otto Strasser of Berlin. His duties were threefold—to speak as an agitator, to edit a new political magazine sponsored by the Strassers, the *National-sozialistische Briefe* (the first issue of which appeared in October 1925), and to attend to organising work in the office.

When Gregor Strasser proposed in August to found the journal, Goebbels' heart leapt up. He saw himself rising to heights in the North German Party group—"headquarters, Elberfeld; senior partner, me," he writes with joy. "A paper to come out every fortnight. Publisher, Strasser. Editor—*moi*! Just as we want it." Now he was all in favour of Strasser's radical interpretation of National Socialism because through it he could channel his ambitions. By September he was absorbed in preparations for the first issue.

Reading the diary quite literally one would be excused for assuming that, apart from Kaufmann, Goebbels was the senior official and responsible directly to Strasser. Yet until Hitler seduced him from Strasser, mainly in the summer of 1926, Kaufmann claims that he held only a very junior position and had no say in Party policy. He was solely the agent of the Strassers and Kaufmann. It was therefore his day-dream of power and his mounting vanity that made him write as if he were the equal of his employers, and after a while in some measure their superior.

Until his later conversion, Goebbels was entirely for the Strassers. For example, in October he writes: "Had a long and comprehensive talk with Strasser, and complete unanimity was reached." "Strasser speaks. Splendid . . . With wit and keenness and irony and everything." "Strasser isn't nearly as much of a bourgeois as I took him to be." In November (at Berlin) Otto has his turn of favour. "Strasser's brother is just as decent a chap. I want to make him my friend." On this same occasion Goebbels was "deeply impressed" by Ludendorff who spoke to him "for a long time". In December he manages to get in a gesture of superiority when he was asked, according to Kaufmann, to do some drafting on a Party programme. Goebbels himself writes as if they had turned to him in despair. *"Strasser's draft is inadequate,"* he writes, underlined. In January, however, it is "complete agreement on everything". In March "Strasser is quite a man!" and "What a wonderful Bavarian type he is. I am very fond of him." After this he was gradually to become more critical as he fell increasingly under Hitler's spell.

In a similar way at first he made up to Kaufmann, the district Gauleiter, to whose staff he was attached. Kaufmann, nevertheless, was slightly younger than Goebbels which put him at some disadvantage. In September he reached the stage of using the intimate term of address with his chief: "Now I am calling Kaufmann *du*. I am very fond of him." In October they helped to celebrate each other's birthdays which happened to fall in the same month. Goebbels was very pleased: "Letter from Kaufmann. Birthday letter. What a dear, kind chap! It's made me very happy. . . . Kaufmann my loyal, good comrade!" However, Kaufmann, unlike the Strassers, had the misfortune of working in the same office as his subordinate, and this soon made him the object of criticism and the subject for intrigue. By November there are references to "having it out with Kaufmann". In January he adopts a new, superior attitude to his chief. "Am worrying about my friend Karl Kaufmann. He is much too unbridled.

Perhaps I can help him. . . . Kaufmann is too good-natured and soft."
On 1st February he wrote: "Kaufmann doesn't treat me as a friend
should be treated, and I stand here with my hands tied."

When confronted recently with the diary, Kaufmann did not know
whether to laugh or be angry. Goebbels, he claims, was an inveterate
intriguer and as jealous as a woman if his chief paid attention to anyone beside himself. The troubles recorded in the diary were mostly
of his own making through his suspicion that he was not for some
reason the centre of Kaufmann's attention, and he could bear no form
of criticism whatsoever. These were the 'differences' that had constantly to be cleared up with Kaufmann inside or outside the office. In
January Goebbels becomes openly scornful: "Am worried greatly
about Karl Kaufmann. He is sometimes so strange and unsure of himself." "Kaufmann seems to be toying with a dictatorship, but he is
much too soft to be a Führer." "I fear," he says at the end of the
month, "that I am going to lose Kaufmann before long." He was
paying too much attention, apparently, to someone else. In February
Kaufmann "is so confused and on edge. Much of it, of course, is his
own fault." February in any case was a month of crisis between Hitler
and the Strassers; Goebbels records 'heart-to-heart' talks with Kaufmann to get things off his chest. "I would like to hug him," he concludes with satisfaction. But by April he goes so far as to think that
Kaufmann is jealous of his success. Goebbels' ambition was beginning
to batten on Hitler.

The secret of Goebbels is always that he must be loved and admired,
a feminine trait in his nature which was so strongly pronounced that
he only loved those who openly and emphatically loved him. Hitler
was astute enough to discover and exploit this weakness, whereas both
Kaufmann and the Strassers grew weary of his intrigues and tantrums.

At the same time they were impressed by his undoubted talents, and
he shared quite genuinely the radical slant to their particular brand of
National Socialism. His experiences had made him antagonistic to the
society that had not recognised him, and his earlier friendship with
Richard Flisges had associated in his mind the excitement of distinction
with the vanity of considering himself an idealist. Even when he
became wholeheartedly Hitler's man, Goebbels was never to lose his

basic radicalism. The Locarno Treaty of October 1925 he notes as a thing of shame for Germany, accepted "because the capitalists want it. They alone have influence nowadays." Later he writes: "My spirit, that is the Socialist spirit, is on the march", "We are Socialists and we do not want to have been Socialists in vain" and "We must be strong, so as to fight for Socialism. *Gut so!*" The memory of his dead friend was associated in his mind with this belief—"Richard Flisges," he says, "taught me its deepest meaning through his own life and death."

Meanwhile he gained great experience as a speaker and agitator. The diary is full of self-praise describing the thousands who flocked to hear him first of all in the towns of the Ruhr district, but soon in many other parts of Germany. Kaufmann and others state that the thousands should read hundreds, and hundreds, tens; Goebbels liked to add rhetorical noughts to his audience statistics. But granted this amiable weakness, there is no doubt that he learned his trade rapidly and well. His theatrical instinct and his desperate need to overcome his subconscious sense of inferiority combined to make him use every means in his power to sway the emotions of his audience. "Yesterday a group-evening. I told them about my growing fame and I had a most devout (*andächtig*) audience." "After three hours, Bamberg. Straight on to the meeting. They receive me with considerable acclaim. I am requested to speak and they listen as devoutly as if they were in Church." "And then I preached (*predigte*) for two hours. A breathlessly spellbound audience. And at the end they waved to me and cheered me to the echo. I am dead tired." "Such an exciting meeting there is not a dry thread on me." "That evening I spoke in Landshut. Everybody raving with enthusiasm. A few very young women seem to be quite crazy about me." Even poor Benno was expected to go to meetings. "Last night I spoke at Düsseldorf and Benno sat quietly with his snout pointed, listening with what seemed considerable interest."

These are the reactions of a performer, not of a man whose prime concern is with his political beliefs. One remembers Goebbels' desire to work in the theatre. As we shall see, he rehearsed like an actor, and was always more concerned with the effect he had on an audience than with the significance of what he was saying. That was merely the script through which he fulfilled his desire to make an overwhelming public appearance. He was a most effective exhibitionist. He wanted to be loved. Almost every page of the diary records his success; only rarely does he spit out because he found an audience which was callous, indifferent or reactionary in the face of his talent. Equally he is contemptuous of most of the other Nazi agitators. After hearing a particularly dull speech he exclaims: "That is not the way to make revolutions. The dash of champagne is missing." Or again: "I refrained from speaking, but someone else talked drivel."

If the dash of champagne meant the capacity to incite an audience, he was himself beginning to enjoy the spectacle of violence. There are constant references to free-for-all fights with the Communists, fights which the Nazis were learning how to promote. On 23rd November 1925 he records that at Chemnitz the Communists were "kicking up a row. At the end of the meeting a ferocious free-for-all. 1,000 beer-mugs broken. 150 wounded, 30 seriously. Two dead." Exaggerated though these figures no doubt are, the police frequently stepped in and banned meetings, and Goebbels was himself more than once interrogated by the police who, he said, wanted to bring charges against him for causing a breach of the peace. Goebbels only cared if they stopped him from public speaking; the violence the meetings provoked was part of his business. "In so many German towns blood is flowing for our ideas," he says. When a meeting in Munich was raided, his comment is: "So what! I don't care a tinker's cuss! After all, we are spoiling for a fight, aren't we? They will get to know us yet."

It is not without significance that he so constantly refers to preaching. "I want," he says, "to be an apostle and a preacher." The apostate who had lost his faith still needed the flamboyance of a belief. He was for the most part incapable of true emotion; his nature did not extend beyond mere emotionalism. Goebbels' only true feeling was for himself, and he was rapidly developing egomania.

Without this understanding of Goebbels it is impossible to appreciate what happened when he finally met Hitler. At first he had followed the Strasser line in opposing the Munich school of Nazism and Hitler himself. For example, in September 1925 he writes: "In Munich some stinking trouble in the movement;" and in October: "Telegram from Munich. Am supposed to speak there. Kiss my arse! Letter to Strasser. Hitler not coming. He has been grousing about me. If he reproaches me on 25th October, I'm quitting. I can't bear this any longer. To give one's all, and nothing but reproaches from Hitler himself! ... In Munich the bastards and intriguers are agitating. Bloody fools couldn't stand having a man with brains near them. Hence the struggle against Strasser and myself ..." and so on, day after day, Goebbels always directly associating himself with the leadership in spite of his junior position in the district office.

He was automatically opposed to Hitler because Hitler was, or appeared to be, against him. However, the famous public attack by Goebbels on Hitler at Hanover never in fact took place. It is merely one of the many legends associated with his name.

During this crucial period in the development of the Nazi movement two conferences important in the history of the Party took place.[1] The first, convened by Strasser, was held in Hanover on 25th January 1926; Hitler was not present but sent Gottfried Feder as his representative. The main point at issue was Nazi policy in the referendum concerning the expropriation or otherwise of the property belonging to the former German royal houses. Strasser's strongly Socialist principles demanded expropriation; Hitler, representing the opportunist and essentially non-Socialist opinion of the Munich school, opposed this. Hitler was by now associating with Hohenzollern princes and members of certain aristocratic families prepared to bring a certain social distinction as well as money to the movement. At the Hanover conference, however, Strasser won hands down and an open revolt was staged against Hitler's attempt to dominate the Party because this faction liked to stress the 'socialist' aspect of National Socialism. It was on this occasion that Goebbels has always been alleged to have said: "In these circumstances I demand that the petty bourgeois Adolf Hitler be expelled from the National Socialist Party." Had he done so, he would have boasted about it in his diary. In fact, he never said the words; they were spoken by Bernhardt Rust, who was nevertheless subsequently to become Nazi Minister for Education. Kaufmann, who was among those present, remembers this quite clearly. The con-

ference, which was attended by some twenty to thirty Party representatives, took place in Rust's flat, and Goebbels was one of the most
vituperative of the speakers for the appropriation of the royal property.
But his principal aim, as Kaufmann recollects, was to achieve a personal
success in the meeting. He was, after all, only voicing the view of the
majority present. The conference was a very excited one lasting for
several hours and Kaufmann claims that Gregor Strasser, who was in
control of the discussion, rejected Rust's proposal about Hitler as out
of order and exaggerated. Feder said nothing except that the outcome
of the meeting spelled trouble.

Goebbels recorded certain reactions to the conference, but not at any
length. He claims to have orated about Russia and "our potential
relations". "I spoke for about an hour with everyone listening in
breathless tension. Then they all agreed with me enthusiastically. We
have won . . . Finish. Feder nowhere. Strasser shakes my hand."

Goebbels was at this time writing articles and making speeches which
implied that although Communism was misguided it was the potential
ally of the brand of revolutionary National Socialism that he was promoting. "We will never get anywhere," he wrote in the *Briefe*, "if we
lean on the interests of the cultured and propertied classes. Everything
will come to us if we appeal to the hunger and despair of the masses."
In an article for the *Völkischer Beobachter* he wrote: "The Soviet system
does not endure because it is Bolshevist or Marxist or international but
because it is national—because it is Russian." Von Pfeffer remembers
thinking that Goebbels at one time had Marxist leanings.[2] If this kind
of sentiment pleased the Strassers, it certainly did not please Hitler,
who was feeling his way to power through other channels besides the
angry proletariat.

The second conference to discuss these differences was convened by
Hitler for 14th February at Bamberg in his own southern territory.
Goebbels was told he must attend along with Gregor Strasser. This
arrangement does not seem to have been very welcome; Otto Strasser
believes he was frightened of going. "*Ich muss danach mit nach Bamberg*"
("I suppose I'll have to go along to Bamberg") is how Goebbels put it
in his diary. But he adds: "In Bamberg we must lure Hitler on to our
terrain." What he disliked really was the prospect of having to speak

at a conference where his views would be necessarily unpopular.

By this time, of course, Goebbels had met Hitler on a number of occasions, and heard him speak. It was Kaufmann who had first introduced him in the autumn of 1925 after a speech which Hitler had made in Elberfeld at the Evangelisches Vereinhaus. The local Party representatives were gathered together afterwards in a small committee room to meet Hitler, and it was then that Kaufmann presented him as Gregor Strasser's secretary who was doing so well with his editorial work on the new Party journal, the *Briefe*. Kaufmann remembers the formality of the introduction and the handshake that followed; Goebbels appeared reserved and distant.

In the diary, however, Goebbels' first account of his reactions to Hitler occurs on the occasion of a subsequent meeting at Hanover. He was evidently greatly impressed. He refers to Hitler's "big blue eyes! Like stars!" He shook Goebbels' hand "like an old friend". "I am *very happy* to see him," writes Goebbels. This was 2nd November 1925, when he belonged, strictly speaking, to the Party opposition. When he heard Hitler speak he was carried away. "That man's got *everything to be a king.* A popular leader born and bred (*geborener Volkstribun*). The *coming dictator.*" Goebbels claims they talked at length ("long disputations") until he had to catch his train to Elberfeld in the early hours of the morning. Three weeks later, on 23rd November, they met again, when Hitler spoke at another meeting. "My joy is great," says Goebbels. "He *greets me like an old friend.* He *speaks to us* all the evening. I *can't hear enough of it.* He *gives me his picture* with a greeting to the Rhineland inscribed '*Heil Hitler!*' . . . I *would love* to have *Hitler as my friend.* His *picture* stands *on my table.* I *could not bear to have to doubt* that man! Good night!"

Such was the background to Bamberg—Goebbels identified with the opposition, yet fascinated by Hitler's magnetic personality. According to the diary Goebbels went to this second conference in a proselytising spirit: "No one seems to have any faith left in Munich. Elberfeld is to be the Mecca of German Socialism." It was then that he added his declaration: "I want to be an apostle and a preacher."

Legends, once they are well propagated, have an adhesive quality in history. Goebbels was subsequently to encourage the story that Bamberg was the great occasion of his public abandonment of Strasser and adherence to Hitler, and this is the account that has so far appeared in all the standard histories of the Nazi movement. But once more the legend is nowhere near the truth.

Goebbels simply records in this private and unedited diary his disgust at Hitler's reactionary views on every major point of policy—restitution to the German princes, the sacredness of private property, the destruction of Bolshevism, Italy and Britain as Germany's allies, the old twenty-five-point programme still the best, and so on. "I am flabbergasted," he writes. "What a Hitler! A reactionary! Astonishingly clumsy and unsure of himself. . . . Brief answer by Strasser. *Ach Gott*, can we cope with these people down here? A mere half-hour's discussion after Hitler's four-hour speech and summing-up. I cannot get a word out. I am quite flabbergasted. We drove to the station. Strasser is almost demented with rage . . . I feel like crying. . . . That was one of the greatest disappointments of my life. I can no longer believe in Hitler! This is the most terrific thing. My faith is shattered and I feel shattered." But Goebbels' opportunism soon reasserted itself before the spectacle of Hitler's social and political success. He contented himself with shouting a slogan or two just to please Kaufmann and the Strassers.

Kaufmann confirms that Goebbels said nothing at Bamberg and that Strasser was angry because his assistant, who was by now regarded as one of their chief spokesmen, had let him down by remaining silent. In Kaufmann's view Goebbels did not speak because he was shrewdly aware that it would not be in his own best interests to do so. What impressed him about Munich was the money that Hitler seemed able to command compared with the poverty of the movement in Elberfeld. Hitler always had cars at his disposal, and Goebbels loved the attention which Hitler seemed ready to show him. And Hitler cunningly arranged for Goebbels to arrive in advance on 15th February to speak at a separate public meeting where he records that he received "considerable acclaim". The extent, therefore, to which Goebbels let the Strassers down at Bamberg was that he did not speak up against Hitler's policy. Nevertheless, within two days Gregor Strasser had calmed down and both he and Otto received Goebbels in Berlin. Otto Strasser admits now that he has in the past exaggerated the degree of the rupture between his brother and Goebbels following Bamberg. He was originally responsible for the slogan "the treason of Bamberg" in connection with Goebbels and in his book *Hitler and I* claims that Goebbels spoke to the effect that Hitler's argument had convinced him and that Strasser was in the wrong. Goebbels himself was subsequently very content to let this apparent act of faith in Hitler stand to his credit. But in fact, he remained in constant touch with both the Strassers and Kaufmann during the ensuing days and weeks, and their intention was to have a further, more private discussion with Hitler to iron things out. "Telegram from Strasser. Must not rush things. . . . The suggestion being that Kaufmann, Strasser and I are to go to Hitler to have it out with him more thoroughly." He still refers to the Munich group as political children, *politische Kinder*. But, he says: "We have the feel of history. History's children . . . that's us!"

But the children in Munich had what Goebbels wanted, a certain amount of money. Hitler lived in a comfortable flat and had a car with a chauffeur. In Elberfeld Goebbels was sure he had less than his due from Kaufmann to whom he kept talking for endless hours until they must all have been glad to see the back of him when he went away to speak—"a great annoyance, what with my being practically indispensable here in Elberfeld". He became intensely jealous of a man called Helmuth Elbrechter, a dentist who was on the fringe of the movement and exercised a certain influence over Kaufmann who was some years his junior.[3] It is very evident that Elbrechter disliked and distrusted Goebbels, who was aware of this and saw at once intrigue against himself as well as lack of his due in appreciation. The diary during the spring of 1926 is filled with vituperation as a result of Elbrechter's alleged intrigues with Kaufmann.

It was at this time that Hitler began to invite Goebbels to speak in other parts of Germany and particularly in Munich and Bavaria. He went to Munich in April with Kaufmann. A car was waiting for them at the station, and later Hitler telephoned them at the hotel and then came round to see them. "He is very, very kind to me and he lends us his car for the afternoon." He addressed two meetings, the last in Hitler's presence, and received the usual ovation. "At the end Hitler hugs me. My eyes are full of tears. I am happier than ever in my life. Through the milling crowds to the waiting car. Thunderous shouts and heils." Then he had supper with Hitler, and could not sleep afterwards for sheer excitement. The following morning, however, Kaufmann criticised the speech. Goebbels put it down to envy. But the truth of the matter was that the lionising treatment given him by Hitler was already bearing fruit. "Well, he may have something in these arguments on foreign policy," writes Goebbels after another session with Strasser and Hitler. "After all he has thought it over a great deal. I am beginning to be quite happy about it. I recognise him as my leader quite unconditionally. I bow to the greater man. To the political genius!"

The honeymoon with Hitler had begun.

Yet he went to visit the Strassers' parents in Landshut and talked again to Gregor. "He is very satisfied. That evening in the soft spring air, wandering through Strasser's home town. What peace! *Ach, du Gregor.*" Then he went back to the magic of Munich. "Ach, those Munich women, so beautiful! And the sun!" Hitler asked him to dinner and produced a girl for company. The next morning Hitler's car came again, but Goebbels by now was equal to the occasion. "I had flowers for him and he seemed ever so pleased." It was like a romance. When he had at last to leave he wrote: "Farewell, Munich! I love thee!" He had to speak in Stuttgart, and Hitler, accompanied by Hess, took him there by car. Hitler arrived clothed in his famous 'autodress', with the leather jacket suitable for motoring in open vehicles in the 'twenties. Goebbels the radical was most impressed by the snobbery of it all. "Lunching in a small inn. He is being recognised. Lots of cheering and back-slapping." He made his speech in Stuttgart as effective as he could to please Hitler. Evidently he succeeded. "He hugs me as soon as he sees me. He praises me to the skies. I think he has really quite a soft spot for me."

His speaking tours were now more widely spread, and among the places at which it was arranged that he should speak was Hamburg. He drove through the amusement quarter, including the Freudlose Gasse that gave its name to G. W. Pabst's famous silent film which appeared about this time. Goebbels' puritan sensuality was roused at

the sight—"The Joyless Street. Tarts standing in front of every door-
way, beckoning. Practically naked, most of them. Some of them
disgusting to look at. To buy a body! How can a man do such a
thing? For money! . . . But whose fault is it? To be locked into that
ghetto of lust! On the streets one can see blonde girls hugging Jewish
pedlars, and the police do nothing about it. In fact, they laugh. Such
is bourgeois society. All of it either lust or business. Oh, let's get out
of here. Back home. But I cannot go to sleep. Is it because I feel as if
I bore part of the guilt?" He was glad to leave Hamburg; he was on
his way back to Bavaria.

Again there was trouble with Kaufmann, who had written to say
that Goebbels was "lacking in the necessary toughness". Goebbels
blamed this on the intrigues in his absence from Elberfeld of his scapegoat Elbrechter, the enemy. "Poor Kaufmann," he writes as if more
in sorrow than in anger. Strasser believes that by now even Goebbels
must have felt some pang of conscience about moving over to Hitler's
faction. Nevertheless, on the train south he was not too worried to
notice "on the side opposite a lovely wench peacefully asleep. Quite a
girl. Yearning? You bet!" He was reading a book about Rasputin.
"How much elementary strength in that fellow, when compared with
sickly intellectuals." It was about this time, too, that he first saw
Eisenstein's film *Battleship Potemkin*, which had recently reached
Germany and was causing a sensation. Kaufmann had strongly recommended it. Goebbels never ceased to think it a masterpiece of propaganda.

Now, however, it was spring. It was Bavaria. It was Hitler. Elberfeld lay on his conscience like a hidden sore, but Hitler played his cards
well. "A two-hours' speech, and in the course of it he praises me to the
skies, and quite publicly too. Later he takes me home in his car. He
seems quite fond of me." It was sour to return to the Elberfeld office
from this. "As for me, no one seems to care twopence. As if I hadn't
done a thing! . . . There is an evil spirit about, making my heart ache,
and somehow I feel Kaufmann is behind it." He wonders whether he
ought to discuss his troubles when he next meets Hitler. Meanwhile
there was always Kaufmann to worry at. "Well, well, people do
repeat again and again an old saying: 'Politics spoil the character.' I

63

would put it better than that: 'Politics teach us what sort of a character a person really is . . .' I *must* have these things sorted out. Can't do a proper job of work otherwise."

On 10th June there appears a significant entry. "There is a lot of talk about sending me to Berlin as a sort of saviour. No thanks! I would hate to live in that wilderness of brick and mortar." This seems to have momentarily frightened him back into Kaufmann's arms. "He is my good friend again. I cannot be cross with him for any length of time. I love persons with a kind heart." But two days later he bursts out: "The whole *Gau* is in a bad way owing to Kaufmann's slackness . . . I am fed to the teeth with the whole bloody organisation. How can we ever make Germany free with rabble such as that? . . . My only hope is that Hitler will take me to Munich so as to get me out of all this muck here. Everything now depends on his decision. Does he want me? . . . Sleep! Oh, if only one didn't have to wake up again at all!!"

And so he was ready for Hitler who was due to speak in Elberfeld. "I revere and love him," he writes gushingly. Hitler arrived, spoke at closed meetings in the district (he was forbidden at this time to speak in public), and consolidated his influence over Goebbels. "Hitler, the dear, old and good comrade. One cannot help being fond of him as a person. And on top of it all, his overwhelming personality. With such a man one can really conquer the world." Hitler invited him to spend three weeks the following month in Upper Bavaria; this announcement in the diary is spaced out from the rest with a flourish. It was apparently intended to be a holiday.

Meanwhile there was to be a delirious meeting along with Hitler at the annual Party Congress, this year staged in Weimar. This was accompanied by a mass demonstration by the Nazis. "I have to shake a thousand hands . . . Berliners arriving in mass formation. They are all so fond of me. A lot of waving and laughing. Then, his motor-car! Hitler arriving. Pandemonium." The following day both Goebbels and Hitler spoke. "My own speech about Propaganda gets them into a frenzy of enthusiasm. . . . Then Hitler speaks. . . . He is so deep it is almost mystical. He knows how to express infinite truth! I thank Fate that there is such a man as he. On the Market Square

64

15,000 S.A. men march past us. . . . A wonderful sight, these 15,000 and a whole forest of flags." He spoke again, to an audience of students, who carried him from the hall shoulder-high. And again the question is debated, whether he should take over the Party organisation in Berlin.

On 23rd July, after what was apparently an agony of suspense and waiting for Hitler in Bavaria, suddenly there was a knock on the door and there was "the Chief" (*der Chef*) arrived by car with Strasser. Off they set through the night to Berchtesgaden, Goebbels sitting in his favourite seat beside the chauffeur. In Berchtesgaden Hitler at this time merely had rooms at the Hotel Platternhof, which was owned by a friend and Party member.

In the lovely mountain sunshine Hitler seemed a god. During the days that followed Goebbels underwent a deep, transfiguring experience as a member of the intimate circle. Love was what he needed, and love was what he found. "Wonderful to be among one's friends and comrades. Rust keeps reminiscing until deep into the night. He seems to be quite fond of me. And now I fall asleep, surrounded by friends and comrades. And I sleep in blissful happiness." It was a mountain idyll, a lullaby.

Hitler himself appeared a genius. "He is the creative instrument of Fate and Deity. I stand by him, deeply shaken. That is how he is. Good and kind, but also clever and shrewd and again at times great and gigantic. What a person. What a man. (*Ein Kerl! Ein Mann!*) He speaks about the State and how to win it and he speaks about the meaning of political revolution. The themes he develops I may have myself thought of from time to time, but never so clearly. After supper we sit in the garden for a long time and he preaches to us about the State and how we are to fight for it. He seems like a prophet of old. And in the sky a big, white cloud almost seems to shape itself into the form of a swastika. Glittering light all over the sky. . . . Is that a sign from Fate?!"

And so the communion went on, for three whole days. "He spoils me like a child. The kindly friend and master! . . . He is absolutely and completely an artist in statesmanship (*Staats-Künstler*). Farewell, my dear Obersalzberg. Those wonderful days gave me direction and pointed my way. In deep anguish I can see a star shining. To him I feel deeply linked. Now the very last of my doubts have vanished. Germany will live! Heil Hitler!"

The parting was no less hallowed. Hitler knew his man.

"We go down into the valley. He singles me out to walk alone with him and he speaks to me like a father to his son. . . . Thanks for everything! Thanks! Thanks!"

Though so beautifully staged, the parting was not for long. They met again in Augsburg four days later, where other supporters showered them with flowers. Hitler prepared a second farewell scene. "Hitler gives me a bunch of flowers . . . red, red roses."

That was 31st July. At the end of August the Berlin post was again in suspense. It was proposed that Goebbels should look after the *Gau* for four months on a provisional basis. However on 28th August he records: "As for the Munich suggestion I should go to Berlin, I have turned it down flat. I don't want to get bogged down in all that mess up there." He had, of course, met the present Gauführer of Berlin, von Schlange, and had liked him, but he knew that the Party organisation in the capital was feeble and ill-disciplined. Berlin might well not prove a good centre in which to shine. He wanted to be with Hitler in Munich.

However on 17th September he writes, in Berlin itself: "In the evening I receive Schlange and Schmidt. Both seem to be well aware of my being all set to take matters in hand." It seems, therefore, that the lure of the titles Gauleiter and Gauführer had begun to overcome his dislike of Berlin. The next day he went to Potsdam, and the aura of Frederick the Great surrounded him as he wandered through the summer residence of the great king. "It is so exciting to go through these rooms. My God! Frederick the Great! That is the big thing about him, that at all times he remained master of himself, that at all times he was the servant of his State. A soldier for seven years. Frederick the Unique."

He was decided. He would accept Berlin. In any case, everything at home was collapsing about his ears. Kaufmann, he learned in September, was thinking of marrying into the same family as Elbrechter, "that swine", his enemy. Strasser, he learned by gossip, "is madly jealous of me", and in October he heard that Hitler had appointed Strasser Head of Propaganda for the Party, the post that Goebbels would dearly have loved to possess. And, lastly, Else had just taken her final leave of him.

Kaufmann gave him a farewell party in Elberfeld, and off he went. Now he had only one master to serve, Adolf Hitler.

It was November. Winter lay ahead in 'Red' Berlin. But at least he was Gauleiter now, at the age of twenty-eight. Berlin was to be his headquarters for the rest of his life.

CHAPTER THREE

Berlin

' A GREY NOVEMBER DUSK falls over Berlin as my train steams into the Potsdamer Bahnhof, and hardly two hours pass before I am standing for the first time on the speaker's platform which is to become the starting-point for our future development. At once I address the Party members."[1]

This was the legend Goebbels himself perpetrated in his book *The Battle of Berlin*, a belligerent account of his first year's work in the capital, but published seven years later in 1934. In order to create the right atmosphere of the beginner who was to make good he allowed another story to circulate: that on his arrival he climbed on to a street bus, a lonely figure from the provinces carrying a simple suitcase, and killed time before the Party meeting looking at the city lights and the pavements covered with strangers. He marvelled, he said, at the size of Berlin; he felt it would swallow him up.

Whatever his real emotions may have been on his arrival—and it seems certain he did not really want to undertake this thankless task— he was no stranger to the city. He had, as we have seen, frequently spoken there at Party meetings, and he knew the previous Gauleiter, von Schlange, whom he was to replace. But Berlin was, of course, the headquarters of the Strassers, and they had secured him a room in the large and elegant establishment of Johann Steiger, who was a member of the editorial staff of the *Berliner Lokalanzeiger*, a right-wing paper controlled by Alfred Hugenberg, the financier. The Steigers, who were ardent Nazis, let off some of their spare rooms and were prepared to give Goebbels good value for very low rent. Frau Steiger had a certain amount of money of her own, and Goebbels not only lived in comfort but was given the use of one of the drawing-rooms for conferences. Otto Strasser met him at the station and took him round to the Steigers' flat to introduce him to his hosts. He did not address a Party meeting for some while after his arrival in Berlin.

He had known for long enough that Hitler was very dissatisfied with the state of the Party organisation in Berlin. The Strassers had been quite unable to maintain order through von Schlange, and such power as there was remained in the hands of the leader of the Berlin S.A., Kurt Daluege, and a man who had already been expelled from the Party, Heinz Hauenstein. Hitler expected Goebbels to face these things alone, purge the membership and begin the work in Berlin all over again. The new Gauleiter was responsible directly to Hitler and not, as he would normally have been, to Gregor Strasser.

Hitler himself has explained why he chose Goebbels, a man with barely eighteen months' experience in the Party, for this difficult task:

From the time I started to organise the Party, I made it a rule never to fill an appointment until I had found the right man for it. I applied this principle to the post of Berlin Gauleiter. Even when the older members of the Party bombarded me with complaints over the Party leadership in Berlin, I refrained from coming to their assistance, until I could promise them that in Dr. Goebbels I had found the man I was seeking. He possesses the two attributes without which no one could master the conditions in Berlin: intelligence and the gift of oratory. . . . When I invited him to study the organisation of the Party in Berlin, he reported in due course that the weakness lay in the junior leaders, and he asked me for a free hand to make the necessary changes and to purge the Party of all unsatisfactory elements. I never regretted giving him the powers he asked for. When he started he found nothing particularly efficient as a political organisation to help him. He worked like an ox, regardless of all the stresses to which the latent opposition must have exposed him.[2]

He had in fact chosen wisely. Goebbels was to make history in Berlin.

The five years 1927 to 1931 were the period during which the Nazis began to consolidate their power in Germany. They won twelve seats in the Reichstag in 1928, when Gregor Strasser, Göring and Goebbels were among those chosen to represent the Party in the House. The allied Control Commission was withdrawn in 1927, and this permitted the German Government to begin a secret policy of rearmament and of the reorganisation of the professional Army, the *Reichswehr*. Nevertheless in the same year Stresemann, the Minister for Foreign Affairs, was awarded the Nobel Peace Prize. But to extremists such as the Nazis Stresemann remained the appeaser, the man who stood by the Versailles and Locarno treaties, the man who signed the Kellogg Pact renouncing war. In Germany itself the internal strife continued between the men of the Left and the *Reichswehr* (who had the police under their control), and this often led to bloodshed. When, for example, in 1929, the workers organised their usual May Day demonstrations in Berlin, they were fired on by the police, who killed no less than twenty-five of the demonstrators. This happened in spite of the fact that men who called themselves Socialists were participating in the Reich Government.

The Nazis, meanwhile, gained in 1929 the help of certain leading industrialists and bankers such as Thyssen and Schroeder, and were able to set up their headquarters at the famous Brown House in Munich. The industrialists subsidised the Nazis because through them and the other Nationalist parties they hoped to establish a counter-revolution which would place Germany entirely in their power. They fostered the semi-military organisations which the Nationalist parties were developing—such as Hitler's Storm Troopers and the German National Party's *Stahlhelm*, a large body of ex-servicemen which was favoured by the *Reichswehr*. When in January 1931 Röhm was put at the head of the Storm Troopers he rapidly developed them into an organisation representing a further half-million men. The Socialists and Communists also had their private armies. Within ten years of defeat, a considerable proportion of the able-bodied men in demilitarised Germany belonged to somebody's private army. In October 1929 Stresemann died to the delight of the Nationalists, in spite of the fact that he had prepared the ground for Germany's resumption of military power. He had negotiated for the Allies to evacuate the Rhineland by June 1930, five years before the time originally fixed in the Versailles

Treaty; he had also negotiated the Young Plan, which lessened considerably the burden of reparations and left the repayment to Germany's good faith.

Opposition to the Young Plan was loudly proclaimed by the Nazis, and on the strength of their outcry they won much greater support in Germany. In the elections of September 1930, they won 107 seats in the Reichstag. They were now a first-class power in Germany's political life.

This had not been achieved without much difficulty. Stresemann's policy had led Germany towards economic prosperity and by 1929 unemployment had been reduced to manageable proportions. What played into the hands of the Nazis was the depression of 1930. Stresemann was dead, but even he could not have prevented the catastrophic effect of this on the German economy. Between September 1929 and January 1933 (when Hitler became Chancellor) unemployment rose from over one million to over six million. Hitler's prophecies of the result of the Government's evil policy seemed to have been fulfilled, and the Party which had only won 800,000 votes in the 1928 Reichstag elections polled 6,401,210 in 1930. Membership of the Party rose— 17,000 in 1926; 176,000 in 1929; 389,000 in 1930; 800,000 in 1931.

As Dr. Bullock points out, the Nazi Party was never a party in any proper sense of the term. It was a conspiracy to gain power, and to achieve this it needed men, money and votes. The men, apart from the leaders themselves, were the Storm Troopers and the Party's paid agents; the money, apart from the minor dues paid by the members, consisted of the subsidies supplied by industrialists who regarded the Nazis as their tool; the votes, apart from those cast by the members themselves, were the results of discontent and uncertainty among the German people. All these elements were essential links in the chain, for Hitler was determined to keep his conspiracy legal and constitutional, winning support from every section of German society—the possessors and the dispossessed alike. At every stage he was against the use of force on a level that would result in a direct clash with the Army and the Police—the legal forces of the State. He confined his use of force to opponents who had no such sanctions at their disposal. For the rest, he relied on the power of propaganda.

When Goebbels unpacked his modest belongings in Berlin, among them was his inscribed copy of *Mein Kampf*. The first part of this extraordinary book was published in the summer of 1925; the second part, written in Berchtesgaden, did not appear until two years later. Among its wilful misinterpretations of history, its ravings in long, turgid and often illiterate German, occur sections which have a certain Machiavellian lucidity, and these are the pages that deal with propaganda.

Hitler prepares his readers for this with precepts that turn on the fundamental principles that enable a leader to impose his personality on the masses. They prefer, he says, like women, a strong man to a weakling. They do not want to read; they need to be influenced by a living presence: "The great masses of a nation will always and only succumb to the force of the spoken word." The leader himself can only generate passion in his followers if he has it himself: passion is the prerequisite of his leadership. He must have the fanatic's view of life. Writers, he says, are seldom leaders. Their attitude to their audience is too generalised and abstract. In his Preface he says:

I know that fewer people are won over by the written word than by the spoken word and that every great movement on this earth owes its growth to great speakers and not to great writers.

It is clear from this that Hitler set great store by oratory and the personal magnetism of the agitator. When he comes, therefore, to the subject of propaganda he treats it wholly from the point of view of a means to an end. It is not, he says, applicable to the intellectual. It is designed for the masses, like a poster or an advertisement:

The art of propaganda consists precisely in being able to awaken the imagination of the public through an appeal to their feelings, in finding the appropriate psychological form that will arrest the attention and appeal to the hearts of the national masses. . . .

The receptive powers of the masses are very restricted, and their understanding is feeble. On the other hand, they quickly forget. Such being the case, all effective propaganda must be confined to a few bare essentials and those must be expressed as far as possible in stereotyped formulas. These slogans should be persistently repeated until the very last individual has come to grasp the idea that has been put forward. If this principle be forgotten and if an attempt be made to be abstract and general, the propaganda will turn out ineffective; for the public will not be able to digest or retain what is offered to them in this way. Therefore, the greater the scope of the message that has to be presented, the more necessary it is for the propaganda to discover that plan of action which is psychologically the most efficient.

Propaganda is not concerned with the truth in general, but the truth as interpreted in the interests of the propagandist:

Propaganda must not investigate the truth objectively and, in so far as it is favourable to the other side, present it according to the theoretical rules of justice; but it must present only that aspect of the truth which is favourable to its own side. . . .

As soon as our own propaganda makes the slightest suggestion that the enemy has a certain amount of justice on his side, then we lay down the basis on which the justice of our own cause could be questioned.[3]

It is interesting after this to note that Hitler constantly singles out British propaganda during the First World War for praise.

In the second volume of *Mein Kampf* Hitler returns to the subject again; he says that he personally took charge of the Party's propaganda when he first joined it. He explains in detail how he learned to master audiences through constant public speaking, and how superior in its effect this method of approaching the public is to mere writing:

These gatherings brought me the advantage that I slowly became a platform orator at mass meetings, and gave me practice in the pathos and gesture required in large halls that held thousands of people. . . .

An orator receives continuous guidance from the people before whom he speaks. This helps him to correct the direction of his speech; for he can always gauge, by the faces of his hearers, how far they follow and understand him, and whether his words are producing the desired effect. But the writer does not know his reader at all. Therefore, from the outset he does not address himself to a definite human group of persons which he has before his eyes but must write in a general way.[4]

In a later chapter he explains how the Party should be organised and differentiates between followers and members. Members are active workers who understand the leadership principle and can practise it within the orbit of the Party. The follower is merely a convert who takes his place in the ranks. The quality of the membership of any Party depends on the degree of struggle there is. Success merely leads to softening and poor quality membership. Strife breeds toughness, keenness and alertness; the Party must always be fighting an enemy. Hitler might well have been writing especially for Goebbels in Berlin when he dictated this paragraph to Hess in Berchtesgaden:

As director of propaganda for the Party, I took care not merely to prepare the ground for the greatness of the movement in its subsequent stages, but I also adopted the most radical measures against allowing into the organisation any other than the best material. For the more radical and exciting my propaganda was, the more did it frighten weak and wavering characters away, thus preventing them from entering the first nucleus of our organisation.[5]

Goebbels' immediate task during his first days in Berlin was to introduce discipline and efficiency. He went round to the office. It was in a disgusting condition:

Our 'office' was a dirty basement at the back of the Potsdamerstrasse. A kind of manager was based there with an exercise book in which he would enter debits and credits as best he knew. Masses of paper cluttered up the place, and in the ante-room numbers of unemployed Party members used to hang around gossiping and killing time. We used to call the place 'the opium den'.[6]

One of the first tasks was to secure a more suitable office:

On 1st January 1927 we turned our backs on the 'opium den' for good and occupied our new offices in Lützowstrasse. According to present standards they would seem extremely modest and primitive, but in those days it meant progress and quite a step forward.[7]

But the *Gau* was in debt and the membership depraved. Schlange himself, who had been Gauleiter before Goebbels, was a Civil Servant and it had been easy enough to get him to resign by arranging for him to be warned that he would lose his main job unless he severed his connection with the Nazis. On the other hand Daluege, the S.A. chief, was just the kind of man Goebbels wanted to protect him at the provocative meetings by means of which he was planning to conquer Berlin for the Party. The Party membership in the capital was about a thousand. Goebbels stripped it down at once to 600 men by getting rid of the more idle riff-raff. He called these men together and told them they must each of them contribute three marks a month. The rest of the money needed to run the organisation he was to get by charging a low admission fee of a few pence to the Party meetings. The unemployed—always the main element on whom the Nazis relied for members—were admitted at half-price. He was determined to make these meetings of such a quality in both speech and action that they would soon be crowded if only initially through curiosity. He was determined to put on a show. As he said early on at a Party meeting: "The Berliners may insult us, slander us, fight us, beat us up, but they must talk about us."[8]

A story told by Otto Strasser shows that Goebbels' character was in no way modified by the weight of his responsibilities in Berlin. At his first public meeting he kept his audience waiting ten minutes or so by arriving late in a taxi. Even then he spread out the time entering the hall and taking the platform. Strasser spoke to him afterwards about the extravagance of hiring a taxi when the *Gau* was in debt. Goebbels replied impertinently. "You don't know much about propaganda," he said. "Taxi be damned. I should have taken two, not one. The other for my brief-case. Don't forget you've got to impress people. And as for being late, I did that deliberately. I always do. You've got to keep them in suspense."

The first task was to organise the kind of publicity which would attract an audience. "I don't mind admitting," Goebbels wrote in *The Battle of Berlin*, "we meant to conquer the street. On the street we had to go for the masses and that was our only road to political power."[9] The tempo of the capital fired him, he adds. He re-designed his posters to be provocative and amusing; they were both designed and worded to incite curiosity. Most posters placed round the *Litfassäulen* (the circular columns at the street-corners) were dully laid out with black and crowded type; this was especially true of the political posters. Goebbels had little money for printing though he was not the man to care whether he was in debt or not at the printers. He used large display type in blood-red ink to score the maximum effect through the space at his disposal, and he forced the eye to continue reading the smaller type by making his main titles extraordinary and inexplicable to read on their own. Passers-by blinked and paused to read more when they saw

THE KAISER OF AMERICA—SPEAKS—IN BERLIN

The rest of the information—an attack on the Dawes or the Young Plan as the products of American capitalism—was infiltrated in small type-face round and through the large-letter words, together with the notice of the meeting at which Dr. Joseph Goebbels, the new Gauleiter of Berlin, was to address all Berliners who would come.

If the posters were red so was the blood that began to flow as a result of Goebbels' organised attacks on the Communists. These were deliberately provoked because the Communists were prominent in Berlin and violence makes news. Goebbels knew that if his unemployed strong-arm thugs were to be kept busy, street-fights and organised demonstrations of violence at the meetings would be the surest and quickest way to bring the Party into the public eye and instil fear into the flaccid, bourgeois soul that he hated, with its love for peace at any price. On a gradually increasing scale the beatings-up began with the Communists as the chosen prey.

On 11th February 1927 Goebbels made one of his larger bids for publicity. He hired the famous Pharus Hall in a working-class district of Berlin. This hall was specially associated with Communist meetings and its choice for a big Nazi rally was in itself a deliberate act of provocation. Every member of the diminutive Nazi Party was ordered to parade with flags before the meeting began. "This was an open challenge," writes Goebbels. "It was meant that way by us. It was understood that way by the opponent."[10] This was to be a *Saal-schlacht*, a battle in a meeting-hall. Hitler had done the same thing for long enough in Munich. The Communists were present in force, and one of their number started the desired trouble by challenging the Chairman (Daluege) on a point of order. He was seized and flung out bodily by a group of Storm Troopers. Then the free-for-all began with bottles, chairs and knuckle-dusters. The water-bottles from the platform, says Goebbels, were flung in self-defence. The police, who had known there must be trouble at such a meeting as this, intervened. The Communists dispersed with their casualties, and Goebbels, as the principal speaker, rose at once to the occasion. He ordered the Nazi stretcher-cases to be put on the platform. He started an oration in which he spoke of the loyalty and the suffering of the Storm Troopers. He used the phrase "the unknown Storm Trooper" as a symbol of the occasion, pointing to one man, Albert Thonak, who lay writhing in agony, suffering itself put on display.[11] Nor was Goebbels finished with this idea for propaganda. He used it again at another meeting, though in this case the wounded men, bandaged and on stretchers, were in reality unharmed actors dressed up for the occasion. But they helped to develop the S.A. man as both hero and martyr. After the Pharus meeting one newspaper called the Nazis bandits. Goebbels was delighted. Next time he laid out a poster he assumed the title Ober-Bandit Joseph Goebbels.

Goebbels now entered upon his second phase as a notorious and out-standing agitator. Soon after his arrival at the Steigers' flat he began to use a huge, three-sided mirror in the drawing-room before which he could rehearse his speeches. Frau Steiger was enchanted by her lodger. He reminded her, she said to Strasser, of Savonarola—so ascetic, so dedicated. Goebbels sat upstairs pondering his speeches. Looking back on this period, he wrote:

More and more I realised how important it is to speak so that people really understand one. And that is how I began to develop an entirely new style of political oratory. When these days I glance at the short-hand transcripts of my speeches in the pre-Berlin period and compare them with my later speeches, the older ones seem to me utterly tame and docile. I had not been caught yet by the tempo and the hot breath of the great city.[12]

He wrote his more important speeches out in full, using multi-coloured pencils to indicate various shades of emphasis and pause. He also developed his capacity for making unscripted, impromptu speeches to catch the spirit of the moment in a meeting.

He was wholly, absolutely self-conscious over his speech-making. He always considered his audience first: how to affect them, how to incite them. He developed little or no personal emotion while speaking, but he gave everything he had, physically and vocally, to rouse emotion in his audience. He pushed his fine, sonorous voice to its limits, and the effort of speaking to mass audiences for prolonged periods of up to two hours cost him a great deal. His small, fragile frame was shaken with nervous energy, and he developed the habit of weighing himself after his more strenuous performances. He claimed that he frequently lost two or three pounds in weight on these occasions. But several of those in a good position to know have admitted that he never expended his own emotions while he spoke. In this respect he was the reverse of Hitler. Goebbels always calculated his effects, and to those he knew well he was prepared to boast about this, saying, for example, before a meeting: "Well, which record shall I put on now?" He also cultivated the capacity to adapt himself to audiences, particularly those likely to be hostile. He became, in other words, completely professional, the master of his audience, proud and vain of his ability to establish himself immediately with the people in front of him. His effrontery dazzled his own adherents and those who came to his meetings out of curiosity. He was a success. The image of the lonely provincial clutching his suitcase on a Berlin bus rapidly faded before the image of the man of destiny standing astride the city of which he was to become the master. He found himself in tune with the spirit of the capital and alive with desire to conquer it.

To make his great public meetings more showman-like he developed Hitler's technique of ceremonial which stirred the hearts of his audience in advance of the speeches. He used banners, processions, marching, music and singing. Street parades normally preceded these meetings. Goebbels himself did not usually appear before the hall was crowded and ready. He would then make a dramatic entrance like an actor timing his cue; he always appeared surrounded by his bodyguard, and the Party supporters in the hall would receive him with prolonged cheering. The emotional ground was well prepared before the speech-making began to insert seeds of propaganda in the human soil.

On 1st May 1927 Hitler made his first speech in Berlin since Goebbels' term of office had begun. This took place at a mass meeting which had to be disguised as a private session for the membership, since at that time Hitler was still banned from public speaking in northern Germany. Goebbels arranged the meeting for him in the Clou, a large and well-known dance-hall in the centre of Berlin.

But Berlin was not composed entirely of men ready to fall at the feet of Goebbels the orator. The police had their eye on him and the more violent members of his Storm Trooper gangs. The main concern of the police was to keep the peace, and one of the easier ways of doing this was to ban demonstrations and public meetings that were likely to become the cause of trouble. On 5th May, four days after Hitler's so-called private conference, the police banned the National Socialist Party in the area of Greater Berlin. When the notice of suspension arrived from the Police Department a receipt had to be signed. But Goebbels knew what was in it and refused to accept it. He claimed that he sent a Storm Trooper in full uniform to return the letter to the police unopened with the remark: "We National Socialists refuse to recognise the ban." Then he put the Party meetings underground, founding local clubs for apparently innocent, non-political ends such as sport and hiking. Although the Party uniform was banned, Goebbels managed to devise other ways of getting his men to dress alike. The ban on the Party (which involved a ban on Goebbels as a Party speaker) was followed by a further prohibition which prevented him from addressing any public meeting throughout Prussia. This was the severest blow the authorities could have dealt him:

Personally I was hit particularly hard by the ban on my speaking in public. At that time I had hardly any other means of keeping contact with the Party comrades. The spoken word to us was at all times more important than the printed word, and in those days we had not many words to print, our press facilities still being very poor indeed.[13]

The only exceptions to the ban on Party members speaking in public were those who were also members of the Reichstag. Goebbels developed the practice of getting up in the body of the hall at meetings where Deputies were billed to speak and making lengthy debating-points. The police soon discovered what was happening; Goebbels persisted and was charged and fined for doing this. His reply to the ban on him as a speaker was to found *Der Angriff* and to initiate in it his campaign of ridicule against Bernhard Weiss, the Jewish Deputy Chief of Police in Berlin.

Der Angriff (Attack) was established as Goebbels' own paper. It began as a diminutive weekly in contrast to the established National Socialist dailies, Hitler's *Völkischer Beobachter* and Strasser's *Berliner Arbeiter-zeitung*. As Goebbels himself wrote, the name of the new journal was a matter of importance:

I never forget how one evening we sat brooding—only a few of us— brooding over the name of our new paper. All of a sudden, I had a brain-wave: surely there could be one name only for our paper: *Der Angriff*. The very name had its propagandistic value, since to attack was really all we wanted.[14]

The editor was a friend of Goebbels, Dr. Julius Lippert. Goebbels used his newly-established poster technique to launch the journal. The first of the blood-red posters announced the title of the paper only, with no explanation. A succeeding poster merely said: "The Attack will take place on 4th July." A third poster announced that *The Attack* would appear every Monday.

One of the first attacks in the new paper was the campaign against Weiss, a humourless man with a pronouncedly Jewish face. He was a gift to Goebbels' crude cartoonists, and Goebbels himself never called him anything but Isidor Weiss—Isidor is to German ears an insulting name with a strongly anti-Jewish connotation—week in, week out, until the public believed this to be his real name and he became a kind of figure of fun. In 1928 Goebbels even published a pamphlet against him, *Das Buch Isidor*. He made Weiss into the scapegoat for every blow he wanted to deliver against the police. He slandered him by inventing endless charges which appeared in the *Angriff*, and when Weiss replied by attempting to defend himself Goebbels delighted in the additional publicity that he gained. He was not afraid of the police courts; they were places where he could show off his insolent wit and gain attention from the press.

Der Angriff in effect became Goebbels' platform now his voice was all but silenced. It was primarily directed at the working class of Berlin, and its writing was angry and waspish. Yet it proved uphill work to sell it, and it was not popular with Hitler or Strasser. It reflected Goebbels' politics rather than Hitler's in its attacks on the capitalists. It was also violently anti-Communist and anti-Semitic. Goebbels always regarded his critics in the press as Jewish-inspired; he represented himself and the Party as persecuted by the Jews, the Communists and the police, led by the Jewish villain of the piece, 'Isidor' Weiss. As for the prohibition on the Party and its meetings, Goebbels invented his own rhyming slogan:

> *Trotz Verbot*
> *Nicht tot!*
>
> In spite of the Ban
> We're not dead!

In *The Battle of Berlin* Goebbels tells the tragic story of the summer of 1927. The circulation of *Der Angriff* was small. There were constant lawsuits to be faced. With no public meetings there was no gate-money for the Party. No one but himself seemed to know how to write. Inexperienced speakers had to be trained against the day when the ban would be removed. It was a matter of ceaseless improvisation and pioneering. The peak event of the year was the Party Congress held in Nuremberg at the end of August. Here the fact that most of the Berlin Party members and Storm Troopers were unemployed men just keeping alive on the meagre official dole made it possible for this event to be supported in full strength. The men marched to Nuremberg—a great propaganda procession and demonstration of comradely solidarity, which took in all some three weeks. Goebbels also describes in *The Battle of Berlin* how he arranged for four private trains to take and bring back those Party members who could afford the special reduced fare of twenty-five marks. At Nuremberg the great rally with its singing, its banners, its speech-making and torch-light processions was beginning to be developed as the highlight among the Party's annual demonstrations. Hitler and the Party leaders took the salute at the march-past. The seed had been sown and the plant was sinking its roots deep into the community. Only too soon now Nuremberg would be the display centre where the Nazis would demonstrate their massive power to the nation and to the world. The Congress of 1927 was a dress rehearsal.

But the police ban on Party meetings in Berlin was maintained throughout the summer, and Goebbels had to go elsewhere to speak. At a congress in the Ruhr held in 1927 he spoke on the value to the Nazis of these large-scale public demonstrations:

Whoever can conquer the street will conquer the State one day, for every form of power politics and any dictatorially run State has its roots in the street. We cannot have enough of public demonstrations, for that is far and away the most emphatic way of demonstrating one's will to govern. It means a darned sight more than election statistics. When we can see our men, thousands of them, marching up and down the streets, that is nothing short of mobilisation for power.[15]

With *Der Angriff* as his chief outlet in Berlin, Goebbels used every means he could devise to increase its sale. It appeared weekly and every Party member was under orders to buy it and increase its distribution. But the sales remained obstinately at a low level of about 2,000. There was little justification for publishing it at all since Strasser's daily paper was already there to serve the interests of the Party. But *Der Angriff* existed to minister to Goebbels' personal prestige, and he would not let it die.

The next stage in the campaign amounted to a press war. Goebbels ordered his Storm Troopers to make life uncomfortable for the Strassers' news-vendors. He imagined he could do this with impunity because the Strassers would be unwilling to take legal action in their own defence and so reveal a split in the Party at this vital stage in the fight for power. All the Strassers in fact could do was appeal to Hitler to intervene, and in the autumn of 1927 he came to Berlin to investigate the matter. Otto Strasser recalls what happened. Hitler came into his office in the Nürnberger Strasse and said that this strife must stop.

"Why don't you say that to Goebbels?" Otto replied.

Hitler hedged and said that what really worried him was that if this recrimination went on a party of Storm Troopers might arrive one day and raid the Strassers' office.

"Then what would you do?" he asked.

"Then I'd shoot, Herr Hitler, and you would lose some of your Storm Troopers," replied Otto, and opened his desk drawer to show Hitler the revolver he kept there. He knew this was the only way to talk to Hitler.

"But surely you wouldn't do that? Not kill my Storm Troopers?" said Hitler, astonished.

"Well, if they *are* your Storm Troopers," said Otto, "just tell them not to come!"

After this Goebbels was less active against the Strassers, and Hitler decided to centralise the policy of the Party newspapers. Otto went to Munich to discuss this and saw for the first time the Party Secretariat at the famous Brown House. A gigantic swastika decorated the front of the building. Inside the main entrance a staff of twenty or so worked at tables behind a long counter; there was the clatter of typewriters and the hurrying of messengers. To get to the rooms of the Secretariat, which was controlled by Hess, and to Hitler's own office it was necessary to go through this hall and across a courtyard. Hitler's room was elegantly furnished and thickly carpeted; in addition to the huge desk there was a round table with a group of leather arm-chairs for small conferences. Hitler normally wore his brown shirt and high boots, and at this stage in his political career carried a riding-whip;

with this he gave added emphasis to his remarks by slapping it against his boots or striking it across the desk or table. On this occasion he wanted to buy up the Strassers' newspapers in the north for himself, and when they refused to sell he became angry. Otto claims that he created a scene by saying that Hitler was wrong. Hitler struck the table with his whip and shouted back: "I am never wrong. Every word of mine is of historic importance." Otto left, leaving Gregor to carry on the conversation at Hitler's request. Hitler knew the value of the Strassers and did not yet want to lose their support; he reverted to his charm in order to placate Gregor.

The luxury of the Munich headquarters was in pointed contrast to conditions in Berlin, where the tramway or Underground was the normal means of transport, not a Mercedes. The Strassers and Goebbels never wore uniform. The absence of money and status rankled with Goebbels, and it was this more than enthusiasm for the Party which drove him on to seek personal power and prestige by whatever means he could—which in the end led him back to his own personality and talents as propagandist, orator and writer.

The celebration of his thirtieth birthday and of his first year in Berlin were almost coincident. The Party members surprised him, he claims, by making a collection which raised 2,000 marks to help the Party finances and producing the names of some 2,500 new subscribers. They also gave him an envelope containing some cancelled I.O.U.s which had involved his personal commitment for money loaned to start *Der Angriff*. But the best present of all came from the police. They raised the ban on his public speaking, provided he obtained permission in advance for each meeting he proposed to address.

1928 was to be an important year for Goebbels. With an intuitive sense of dedication to the future he gave a speech on perception and propaganda early in January. In the course of this he emphasised first that propaganda should use any means to achieve its ends and that the creation of propaganda is not a matter for talent alone, but for the kind of genius that inspired the great religious teachers. Propaganda, he pointed out, has always been promoted most effectively not by writing but by word of mouth, where the personality of the speaker achieves its own mastery of the audience:

There is no theoretical way of determining what kind of propaganda is more effective and what kind is less effective. The propaganda which produces the desired results is good and all other propaganda is bad, no matter how entertaining it may be, because it is not the task of propaganda to entertain but to produce results. . . . Therefore, it is beside the point to say your propaganda is too crude, too mean, or too brutal, or too unfair, for all this does not matter. . . . The moment I have recognised some truth or other and begin to speak about it in the tram—I am making propaganda. This is the moment when I begin to search for others who, like myself, have recognised the same truth. Thus, propaganda is nothing but the predecessor of an organisation. Once there is an organisation, it becomes the predecessor of the State. Propaganda is always a means to an end. . . . You are either a propagandist, or you are not. Propaganda is an art which can be taught to the average person, like playing the violin. But then there comes a point when you say: "This is where you stop. What remains to be learned can only be achieved by a genius. . . ." If they say, "But you are only propagandists," you should answer them: "And what else was Jesus Christ? Did he not make propaganda? Did he write books or did he preach? And what about Mohammed? Did he write sophisticated essays or did he go out to the people and tell them what he wanted? Were not Buddha and Zoroaster propagandists? . . . Look at our own century. Was Mussolini a scribbler, or was he a great speaker? When Lenin went from Zürich to St. Petersburg, did he rush from the station into his study to write a book, or did he speak before a multitude?" Only the great speakers, the great creators of words have made Bolshevism and Fascism. There is no difference between the speaker and the politician. . . .[16]

At the end of March it was announced that there would be an election for the Reichstag on 20th May. Simultaneously the ban on the Nazi Party was raised by the Prussian Government. Goebbels' platform was free again. Now was his chance.

Goebbels, who had formerly been hostile to the Party involving itself in the Reichstag since attack seemed to come better from without, now changed his mind. The Reichstag would provide a prominent centre from which to work to bring the Party to power. Goebbels applied his phenomenal, dedicated energy to winning votes for the Party at the election. He made his attitude quite clear:

We will move into the Reichstag to supply ourselves at the arsenal of Democracy with its own weapons. We will become deputies of the Reichstag to paralyse the Weimar way of thinking with the support of Weimar. . . . If we succeed in planting in parliament sixty or seventy of our own agitators and organisers, then the State itself will equip and pay for our fighting machine. Whoever is elected to parliament is finished, but only if he plans to become a parliamentarian. But if, with his inborn recklessness, he continues his merciless fight against the increasing scoundrelisation of our public life, then he will not become a parliamentarian but he will remain what he is: a revolutionary. Mussolini also was a member of parliament. In spite of that, not long afterwards, he marched on Rome with his Blackshirts. . . . The agitators of our Party are spending between six hundred and eight hundred marks a month on train fares in order to overthrow the Republic. Is it then not just and fair that the Republic should reimburse their travelling expenses by giving them free railway passes? . . . Is that the beginning of a compromise? Do you believe that we would lay down our arms for free railway passes? We, who have stood in front of you a hundred and a thousand times in order to bring you faith in a new Germany? . . . We do not beg for votes. We demand conviction, devotion, passion. The vote is only an expedient, for ourselves as well as for you. . . . We do not care a damn about co-operation for building up a stinking dung-heap. We come to clean out the dung. . . . We do not come as friends or as neutrals. We come as enemies.[17]

The Nazis were still too young and too suspect a party to win any substantial backing from the German public. Their supporters were almost entirely confined to the Party membership, and they polled in 1928 only 800,000 votes. Nevertheless, this entitled them to twelve seats in the Reichstag, and the indefatigable Goebbels was allocated one of these seats. Within three years of his appointment as Gregor Strasser's secretary he had risen by his own energy, invention and sheer insolence to becoming a member of the House of Government. Whether they liked him or not, the Nazi leaders had to admit he was one of the best and most active men in the Party. And he evidently enjoyed the special favour and protection of Hitler. Goebbels celebrated his election by writing a broadside against the dignity of office in the Reichstag:

Maybe the representatives of the other parties regard themselves as representatives; I am not a member of the Reichstag. I am an I.D.I. and I.D.F.—*Inhaber der Immunität* (possessor of parliamentary immunity) and *Inhaber der Freifahrkarte* (possessor of a free railway pass). . . . The I.D.I. is a man who may speak the truth from time to time even in this democratic Republic. He distinguishes himself from other mortals by being permitted to think aloud. He can call a dung-heap a dung-heap and needn't beat about the bush by calling it a State. . . . This is but a prelude. You're going to have a lot of fun with us. The show can begin.[18]

Hitler's faith in Goebbels was confirmed later in the year when he appointed him in November as Head of Party Propaganda. Strasser, who had formerly held this office, was still close to Hitler at the top of the hierarchy, and had been placed in charge of the Party organisation.

Goebbels now had national status both inside and outside the Party, and he proceeded to use it. Throughout the country in the next four years he was to concentrate on political meetings, demonstrations and ceremonies. For at all the principal meetings ceremony, with its emotional stimulus through singing and the parades of flags and banners, always prepared the audience to receive the spoken word. It was in this manner that Goebbels presented Hitler at a great gathering in the vast auditorium of the Berlin Sportpalast in September 1928. The Sportpalast and the Stadium at Nuremberg were to become the two favourite centres for massive Nazi demonstrations. On this occasion Hitler ranted for nearly three hours.

Goebbels, it must be remembered, had in 1929 neither the radio nor films at his disposal. All his propaganda had to be effected through the press and public demonstrations or meetings. Occasionally, however, he was able to take advantage of some special event to supplement the routine of his normal methods of work. Such events were the death of Horst Wessel in February 1930, which Goebbels managed to turn into a political *cause célèbre*.

Horst Wessel was a pimp who died as the result of a brawl with another pimp called Ali Hoehler. Hoehler was put up on trial and given a lengthy sentence for manslaughter. But for Goebbels Wessel had two useful claims on his attention. He had been a member of the Party (and a noted street-fighter until he took to living on the earnings of a prostitute), and his death could quite easily be developed into a political martyrdom. But in addition he had written a little political verse for *Der Angriff* which happened to go well with the tune of a song popular among the Communist youth. This became the famous Horst Wessel Lied. Goebbels took the story of this young reprobate's death and built it up through *Der Angriff* into a major tragedy; Wessel's funeral ceremony was taken over by the Party and Goebbels himself gave the customary oration. Indeed, he was to become a master in the exploitation of funerals. The Lied was sung for the first time in public and formally adopted as the Nazi anthem. Wessel himself was sanctified as the warrior crowned in death. The tune, with its hymn-like sentiment, was undoubtedly effective, and Goebbels' instinct for the religious saw that it would both dignify and hallow Nazi ceremonial in the future. In fact it became the theme-song of the movement and lasted as long as the régime itself.

In 1930 the old trouble between the Strassers and Hitler was revived. It is wrong to imply that Hitler's brand of National Socialism was right-wing and the Strassers' left-wing. Hitler's politics were wholly in terms of power not policy, and he had found that the men on the Right—the aristocracy and the industrialists—had the money and the influence he needed. He had found out that it would pay to work along wholly constitutional lines, and to play down any references to a social revolution. The Strassers, on the other hand, looked mainly to the workers and the unemployed, and their politics were accordingly left-wing and pseudo-revolutionary in approach. With Gregor working now in Munich, Otto developed a strongly radical line in the northern Party press that he controlled, including support for a strike that occurred in Saxony and which Hitler, under pressure from the industrialists, ordered all Party members to boycott. Otto and Hitler met in Berlin to hammer out their differences. Hitler remained adamant in seeking power the way he chose, which meant adopting legal and constitutional means to increase the Party's stake in the Government and, when expedient, full collaboration with the Right. No agreement was reached, and when Hitler returned south he ordered Goebbels, who had not been present at these conversations, to expel Otto and his supporters from Party membership. While Gregor for the time being sided with Hitler, Otto set up his own break-away party called the Black Front.

This happened in June. The following September there were fresh elections for the Reichstag and it was now that Hitler's stand for right-wing National Socialism scored its astonishing victory. The Nazi propaganda machine developed so well now by Goebbels went into full swing with its tub-thumping nationalism and its particular brand of middle-class revolution which managed to secure the capitalist while at the same time satisfying the impoverished imagination of the bourgeois artisan and working-class voter. The economic crisis through which Germany was about to pass played into his hands. What the Nazis did was put on a show and make an energetic jingoistic noise rather than debate serious politics. Hitler found scapegoats for the wounded pride of Germany—the rich Jews, the Allies, the Treaty of Versailles, the big trusts and monopolies, the Communists. With the Nazis yelling at them from every possible platform, with bands and processions and marching men, the 1930 elections were swung violently in Hitler's favour. The widespread and growing unemployment played directly into his hands. The Nazi vote leaped up to some 6,400,000, and the Party's seats in the Reichstag from 12 to 107. The Nazis rose to prominence overnight as the second party in the State; the bit was between their teeth in the race for ultimate power. They were now important people who could throw their weight around in the Reichstag. Goebbels, of course, retained his seat in the House.

But the Party still had to reckon with the dissident element. The Storm Troopers had mainly been recruited from the unemployed and unemployable. They enjoyed their violence, their street-fights and the fun of being feared, and they began to resent bitterly the lack of any reward from Hitler for their loyal gangsterism. They received no formal payment; all they had were frequent rounds of free beer and sausages. In September, about the time of the elections, they raided Goebbels' office in Berlin. He had to call in his old enemies, the police, to restore some order, and Hitler had to intervene in person to clear the matter up. He held out to them the hope that they might one day be rewarded for their services as the result of a levy on all Party members; he made himself their supreme Commander and appointed Röhm as Chief of Staff. Order was thus restored for a while. But suspicion was still alive that neither bread nor circuses were on the way. What the S.A. really wanted was fun and games at the expense of the community now that their party was so near the top. They could not understand that the last thing Hitler wished for was street-battles and the scandal of beatings-up, and that he must retain his reputation for 'legitimacy' in order to bring off his final ascent to power. What the S.A. enjoyed was the kind of organised hooliganism that Goebbels devised to secure a ban on the screening of the film *All Quiet on the Western Front* that had been adapted from the German novel by Erich Maria Remarque. Goebbels distributed to members of the S.A. a considerable number of tickets for the theatre where the film was playing. The Nazis crowded into the place on the second day of the projection, armed with white mice in cages and an arsenal of stink-bombs. The mice were released in the darkness and the stink-bombs set off. The police were called but by that time could trace no obvious culprits. Everyone present merely stated that he wanted to see the film. But the following day *Der Angriff* was full of the story, and the Government banned the film as likely to be the cause of more rioting.

Goebbels had since 1928 enjoyed immunity from police interference and prosecution as a Reichstag deputy. On 13th October, when the Nazi deputies in the new House took their seats for the first time, he arranged for Storm Troopers in civilian clothes to smash the windows of Jewish-owned shops in Berlin. This was to be a sign of the wrath to come. But Goebbels lost his immunity the following February when the Nazi deputies marched out of the Reichstag in a body; at once he became subject to prosecution. He was accused of being responsible for the window-smashing campaign the previous October. In court he refused to testify and adopted the tactics of raving at the judge and the prosecution. It is typical of the fear the Nazis were beginning to inspire in the hearts of law-abiding democrats that he was merely fined 200 marks for this flagrant case of contempt of court.

The trouble with the S.A. flared up again. On 20th February Hitler formally prohibited the Storm Troopers from taking part in street-fights and so lowering the tone of the Party. Meanwhile the leader of the S.A. for northern Germany, Captain Walter Stennes, in association with Otto Strasser's Black Front, was planning an organised revolt in the hope that a major demonstration by the radical wing of the Party with its discontented and neglected forces might swing Hitler round to the Left. Otto Strasser mentions that Goebbels knew in advance of this action which was planned to take place during the Easter period of 1931, and deliberately went south to Munich in order to leave the field clear. Had Stennes succeeded he would probably have supported him when it came to an argument with Hitler. Stennes, however, delayed his action and merely effected a token occupation of the Berlin Party offices. According to Strasser, when Goebbels saw that Stennes was unlikely to be successful he supported Hitler's action in dismissing him from the Party.

Goebbels had by now been Gauleiter of Berlin for four and a half years, a Reichstag deputy for almost three years, and Head of Party Propaganda for two and a half years. He was only thirty-three, but he was consolidating in these days of success the special character he had developed during earlier and harder times. He never lost his need to assert himself, to compensate for his lack of strength and stature and for the rejection of his talents when he was young. He practised his violence and his sarcasm on everyone, whether opponent or assistant. A portrait of him in action at this period has been given by Erich Maria Berger, a member of the staff of *Der Angriff*, whose offices Goebbels visited weekly, where he liked to direct policy and make his presence felt both as their master and their superior in talent and professional insight.[19] Goebbels would sit in the Editor's chair, displacing the

Editor, Dr. Julius Lippert, who had to stand around with the rest of his editorial staff. Goebbels would habitually take off his wrist-watch and place it on the desk in front of him, saying that he could only spare seven or perhaps eight minutes. Berger remembers him taking a crumpled page from the previous day's paper out of his pocket and starting to speak in his maddeningly polite but venomous way. "Herr Lippert, you are the Editor of this paper, are you not? Well, if you want me to believe that this piece here is what you call journalism, I am very much afraid that it shows a degree of naïveté which is almost criminal—or would you prefer me to say insane?" Then, while Lippert blushed at being so criticised before his own subordinates, Goebbels would trounce the subject and presentation of the article with slow and deliberate sarcasm—once even insinuating, Berger remembers, by making a pun out of the word *Wirtschaft* (which has the unfortunate double meaning of economics and a tavern) that the Editor understood drinking better than the economic situation. After this had been done to his satisfaction, he would glance again at his watch. The seven—or was it eight?—minutes were exhausted. He would get up to go.

Once, after one of these embarrassing conferences, he limped quietly out to his car, calling Berger to come with him because he had to speak at a funeral but still wanted to deal with some further editorial matter. On the way to the cemetery Goebbels explained certain other points which were wrong and demanded improvements. Then he went into typographical details. His instructions continued in a whisper as he and Berger walked past the columns of Storm Troopers on parade for the funeral. Then, the open grave before him, he launched into an apparently emotional oration on behalf of the dead comrade. The moment they were back in the car, Goebbels resumed his typographical discussion like an actor who had just come off the stage. He even went so far as to admit he had forgotten who the man was whose virtues he had extolled.

One might say that Goebbels never, in fact, left the stage. Even though he was as professional at his work as any man has ever been, he still had to play the part of being the great professional as well, in order to assuage his unending vanity.

Of his relations with women at this time little is known. Otto Strasser asserts that Frau Steiger, at whose house Goebbels stayed when he first came to work in Berlin, complained that her Savonarola had seduced the prettier one of her two maids. However that may be, in December 1931 Goebbels married Magda Quandt, a woman who had divorced her husband, a wealthy industrialist, in 1929. She already had a son by her former marriage, Harald Quandt, a boy ten years old.

Magda Goebbels had for some while been doing voluntary work for the Party at the Berlin office, and Goebbels, attracted by her wealth, her social position and her outstanding blonde beauty, had given her special work which involved handling his more secret files. Magda was fascinated by the dynamic qualities of National Socialism as represented by the charming, smiling Joseph Goebbels, and she fell in love with him.

Goebbels himself by now was far better placed financially than in his earlier days with the Party. He earned 400 marks a month as Gauleiter, and a further 500 marks a month as a member of the Reichstag. He was comfortably housed in a two-roomed flat in Steglitz, but Magda, who had a lavish allowance from Quandt of 4,000 marks a month, had a luxurious apartment which she rented in one of the best residential quarters of Berlin.

Magda was impulsive and emotional, a simple-minded rather than a sophisticated woman. But she was used to luxury and she liked it. Her mother, who was also strikingly good-looking, had been three times married: first to Magda's father, a diplomat called Rietschel, secondly to a Jewish business-man called Friedlaender, and thirdly to a man called Behrendt. Magda, born in 1901, had been educated first in a Belgian Catholic convent, and later in Berlin. She had married in 1921 her first husband, Günther Quandt, against everyone's advice, for he was in his forties and had already had two sons by his first wife, while Magda was only nineteen. The marriage had failed largely through the disparity of years, and Magda, after using a little moral blackmail, had secured for herself the handsome allowance of 4,000 marks a month so long as she did not remarry. She was known to have been in love with a young student, but the attraction of Goebbels was too much for her, and she gave up her lover for the man whose personality and political views she found so fascinating.

When they married on 12th December 1931 Hitler was present and acted as best man. He very much approved of Magda's social position and wealth. It was the beginning of a close personal friendship, and there are those who claim that Magda had really wanted to marry Hitler himself.[20] She was to remain for the rest of her life a member of the intimate circle of women friends who gave Hitler the platonic relaxation for which his particular form of masculinity craved. To her he was '*mein Führer*'; she was the '*gnädige Frau*' whose hand was always kissed. She was utterly devoted to the Führer and through him to the power politics of the Nazis; she came to identify herself completely with the régime. Hitler was charmed by her elegance, her femininity, her wit and good humour, and he respected her proud devotion as a mother.

She was an excellent hostess and she delighted in her capacity to draw Hitler to her hearth. He was to be alternately her guest and her host until in the years of tribulation he gradually isolated himself and became a recluse. But in 1932 these sterner years were far ahead and never anticipated. Goebbels' happy bride opened her luxurious flat to her husband's friends. It was situated on the Reichskanzlerplatz which was only too soon to become the Adolf Hitler Platz. With the Kaiserhof it became for a while the chief centre for the intrigues that led to the victory of 1933.

CHAPTER FOUR

The Fight for Power

SECOND in the series of Goebbels' published diaries—and the last, in fact, that he was to edit for publication himself—comes *Vom Kaiserhof zur Reichskanzlei*, which first appeared in 1934 from Hitler's own publishing house, the Eher Verlag. This diary covers the critical period in the history of National Socialism, from 1st January 1932 to 1st May 1933, when Hitler agreed to Goebbels' idea that the great day of Communist celebration should also become the day set aside for public rejoicing at the advent of the Third Reich.

This period was to be one of the hardest in Goebbels' life of service to his master. It could be reasonably debated that Hitler might never have gained the position to manœuvre himself and the Party to power without the outstanding ability, tireless energy and political acumen of his campaign manager. There is no doubt that during this time, with its strange atmosphere of mingled success and frustration, Hitler leaned heavily on the man dedicated to help him. He spent endless time in the Goebbels' flat on the Reichskanzlerplatz. Within twelve months the Nazis fought five major election campaigns. Those for the Presidency involved two successive ballots on 13th March and 10th April 1932; in the first Hindenburg failed to get the absolute majority he needed; in the second Hitler was finally defeated, obtaining 36.8 per cent as against Hindenburg's 53 per cent of the votes. Then the Nazis fought three hard campaigns to increase their representation in the State administrations and the Reichstag. In these further contests their fortunes varied. In the State elections of 23rd April 1932 they became the strongest party in the Prussian Diet, but fell short of a majority in Würtemberg, Bavaria and Hamburg. In the General Election for the Reichstag on 31st July, the Nazis won 230 seats, making them the most powerful single party in the Government, but without an absolute majority. This majority was still held by the other parties, and in particular by the Social Democrats. Göring became Speaker and attempted on 12th September to out-manœuvre Chancellor von Papen's determination to dissolve the Reichstag for failing to give him its vote of confidence, by preventing him from speaking. However, the President supported the dissolution, and a further General Election took place in November 1932. In this election the Nazis lost ground, their representation falling to 196—they dropped in all two million votes. It is significant that the crisis in unemployment had reached its peak by the middle of 1932, when the Nazi vote was high; now that unemployment was reduced the Nazi vote declined. Nevertheless, they remained the largest single party in the Reich Government. On 17th November, von Papen resigned as Chancellor, and there then followed the final struggle for power between Hitler (who laid his terms for an authoritarian government before Hindenburg on 23rd November) and von Schleicher, who in fact became Chancellor for a few weeks on 2nd December, only to be forced to resign on 28th January 1933. On 30th January Hitler himself was appointed Chancellor by Hindenburg, and there began the long reign of terror which was to end only in the rubble of Berlin twelve years later.

Behind this list of cold facts with their neat succession of dates lay one of the most bitter struggles of our time. Excitement, intrigue, the traditional calculation of the old-style diplomats pitted against the determination of Hitler to out-manœuvre them, shaped what was happening immediately beneath the surface. The vast, aged father-figure of Hindenburg presided over this political melting-pot from which the future of Germany was to be cast. In the foreground were the statesmen and militarists opposed to the upstart Hitler though prepared to use him, as they hoped, for their own purposes, men such as Chancellors von Papen and von Schleicher; in the background were the various pressures exerted by the bankers, the industrialists and the trade unions. The political problems round which the struggle for ascendancy turned included the payment of reparations, the un-balanced budget at home and the cost of unemployment, and Germany's anxiety at what she regarded as a dangerous and undignified state of disarmament. As far as German militarism was concerned, von Papen hoped that out of the disagreements of the Disarmament Conference at Geneva (which opened on 2nd February 1932 and dragged on for months) Germany might gain a recognised right to the rearmament that the *Reichswehr* had in fact already achieved more or less in secret. Meanwhile, the private armies of Hitler, the S.A. and the S.S., were themselves the subject of much internal dispute. The Reich President directed by an Emergency Decree dated 13th April 1932 that these semi-military organisations were in future to be prohibited. Two days later he further prohibited the Red Front organisation that had been set up by the Social Democrats, the Republican *Reichsbanner* formations and the trade unions to oppose Hitler should he drop his mask of legality and resort to force in order to gain the ultimate power. Later, no 14th June, the ban on the S.A. was revoked by von Papen, who had just assumed the Chancellorship and desired to make what terms he could with the National Socialists. As the German Government drew further to the right, Hitler became increasingly in their eyes a man to win over to their own particular authoritarian camp. Indeed, they were eager to avail themselves of the nationalistic mass movement which Hitler had managed to build up, and which they hoped to exploit for their own ends. However, it was to become clear in the long run that only one thing interested the Nazi leader—absolute power for himself. He played the game of diplomatic intrigue with von Papen because it suited him to gain the final ascendancy by overtly legal rather than by overtly illegal methods. Like a magnet, Hitler gradually drew power towards himself, negotiating at this crucial time with an intuitive skill. In the summer of 1932, when Hitler's voting strength was at its peak, there were seven million men on the dole; half the nation could be said to be living near starvation level and many were ready to turn to a leader who offered them some revolutionary form of change in their status.

Behind all this intrigue, the active little figure of Goebbels ceaselessly planned and worked for Hitler. If the Kaiserhof Hotel was the Party's administrative headquarters, Magda Goebbels' comfortable flat in the Reichskanzlerplatz became Hitler's centre for relaxation, conversation and discussion of future ideas and tactics. Goebbels gave endless advice and counsel, and once a decision was reached that affected him sprang into action day or night. He was chiefly concerned with the election campaigns, the planning of propaganda, the writing of articles and the ceaseless travel that his arduous speaking tours involved. He was for the most part in a buoyant mood, as well he might be. Barely eight years before he had been a penniless and rejected author. Now he had already been a member of the Reichstag for four years, and he was the devoted confidant of his leader at the time when the Party was within sight of gaining supreme power. To add to all this, he had recently married a wealthy and attractive woman. The lonely life in rooms was over. He could write down 1st January 1932 in his diary with happiness and confidence.

It was, he claims, he himself who urged Hitler to test his personal standing with the German people by running for President.[1] One can well imagine him leaning forward pressing his case. "I strongly urge him to come forward as candidate himself," he writes on 19th January. Hitler remained silent, only giving his decision to stand at the end of the month. This turned out, however, to be provisional; Hitler was still hesitating even by 12th February. There is no doubt that this hesitancy was largely strategic. Hindenburg himself did not announce his candidacy until 15th February. Hitler finally decided he would do the same on 22nd February. "The chief thing is now to break silence," writes Goebbels. "The Leader gives me permission to do so at the Sportpalast tonight. Thank God!" The long interval of indecision had been a propagandist's nightmare—"this everlasting waiting is almost demoralising", he laments. Now he could go to town at last:

Sportpalast packed. General meeting of the members of the northern, eastern and western districts. Immense ovations at the very outset. When after about an hour's preparation I publicly proclaim that the Leader will come forward as candidate for the Presidency, a storm of deafening applause rages for nearly ten minutes. Wild ovation for the Leader. The audience rises with shouts of joy. They nearly raise the roof. An overwhelming spectacle![2]

Thus Goebbels lived closely to the events themselves and played his daily part in shaping them. He was never to be so close to Hitler again until the last tragic days drove them underground together, seeking what little comfort they could from Carlyle's story of the miraculous delivery of Frederick the Great from the shadows of defeat.

Goebbels' adoration of Hitler reached its height at this time, as well it might. His own ambition fed on Hitler's; he played the prophet to Hitler's God, before whom his personal vanity turned into that of the devoted servant aware of his genius for service. His attitude to Hitler is rather like that of a head prefect who is specially favoured by the headmaster. He basks in the sunshine of favour which is all the sweeter because Hitler spends his evenings in Goebbels' own home, or the home with which his new wife had presented him. He delights in the confidences which Hitler gave to him, and to him alone:

Return to Munich with the Leader. It is delightful to be alone with him, when he can speak freely and naturally. He is the best story-teller I know.

He is splendid to work with, and belongs to those few who, once having given their confidence, leave one to carry on freely by oneself, untrammelled. . . . The hostile press depicts him quite falsely and gives rise to a very erroneous idea of him. There is nobody in the world less qualified for the rôle of tyrant than Hitler.

Not only has he the gift of rapid and correct decision, but personally he has an indescribable aura about him of kindness and hearty good fellowship, and so captivates everybody who approaches him.[3]

Magda in her turn mothered Hitler, encouraging him to spend his nights at her home in endless talk. She even prepared meals for him herself and took them to the Kaiserhof when in 1932 he feared there was a plot to poison him.[4]

The picture of Hitler that Goebbels builds up for the public is that of a hero, a mythological figure. And yet the figure is, of course, deeply human—talking at night to his friends, visiting Magda in hospital during her illness, when her husband has to be away on duty, responding to children who "stretch up their tiny hands to him", clasping the hand of a dying man of the S.A., and, moreover, the sensitive, artistic man who delights to hear music with a little circle of his friends at night. This particular form of heroism acts as a cushion against which Hitler the politician and Hitler the knight-at-arms can rest in the imagination of his public. For Goebbels also observes, on 4th February 1932, virtually a year before the Chancellorship, "how surely and unerringly the Leader adjusts himself to coming power. He has not the slightest doubt about it, but speaks, acts, and feels as if it were already ours." When Hitler loses the Presidential election, Goebbels telephones him knowing how composed his Leader will be. Hitler merely tells him the fight must go on. "That gives us all new courage," writes Goebbels. "If the Leader does not weaken neither will the Organisation. He is masterly at a crisis." [5]

And so the legend is built up. Hitler, the crack shot, at private pistol practice; Hitler, the mountain-lover of Berchtesgaden, making momentous decisions away from the crowds in the cities; Hitler, the great orator, descending from the clouds in his aircraft as part of Goebbels' scheme for establishing his omnipotence.

It is with pride that Goebbels notes that, while other passengers inhaled oxygen, Hitler remained serene and unperturbed at the height of six thousand metres. Shared with Hitler, the heights were "radiant and luminous".

For the activities of the other leaders among the Nazis—all except Gregor Strasser—Goebbels has little space; Göring is allowed a passing tribute as a "valuable help" to Hitler. But it is characteristic that the diary form of record so beloved by Goebbels permits his own personal share in these momentous events to take precedence over everything else. To Strasser alone, his former employer, the man who had brought him into the Party, he constantly returns in order to revile him for his defeatism. He is accused of disloyalty, of becoming the centre of the clique anxious to give up the fight, of ineffective speaking in the Reichstag, of popularity with the enemy, of attempting to disintegrate the Party, of being sunk in pessimism. He is, says Goebbels, "the chameleon of National Socialism". [6] On 8th December 1932 he resigned all his posts in the Party, opposing Hitler's policy of 'useless opposition' and advocating compromise with the Government. Behind these accusations is the certainty in Goebbels' mind that Strasser wants to replace Hitler as Head of the Party. "Treachery, treachery, treachery," he cries out:

For hours the Leader paces up and down the room in the hotel. It is obvious that he is thinking very hard. He is embittered and deeply wounded by this unfaithfulness. Suddenly he stops and says: "If the Party once falls to pieces, I shall shoot myself without more ado." A dreadful threat, and most depressing.[7]

In the final downfall of Strasser, Goebbels without doubt played a significant part. After the setback to the Nazis in the November election, there was a real opportunity to get rid of Hitler and secret discussions were going on to bring about a relatively left-wing coalition between Schleicher, the Chancellor, Leipart, representing the trade unions, and Strasser, representing the wing of the National Socialists prepared to bring into a coalition Government all that could be called rational in the Party. This would have meant the end of Hitler's all-or-nothing attitude, and the passing of the leadership of the Party over to the more moderate Strasser, who regarded National Socialism as a revolutionary movement for the good of Germany and not, like Hitler, as a channel through which to gain a personal dictatorship for himself. Goebbels was determined at all costs to smash what he regarded as a conspiracy within the Party, all the more when, on 3rd December, a local election in Thuringia showed a drop of about 40 per cent in the Nazi vote.

On 5th December Goebbels convened a conference of the Party leaders at the Kaiserhof on Hitler's behalf, sending a telegram to all the Reichstag deputies to attend. Here the whole business of coalition was hotly debated, and Hitler refused to let Strasser discuss any terms with the new Chancellor, Schleicher. Two days later, on 7th December, Hitler and Strasser confronted each other at the Kaiserhof. Hitler accused Strasser of disloyalty and of scheming with Schleicher behind his back, and staged one of his great outbursts of fury, refusing to listen to Strasser's assertions that he had been loyal to the Party. At last Strasser challenged him:

"Do you really mean what you are saying?"

"I do," shouted Hitler, nodding his head vigorously.

Strasser simply reached for his brief-case and left the room. He was white with rage. At his hotel he wrote his letter of resignation, got into his car and drove away south from Berlin. He took no further action in the Party's politics, and every attempt to get him back proved hopeless. Messenger after messenger was sent in vain by his friends and supporters urging him to return to renew the fight. Goebbels then set about destroying the remnants of support for Strasser's policy of coalition. It was thought that about a third of the Reichstag National Socialist deputies were among those initially prepared to support him.[8]

The one thing Hitler did not want was the Reichstag to be dissolved yet again, and his almost bankrupt Party to be faced with the cost of yet another election. It was about a month later that the celebrated lunch took place on 4th January at which Hitler met von Papen at the house of Kurt von Schroeder, one of the most prominent bankers in Germany. This lunch proved to be yet another turning-point in the developments which led to the rise of the Nazis to power, though von Papen has sworn on his word "as a Christian and a gentleman" that the meeting proved to be of no importance whatsoever, but was merely an attempt by Schleicher to get him disgraced in the eyes of Hindenburg.[9] Otto Strasser, however, claims it was at this lunch that Hitler learned the President had no intention of dissolving the Reichstag, and so was encouraged to persist with the intransigent attitude which only three weeks later was to give him the Chancellorship. Goebbels did his best to keep the meeting secret, but the press learned of it and blazoned it on the front pages of the morning papers.

After this lunch it was only a matter of three weeks before Hitler was to be Chancellor with von Papen in his Cabinet.[10] Hitler was prepared to compromise to the extent of bringing certain members of the opposition into his Government. He knew that once he was in power he could shape the destiny of Germany and the nature of her Constitution as he willed. Meanwhile, the policy so persistently advocated by Goebbels had triumphed, and the main struggle was almost over, for all that remained to be done now was to ease out the

Ministers who for the time being gave an air of coalition and legality to Hitler's Government. Von Papen and his eight colleagues in the Cabinet, who faced only three National Socialist Ministers, had yet to learn how worthless their apparently overwhelming majority was in fact to prove.

In his own specialised field in the development of Nazi policy, the department of propaganda, Goebbels was prepared to admit only Hitler as his superior. Otherwise, he himself, of course, was supreme artist. In the diary he constantly states his views about propaganda methods, party tactics and the principles of authoritarian rule. In all these matters he experiences a Machiavellian delight in thinking up ways and means of being successful. The only thing of which he is scarcely conscious is the despicable self-portrait that so frequently emerges from his own self-satisfaction.

He records with pride the praise given him in March 1932 by a visiting representative of the *Popolo d'Italia*. The journalist, he says, was dumbfounded and exclaimed that Goebbels had created "the vastest and most up-to-date propaganda in Europe". For Goebbels "propaganda must be raised to a political art". Already in January 1932 he claims that he was discussing with Hitler the idea of founding a Ministry for Popular Education with full control of the press, cinema, radio, educational establishments, the arts, culture and the machinery of propaganda.

Meanwhile, as the Party's Head of Propaganda, he used every device, old or new, to impress the German people. "I hope," he says in February, "to achieve a masterpiece of propaganda for this year's elections." In May he writes that he considers "the main burden of the work will rest on the propaganda. Our technique has to be worked out to the minutest particular. Only the most up-to-date and expert methods will help us to victory." When it was all over and Hitler safely installed, he boasts: "Our propaganda is acknowledged not only by the German, but also the international press, to be a model, and unique. We have gained such extensive experience in this matter during the past election campaign that we are able to win a victory over our adversaries without difficulty by our superior methods".[11] Chakotin, in his book *The Rape of the Masses*, quotes Goebbels' claim that in the presidential campaign he would use "American methods on an American scale", although when Hitler was in fact defeated he raged that the other side had used these same American methods at the instigation of the Jews and with the help of Jewish money.[12] Throughout 1932 he constantly complains of the lack of money to develop his ideas and staff his department, and he appropriated for his purposes every financial windfall on which he could lay his hands. Like an advertising agent, he would ponder for hours to get the right kind of slogan for the posters. He liked the abruptness, for example, of "Make an end of it!" The Party, of course, had its fighting newspapers, such as Goebbels' own paper, *Der Angriff*, which now appeared daily. But in addition to these obvious means of propaganda, Goebbels, whenever the money came his way, resorted to additional modern methods to reinforce his campaigns. In February 1932 fifty thousand midget gramophone records attacking the Government were released; they could be slipped into an ordinary envelope. This device was successful enough to be repeated later. Although talking-films were barely established in Europe, Goebbels had himself filmed making a ten-minute speech for open-air projection in the public gardens and squares of the larger cities. This device, too, proved successful and became standard practice. He did not need the Russian cinema of Eisenstein and Pudovkin to teach him what this medium could do in the hands of a propagandist of genius. In January 1933 he writes:

In the evening we go to see the film *Rebel* by Luis Trencker. A first-class production of an artistic film. From it I can imagine the film of the future, revolutionary in character, with grand mass-scenes, composed with enormous vital energy. In one scene, in which a gigantic crucifix is carried out of a small church by the revolutionaries, the audience is deeply moved. Here you really see what can be done with the film as an artistic medium, when it is really understood. We are all much impressed.[13]

But the Party's financial resources at this stage did not permit the full use of the cinema; that was to come. Radio, again, was difficult for the Party to use. None the less in September Goebbels reports that his "broadcasting organisation" is working finely, except that it has not got the use of a transmitter! The following year, soon after Hitler had become Chancellor, he writes:

As an instrument for propaganda on a large scale the efficacy of the radio has not yet been sufficiently appreciated. In any case our adversaries have not recognised its value. All the better; we shall have to explore its possibilities.[14]

His imagination was fired by the possibilities of film and radio once he was in contact with them, but he had to content himself now with the more startling development of the resources he could afford. His placards and posters flared out to such an extent that he frequently ran into censorship trouble. In Berlin, on 4th April, he claims the city "is hardly recognisable". "Our posters blaze forth on every advertising pillar." In June he boasts that he has composed "placards, which, unless they are forbidden, will turn the entire city upside down". He still used red colours so that his posters should stand out boldly against the conventional black of the rest of the circular street hoardings.

At one celebrated public meeting he used an ingenious method to score a victory over the Government. He issued a challenge to Brüning, the Chancellor, to take part in a public debate with him. It was most unlikely that a man in the Chancellor's position would have accepted such a challenge, but in fact Goebbels never gave him a chance to do so. The big posters announcing the Chancellor's refusal were out within an hour of Brüning's first knowledge of the challenge. For Goebbels had his own idea about how the debate was to be conducted. When he appeared that evening, a number of large suitcases were brought up on to the platform after him, and he set his audience laughing when he said that, in spite of the Chancellor's refusal to appear, he had brought him along none the less. As his assistants began to unpack the suitcases, Goebbels added: "In here I have got Herr Brüning, or at least all that matters of him!" The cases contained large disc recordings of Brüning's speeches, and from then on Goebbels conducted a debate with the absent Chancellor by switching the recordings on and off. This original kind of performance delighted the audience and scored a propaganda victory as sheer entertainment. Incidentally, the B.B.C. was later to adopt the same device in its broadcasts to Germany during the war, using recordings of Hitler's propaganda speeches and broadcasts against him with interpolations of the truth.

Another example of strategy was Goebbels' handling of the elections in the smallest of all the German states, Lippe-Detmold, the population of which was only some 150,000. This election came early in January when the Nazis were still smarting under their defeat in the November elections. Goebbels realised that during this period of stalemate with the Government what the Party needed was a resounding victory in a local election; only a few weeks before they had dropped nearly 40 per cent of their votes in Thuringia. So he decided to concentrate all his propaganda resources on this minute section of the German population. Hitler, Göring and other leaders went round, speaking in inns and village halls, and even canvassing for votes from door to door. Thousands of Storm Troopers invaded the neighbourhood, and every opposition poster was torn from the walls. Although Magda, his wife, was seriously ill in Berlin, Goebbels concentrated for two weeks on the conquest of the Diet of Lippe. He won. In *Der Angriff* of 20th January he wrote: "The decision of the citizens of Lippe is not a local affair. It corresponds to the sentiment prevailing throughout the country. Again the great masses of the people are on the move— in our direction."[15] It was a brilliant idea, and it succeeded. The German press, which had laughed at the whole affair, found their laughter turned against them.

The National Socialists were also masters of the art of ceremonial. Their genius for pageantry and for the generation of mass emotion through the combination of elaborate processions, stirring music and dramatic speech-making has probably never been equalled; it reached its height in the great Nuremberg rallies of the pre-war years. Goebbels himself was not only an eloquent orator on such occasions, but an adept at exploiting the easy emotions that are available to the propagandist when people are gathered together to do honour to this or that. For example, Goebbels loved funerals. During 1932 he saw to it that every funeral possible of an S.A. or S.S. man who had been killed in street-fights or ambushes was turned to advantage. "In the churchyard by the graveside I give full vent to my grief and indignation" (26th January 1932). "At noon we bury our murdered comrade, Koester, in a churchyard outside Berlin. Our S.A. men are pale with rage and indignation . . . I express all the hatred and rage that weighs upon my heart. Ten thousand people listen with boundless resentment" (25th June 1932). But he went even better on 11th November:

At Schöneberg (suburb of Berlin) we bury Reppich, the Storm Trooper who was killed during the strike. Forty thousand people are present at the funeral. He is being laid to rest like a prince. Over the cemetery aeroplanes are circling with Swastika flags swathed in black as a last greeting to the dead. The Storm Troopers present are much moved.

Most useful of all were the funerals of the Hitler youth. In January 1933 Goebbels claimed the "whole population of Berlin" followed one boy to his grave. "We march behind the coffin of this murdered boy through eternal walls of men for two and a half hours." The sixteen-year-old youth sacrificed to Hitler is returned "to the motherly bosom of the earth". Even more effective, though much simpler, was the funeral of a small boy of the *Hitlerjugend* who was stabbed a year earlier in the Moabit suburb of Berlin, the district with strong Communist associations. Goebbels refers repeatedly to the marks made on a white wall by "his little bloodstained hands". These marks, he says, are like the *Mene Tekel* at Belshazzar's feast. Although at that period prohibited from speaking in public by Berlin's Deputy Chief of Police, who was still the famous 'Isidor' Weiss, Goebbels could scarcely be stopped from orating over the grave of this poor child.

We bury the "Hitler boy" Norkus on a biting cold day. From the bottom of my heart I speak to the children and the men gathered round the narrow coffin. The boy's father, a simple workman, is brave beyond words. Grief-stricken, with an ashen face, he raises his hand in salute to the strains of the Horst Wessel Lied and sings with bitter pride and deep wrath "Hold high the flag!"[16]

Although there was at times little to choose between the methods used by the Communists and the National Socialists to exploit the political situation, Goebbels did everything he could to dramatise the violence he himself incited in the bitterest of his opponents. The Nazis always deliberately provoked trouble.

The following October he boasts of how he organised the break-up of a political meeting. Hundreds of National Socialists were issued with forged passes to a joint debating session staged by the Nazis together with the Nationalist Party, most of whose own members were left outside the hall waving their genuine passes in indignation. This meant, in effect, that the hall was virtually filled with National Socialists long before the debate was due to start. Goebbels then arrived with his entourage and was carried shoulder-high into the hall amid shouts and cheers. "I myself," he writes, "am surrounded by a ring of S.A. men, stout as oaks. It will be no pleasure surely for the Nationalists to make a speech against the Nazi Party in this hall." In the end, the Nationalist speakers were howled to silence, and the chairman of the meeting had to call on Goebbels to restore order. Outside the sound of the Horst Wessel Lied left no doubt which of the two parties was the better and less scrupulously organised. Goebbels, elated with his success, rushed round to ensure that a million (Goebbels' figure) extra copies of the National Socialist papers would be on the streets to reinforce the victory.

The violent break-up of meetings extended even to the Prussian Diet, where on 25th May Goebbels was among those who incited a bloody battle with the Communists who were flung bodily out of the Assembly. The victorious Nazis sang the Horst Wessel Lied on the scene of their triumph. 1932 was also a year of violent street-fighting between the Communists and the National Socialists. In Prussia alone 461 political riots took place in fifty days, 1st June-20th July, with 82 killed and 400 seriously wounded. The Ruhr was another centre for violence, and on Sunday 10th July a pitched battle between the Nazis and Communists took place in Altona, a suburb of Hamburg, in which nineteen people lost their lives and nearly 300 were wounded. Goebbels himself describes the violence of his reception in Elberfeld and Düsseldorf, his old district as a Nazi organiser:

We fight our way through the seething mob at Düsseldorf and Elber-feld. A wild trip! We had no idea that the situation would turn out to be so serious. Innocuous, we drive into Hagen quite openly, uni-formed, and in an open car. The streets are swarming, full of the mob and Communist rabble. They block the thoroughfare so that we can neither advance nor go back. There is nothing for it but to drive straight ahead at full speed and give them to understand we don't care a fig for them! We dash straight through. Each of us has his revolver ready and is decided to pay for his life, if needs be, as dearly as possible.

The meeting place lies on a hill with a wood in the background. The Communists have ingeniously set fire to this wood, so that the holding of the meeting is rendered impracticable. But speeches are delivered, in spite of this. The enemy is not to have the fun of beating us. Ten thousand are present on the hillside. Our S.A. men blanch with rage.[17]

On 15th July he was stoned out of Rheydt, his native town. He was not to forget this insult in a hurry.

Yet the Communists were turned to account in the final dealings with Schleicher, who was convinced in the end that National Socialism must not be allowed to disintegrate. Were it to do so, he realised all too well that the only place appropriate for the rowdies of the streets, the private armies of unemployed men and hysterical youths would be in the ranks of the Communist Party itself. Goebbels hastened to point this out to the wavering democrats. Without National Socialism, he alleged in January 1933, there would be twelve million more Com-munists in Germany. But the unemployed rabble that made up the greater number of the Storm Troopers were quite unfitted to accept the strict ideological discipline imposed by the Communists.

Goebbels still recognised that speaking, not writing, was the essence of effective propaganda. Hitler had said so in *Mein Kampf*, and it was indeed fortunate for Goebbels that his personal ambitions were equally divided between recognition as a great orator and as a great writer. The Nazis were never to succeed with the printed word to the extent that they succeeded with the spoken word, where the situation was totally different because the dramatic utterance of the living performer could be designed to steal the attention of an audience excited by the contagion of mass enthusiasm. Like Hitler, though so different in his style and manner of speaking, Goebbels was perhaps happiest before an audience. In any case, he claimed that though the National Socialists had many good speakers at their disposal they had virtually no good journalists. Then he makes a revealing statement (1st October 1932):

In many cases our journalists do not understand that in election times papers have to give themselves up to propaganda almost exclusively. These writers are generally too sincere and more like scientists than propagandists.

Our propagandists are better. Day by day, and evening by evening, they are in direct contact with the masses. They are masters of their job, the élite of our Party. The best platform speakers that Germany has ever produced are to be found on our side.

Goebbels had no illusions about the nature of propaganda. If journalism was degraded to a science, propaganda was raised to an art! The thirteen months from 1st January 1932 to 30th January 1933 saw an orgy of speech-making. Goebbels turned the whistle-stop system of American campaigning into the flight-stop system of the Nazis. "A critical innovation," he writes in March. "The Leader will conduct his next campaign by plane. By this means he will be able to speak three or four times a day at various places as opportunity serves, and address about one and a half million people in spite of the time being so short." The flights were often terrible, but Hitler seemed to enjoy them. On 8th April, when storms grounded all aircraft over western Germany, Hitler flew to Düsseldorf to fulfil his engagement to speak. "The small sporting monoplane leaps and tosses," complains Goebbels, on the way to Dresden, six months later. But the Leader came down safely from the clouds to address an audience claimed to be thirty thousand at the Stadion. These 'propaganda flights' were Goebbels' idea; they were minutely planned by him and carried out with the help of the National Socialist Flying Corps.

But the greatest meetings of all were those staged by Goebbels in the Sportpalast, the vast arena in Berlin, which held some 12,000 people. The Nazis adopted it as their principal platform. Goebbels writes:

The Sportpalast is the great political platform of the capital, and we have made it into what it now is. There is something quite unique about it. When one enters it on an overcrowded occasion one is immediately affected, as it were, by the mass emotional content of the place.[18]

Later he claimed that "the use of the Sportpalast is having a lasting effect on public life. Its platform is truly the platform of the people." It was here on Sunday 22nd January that Hitler made his last public speech, an address to the Storm Troopers, before he became Chancellor. This followed a day of marching directed against the Communists, who had planned a counter-march which seemed to make a street-battle inevitable, especially as the Nazis intended to begin their demonstration outside the Communist Party headquarters. Schleicher, faced with the problem of public safety, prohibited the Communists from assembling, but permitted the Nazis to do so. With armed police protection and escorted by armoured cars, the Nazis flaunted their victory in the face of the Communists on their own ground, the Bülowplatz. Goebbels could afford to laugh; he knew now that Schleicher's days were numbered and that it was only a matter of waiting impatiently for the President to call on Hitler to become Chancellor.

Behind the propaganda, the demonstrations, the street-fights, the funerals and the shouting lay the philosophy of Nazism itself—if it could be called a philosophy. It sharpened itself against the whetstone of both its success and its setbacks. It was completely opportunist. But certain principles underlie Goebbels' presentation of the Nazi case in their relentless pursuit of power. Goebbels says significantly that it is always necessary to be "strict in principle" but "elastic in application". "Tactics," he explains elsewhere, "are more a matter of intelligence and instinct than of character. One sometimes has to go a roundabout way to attain a great goal. Most people," he goes on, "do not understand the difference between strategy and tactics."[19] What he seems to mean by this is that you must as a tactician use any means you can devise to gain your ultimate objective as a strategist!

What the Nazis wanted was a single simple act—an Enabling Bill giving Hitler dictatorial power—"the contest for power, the game of chess", as Goebbels calls it.[20] This they eventually achieved in March 1933. It was the sound barrier through which the Nazi machine had to penetrate, and the way through was opened when Hitler became Chancellor. Until that time the heat had to be kept full on. "The Party must always be kept with the steam up," says Goebbels.[21]

The policy was one of attack. Attack represented strength. "We must make up our minds to live dangerously," he writes.[22] And again: "We are always strongest in the offensive."[23] It was right to be "everlastingly worrying on the heels of the Government".[24] In any situation, however adverse, aggression was the rule. On one occasion Goebbels found a policeman had confiscated his car because it was parked in front of an hotel entrance. He immediately created a scene, lost his temper and turned the situation into a public exhibition in which he called the policeman a Communist and began to incite the people attracted by the shouting against the Government. The result of this, he boasts, was that the police thenceforth left his car strictly alone. Aggression pays! "One must never allow oneself to fall back on mere defence."[25] The Party, therefore, was constantly being rallied, and enemies created for it to fight. The enemies were the Government, the Communists and the Jews. Meanwhile, to overawe them and the weak and vacillating bourgeois ("who is unable to understand the present situation") came the arrays of marching men ("two hours of eternal marching, tall, fair, the best of our German youth . . . with them one can achieve a revolution").[26] And behind the marching men came the sudden violences—"outside in the corridor the slandered Klotz is being flogged by a few hefty members of the Party".[27] "A National Socialist only feels himself when he is at liberty to make a fight of it."[28] Violence had always to be engineered against the Communists in the streets and alleyways and meeting-halls. Bloodshed became normal.

The Nazis made great play with their direct contact with the people. "We must appeal to the primitive instincts in the masses,"[29] writes Goebbels, and throughout the diary he never stops emphasising that the Nazi strength lay in its direct dependence on the will of the people. Just as enemies had to be incited to give the S.A. and the S.S. someone to fight, so the ambitions of the Nazi had to be made to seem dependent on the support of a proletariat. "One must never fall out of touch with the people," says Goebbels.[30] "The people are the beginning, middle and end of all our endeavours." The people did not include, of course, the Jews, the Communists, the Social Democrats and the bourgeois. They were those who could be induced, bribed or brow-beaten into supporting the ambitions of Hitler and his associates. "The Poll! the Poll! It's the people we want" expresses exactly the reason for these constant references.[31] But the Nazi proletariat had its symbolic representatives. "A simple workman comes up to the plat-form and hands me his wedding-ring. It is a wonderful people for whom we are fighting!"[32]

The attitude of the Nazis to both the industrialists and the intelli-gentsia was equally opportunist. Power, as Goebbels remarks wryly, begets money; but when you have not yet achieved power you are always in need of it.

Deliver an address to the leaders of industry in the afternoon. The more desperate their situation, the better they understand us.

Speak to the working classes in the evening. The S.A. takes forty minutes to march in.[33]

Goebbels was careful to adapt his style when he was called upon to handle the selected audience of influential people.

In the evening at the Hotel Prinz Albrecht. I address a small circle of invited guests. Here, also, problems of National Socialism are begin-ning to attract interest, although these people approach them in their own manner, with a slight degree of hauteur, and from a considerable distance.

They seem utterly unable to grasp that we really embody something essentially new, that we cannot and will not be compared with any other party, that we are aiming at a totalitarian State, and must attain absolute power in order to achieve our aims.[34]

Goebbels makes some interesting remarks about the ideal human material for whom the Nazis were searching to increase their supporters. "A man of good character," he says, "without necessarily great insight into things is always better than an intelligent man without much character."[35] And again: "Politics turn far more on character than on intelligence: it is courage that conquers the world!"[36] Seeing that Goebbels had no doubt at all of his own intelligence, it is clear that all the Nazis wanted were malleable men who once their sights had been levelled allowed themselves to be used as human weapons against their nation's opponents. "A few flames burn brightly, the others only reflect their light."[37]

The brightest flame was, of course, Hitler himself. "The Leader is great just because he follows one sole end with dauntless tenacity, and is ready to sacrifice everything for it."[38] One night at the Kaiserhof Hotel Goebbels spoke to his colleagues about nobility. Nobility has value "only if its privileges are based upon greater duties towards the nation". In any case, as Goebbels put it, "the Movement had grown under divine protection, and all that was, has had to be, so that we might reach the point where we are now".[39] One could not say fairer than that.

Goebbels himself, both consciously and unconsciously, draws his own self-portrait in this undoubtedly much edited book. There are, of course, none of the revealing glimpses of his private life such as those set down by his own hand in the diaries of 1925-26. This is the public Goebbels, the man in the Nazi mask. He represents himself as boundlessly energetic, ceaselessly efficient, continuously overworked, a relentless campaigner for Hitler. Much of this we must admit to be true, however coloured the self-portrait is by Goebbels' vanity. At the time the published diary begins he had just got married, and Magda is represented as never very far from his thoughts. Hitler, as we have seen, was a constant visitor, talking into the night. ("It is delightful to be alone with him.") Magda gave birth to a daughter, Helga, on 1st September 1932. But by the following Christmas ("The feast of the Divine Love is drawing near," writes Goebbels) Magda is seriously ill in hospital. "A sad Christmas! My heart is full of grief. The only consolation is that little Harald is with me."[40] Harald was Magda's son by her first husband. "We light up a Christmas tree, and have a sad little Christmas by ourselves. . . . The Leader has sent a very kind telegram to the hospital. He, too, will be quite alone on Christmas Eve." After this he plunged into the Lippe election campaign, keeping in touch with the hospital as best he could by telephone. Magda did not return home until 1st February. Hitler visited her in hospital, and sent her flowers.

With these occasional glimpses of a domesticated Goebbels we have to remain content. He likes to refer to the relaxation of music after the long day's work—"Music lifts us out of the humdrum of every day, and makes us feel, afresh, the higher inspiration of our work."[41] Goebbels had, after all, as the Minister responsible for culture as well as for propaganda by the time his diary was published, to maintain the correct kind of self-portrait before the German public. Wagner, Hitler's favourite composer, always stimulated him. Wagner's kind of music could so easily be linked with German nationalism. There are many references in the diary to Wagner's "eternal genius". After hearing a performance of *Die Meistersinger* Goebbels writes:

The giant Wagner stands so high above all modern musical nonentities that it is unworthy of his genius for them to be compared to him. As the great 'Awake' Chorus begins you feel the stimulation in your blood. Germany, too, will soon feel the same, and be called to an awakening.[42]

But the main picture of himself that he presents in the diary is of the worker and strategist, tirelessly pursuing campaign after campaign. "We live for nothing but this drive for success and political achievement."[43]

Once more eternally on the move. Work has to be done standing, walking, driving, flying. The most urgent conferences are held on the stairs, in the hall, at the door, or on the way to the station. It nearly drives one out of one's senses. One is carried by train, motor-car and aeroplane criss-cross through Germany. One arrives at a town half an hour before the beginning of a meeting or sometimes even later, goes up to the platform and speaks.[44]

"I am so dead tired and exhausted that I can hardly stand," he writes elsewhere. And with a suitable touch of pathos to win the admiration of the reader relaxed in his armchair: "I *must* break off a little just for an hour's rest." Even when he is ill with a high fever he presses on. "I give an address in each of the two halls. The audience has no idea how bad I feel."

With Goebbels the pose is never very far from the man. Much of what he claims for himself is just, but he is so vain of his achievements that he basks almost indecently in the sunshine of his self-assumed virtues. No one questions his ability, though he was, like other very able men in politics, to miscalculate sometimes, more especially when he came to power. No one questions his energy, though if his self-interest was not fired he could be listless and lazy, as he admits in his earlier writings. His loyalty to Hitler was without doubt linked subconsciously to this same instinct to gain power and glory for himself, but even so there is no need to question the sincerity of his devotion as far as it goes. Hitler was a success partly through Goebbels' own intelligent promotion of him. His success was a measure of Goebbels' own power. Loyalty to Hitler was loyalty to himself.

Goebbels' greatest self-appreciation lay in his talents as a speaker. He knew he was good, and he was good. There are constant, revealing references to his experiences as agitator and orator. "Am received by hooting. When I leave there is either silence or applause."[45]

But there was no pleasure to equal the enjoyment of a completely successful performance before an already excited audience in the Sportpalast.

To address such an audience is a real treat. One forgets time and space. I speak for two and a half hours or more, and launch attack after attack against the Government. It all ends with prolonged cheering. A strange experience to leave the seething ocean of humanity at the Sportpalast, drive through the wildly cheering crowd in the Potsdamerstrasse, and find oneself sitting in the quiet of one's home a few minutes later. One arrives late and tired, and tumbles into bed like the dead.[46]

Examples of Goebbels' publicity in Berlin. *Left above and below* poster layouts, printed in red. *Right, above,* a *litfassäule* displaying a Nazi poster. *Right, below,* the front page of the first issue of *Der Angriff.*

Otto Strasser, 1932

Gregor Strasser, 1932

Goebbels defending himself in a
court of law, 1931.

Goebbels, 1932

He also had to master that most difficult of techniques, the art of addressing a large audience from a platform while at the same time using a microphone for the transmission of the speech over the radio. For the skilled orator direct address to an assembled audience is a matter of establishing the correct level of vocal projection that will give him complete mastery over his hearers' attention. Goebbels was, of course, thoroughly experienced in this largely instinctive technique. But to effect the right degree of projection to suit a microphone only two feet from one's face while at the same time endeavouring to reach out with his voice to the boundaries of a packed hall is a matter of highly skilled technical compromise, as Goebbels himself found.

For twenty minutes at the microphone speak to the audience in the Sportpalast. It goes better than I had thought. It is a strange experience suddenly to be faced with an inanimate microphone when one is used to addressing a living crowd, to be uplifted by the atmosphere of it, and to read the effect of one's speech in the expression on the faces of one's hearers.[47]

Once the Nazis were in power the radio (then only a few years old as a public medium) was at their disposal, and new techniques of speaking had to be learned. Goebbels was soon to become an expert broadcaster.

The emphasis of the rest of Goebbels' self-portrait is on the aggressiveness and violence that was part of the Nazi character. He encourages and looks for insults in order to avenge them. "Perhaps the best way would be to have one of those scurrilous scribblers dragged out of the office by some S.A. men and publicly flogged," he writes when he has been attacked in the *Acht-Uhr Abendblatt*.

If hot water is the revolutionist's element, as Bernard Shaw's rebel, Jack Tanner, claims, then Goebbels was fortunate during this period. In January 1932 he was called as a witness in a case of assault against some Jews of which Count Helldorf, the S.A. Leader in Berlin, was being accused; Goebbels was thought by the police to have been involved himself. After refusing for a while to give evidence at all unless the police revealed the source of their information against him, he eventually appeared:

I then direct my attention to the Attorney-General, and overwhelm him with my indignation. At last I give my evidence as insolently as I can, and am dismissed after having been fined 500 Reichsmark for contravention of a regulation. The defendant S.A. men shook with laughter.[48]

Immediately after the case Goebbels was prohibited from speaking in public by his old enemy Weiss for a period that amounted to about three weeks. This did not, of course, stop him speaking elsewhere. In February he was excluded from the Reichstag for causing an uproar and (falsely, as he claims) insulting the President. In April the Supreme Court of Justice indicted him for high treason. ("The accusation covers forty pages. A bothersome affair!") He made himself immune from proceedings for a while by accepting the mandate of the Prussian Diet —that is, the privilege accorded to a Party member who has been allocated a seat in the Government. In May the case was dropped. In July he was stoned out of his native town of Rheydt. In September he claims that the "bourgeois press" had obtained a decree threatening to fine him 300,000 Reichsmark and to have him imprisoned because of his organised boycott by the Nazis of all papers that were consistently attacking the Party. This case also came to nothing. In November the Government forced *Der Angriff* (which was frequently suspended from publication for the tone of its articles) to publish a special edition on the eve of the General Election with an appeal of an anti-Nazi nature in it. Goebbels agreed to publish the edition, but had the whole issue secretly thrown into a canal in the night. "Let it sink!" he wrote. No doubt the water was hot.

But ceaselessly aggressive tactics paid in the end. On 30th January 1933 Hitler became Chancellor, and the balance of the world was changed overnight. Those who had brought this change about thought, no doubt, that they could control it. Hitler's first Cabinet had only three Nazi Ministers in it. But the days of both the Cabinet and the Reichstag, as representative of democratic government in Germany, were numbered. As Goebbels put it less than three months later, on 22nd April:

The Leader's authority is now completely in the ascendant in the

Cabinet. There will be no more voting. The Leader's personality decides. All this has been achieved much more quickly than we had dared to hope.[49]

The intermediate weeks saw the rapid stripping of German democracy, such as it was. Göring, in a powerful position as head of the Prussian Ministry of the Interior, set about reform with a will. Anti-Nazis were removed from offices of importance both centrally and regionally. The heads of the police force were replaced by Nazis. Papers which had consistently attacked the Party (such as *Vorwärts* and the *Acht-Uhr Abendblatt*) were prohibited from publication and on 24th February the police raided the Communist headquarters in Berlin. Then, on 27th February, the sinister affair of the Reichstag fire took place, followed by Göring's immediate suppression of the "entire Communist and Social Democrat press" (as Goebbels puts it) and a direct attack by the Nazis on the Communist Party with the aim of its complete elimination. The Nazis claimed that the Communists had been about to stage a revolution of their own.

Goebbels' account of the fire itself is brief, and his view of its cause succinct:

Work at home in the evening. The Leader comes to dine at nine o'clock. We have some music and talk. Suddenly a phone call from Dr. Hanfstaengl: "The Reichstag is on fire!" I take this for a bit of wild fantasy and refuse to report it to the Leader. I ask for news wherever possible and at last obtain the dreadful confirmation: it is true! The great dome is all ablaze. Incendiarism! I immediately inform the Leader, and we hasten at top speed down the Charlottenburger Chaussee to the Reichstag. The whole building is aflame. Clambering over thick fire-hoses we reach the great lobby by gateway number two. Göring meets us on the way, and soon von Papen also arrives. That this is the work of incendiaries has been ascertained to be the fact at various spots. There is no doubt that Communism has made a last attempt to cause disorder by means of fire and terror, in order to grasp the power during the general panic.[50]

This atmosphere of domesticity disturbed and shocked by a surprising event is borne out by Hitler's friend and photographer Heinrich

Hoffmann,[51] who was present at the Goebbels' flat when the fire was discovered. Hitler, accompanied by Goebbels, went to the offices of the *Völkischer Beobachter* and issued a new editorial demanding vengeance.[52]

There can now be no doubt at all that Goebbels himself was implicated with Göring in the Reichstag fire plot.[53] They needed some incident which would afford the Nazis an excuse for suppressing the Communists in the cause of public safety. The Communists still commanded some six million votes in Germany. This, it appears, is what happened. There was an underground passage linking the Palace of the President of the Reichstag with the Reichstag building. During the night of the 27th, members of the S.A. led by Karl Ernst, trusted assistant of Count Helldorf, Leader of the S.A. in Berlin, entered the Reichstag along this passage and prepared certain furniture and fittings for the flames with a chemical solution; a young madman, van der Lubbe, an alleged Communist, immediately admitted incendiarism when he was found half-naked in the burning building. He was a willing tool of the S.A., and longed for fame and martyrdom. The Nazis saw to it that the Reichstag fire was regarded as a symbol of the incipient Communist revolution which their vigilance had frustrated. Hitler himself wanted an immediate Communist blood-bath, but was restrained by his Cabinet. Yet when the trial connected with the fire was held later in Leipzig, all four of the Communist leaders accused of implication were acquitted, and only van der Lubbe, who had admitted his guilt from the start, was sentenced and executed. All the Reich Court permitted itself to say was that the fire could have been an act perpetrated by Left radical elements with a view to overthrowing the Government and seizing power. But the fire served its purpose well, and the first stages in the establishment of a police state were secured. Hindenburg, as President, signed an emergency decree "for the Protection of People and State", and Göring, as the Minister in charge of the police, took over. Communists were arrested by the police, or, what was far worse, seized by the S.A. and viciously maltreated. The Communists were the excuse for a temporary suspension of civil rights which was to become permanent. They were only the first on the list of parties and organisations to be suspended.

Karl Ernst was subsequently to be killed by the Nazis during the Röhm purge the following year. Gisevius, the former Gestapo official who was to become one of the leading agents among the German underground, gave evidence at the Nuremberg Trials which affirmed that it was Goebbels himself who had planned the whole operation of the fire with Ernst on 18th February, supervised the selection of the S.A. men to take part and advised Ernst that the police would not investigate any use to which the President's passage to the Reichstag might be put. After all, the President was Göring himself.

Goebbels, like Hitler, wanted to make the fire the occasion for a blood-bath. Later he boasted that it was he who had advised Hitler to hang van der Lubbe in public in front of the gutted building.

Curt Riess ingeniously reminds us that Dostoevsky's nihilist hero Pyotr Stepanovich Verhovensky in *The Possessed*, which Goebbels had read with so much enthusiasm ten years previously, was himself an incendiarist by inclination. Did Goebbels, he queries, get the idea originally from his reading of Dostoevsky?

While the excitement about the fire was at its height, the elections for the Reichstag came round once more. Goebbels arranged a vast torchlight procession to act as the culmination of the month's campaign for votes in which every device of processions, demonstrations, marching, orations to cheering crowds and the sinister intimations of violence and beating-up had been used to effect a favourable poll. The results could only be described as disappointing for the Nazis, the more so considering that their opponents had been deprived by violence of any effective campaign. The Nazis polled only 43.9 per cent, or just over 17 million of the 39 million votes cast. Coupled with the Nationalists, Hitler was only able to muster a bare majority in the House. But with the Communist representatives proscribed, they had now in fact little to fear, and Goebbels in his diary has no qualms about presenting the vote as an overwhelming victory: "The victory is ours. It is far greater than any of us had dared to hope. But what do figures signify any longer? We are masters of the Reich and of Prussia; all other parties have been definitely beaten."[54]

Events followed quickly. On 14th March Goebbels was appointed Minister for Propaganda and Public Enlightenment.[55] The Ministry he had spent so much time planning when its existence was still a dream had now at last materialised. In a speech made only two days after his appointment he explained why propaganda was so necessary to the régime. "A government such as ours which has to take such far-reaching measures . . . must make propagandistic preparations in order to draw the people to its side . . . Public enlightenment is essentially passive; propaganda is active . . . we are determined to work on the masses until they have fallen to us."[56]

There is some evidence that Goebbels would have preferred a ministry with greater executive power, and later he was continually to show his ambition to control the internal affairs of Germany. He remained Gauleiter for Berlin for the rest of his life, and this office, especially during the war, enabled him to control the civil population in certain respects. But Hitler recognised that Goebbels could serve him best in the field where his real genius lay, and the new ministry was created especially for him. He was given the Leopoldpalast on the Wilhelmplatz, opposite the Chancellery, in which to set up his Government department. It was here that he built up the network of controls that made him master of every medium of expression Germany possessed.

CHAPTER FIVE

Minister for Propaganda and Public Enlightenment

THERE WAS DUST in the curtains of the house on the Wilhelmstrasse which had once been a royal residence. "A beautiful building by the great architect Schinkel," writes Goebbels, "but so old-fashioned we shall have to have it adapted to our requirements."[1]

Goebbels decided that this beautiful house had to be stripped as clean as Germany herself by the revolution. Down with the curtains, and off with the stucco—"I cannot work in the twilight." The horrified officials of an older régime stood around, hindering, expostulating, holding up the builders whom Goebbels had rushed in. No matter.

I simply take a few bricklayers from the S.A. and have the stucco and wainscoting knocked off during the night; newspapers and documents as old as the hills are taken down from the shelves, where they have lain musty and dusty for years and are flung downstairs pell-mell. Only clouds of dust attest the bygone splendours of bureaucracy! The worthy gentlemen who come next to be evacuated are much astonished by what they find next morning. One of them, horror-stricken, stammers: "Herr Reichsminister, do you know you may be put into prison for this?"[2]

Goebbels just laughed. Dismissals were easy enough to effect just now. This was a time for new men. "Here and there an official offers resistance, but slight pressure suffices to bring him to his knees." It was all done in no time.[3]

Everyone was tense with the excitement of opportunity. "Is it not as if the wings of History touched us!" murmurs Goebbels as on 12th March he watches the Leader ("trembling with the emotion and solemnity of it all") reading a proclamation that new flags with swastikas on them are to be "flown over the nation."

These early days were filled with public events that served in some measure to hide from people who were not yet ready to accept the Nazi regime the radical transformation that was in fact going on. Arrests, dismissals and reappointments of reliable Nazis in positions of authority were daily occurrences. Goebbels was well aware even before the creation of his ministry gave him immediate powers that the radio and the press were the first problems to tackle. The Nazis, though constitutionally still holding less than half the seats in a democratically elected Reichstag after the election in March, skilfully used the powers that they had acquired to frustrate any attempts at opposition. "Göring is cleaning out the Augean stables," says Goebbels. "Names of great importance yesterday fade away today to nothing."[4] Both before and after the election the Nazis carefully alternated public ceremony and rejoicing with various acts of suppression and oppression, especially of men remaining critical of them in positions of influence in the press and the radio. "One ban follows another very quickly," he writes on 15th February. By the end of the month some 60 Communist and 71 Social Democrat papers had been suppressed and their leading editors and writers confined in Göring's prisons and concentration camps. By the end of April virtually all but Nazi papers had disappeared.

Of particular significance, so it seemed to Goebbels, was the annual Potsdam ceremony associated with Frederick the Great. The father-figure of Hindenburg ("What a happiness for all of us to have this venerable and remarkable man still over us,"[5] says Goebbels with suitable reverence, for Hindenburg helped the Nazis to seem respectable) was to stand side-by-side with Hitler in what was planned by the new Minister as a ceremony "to be held for the first time after the National Socialist style. . . . At these great State festivals the most minute details are important." This was on 21st March; on 20th March Hitler had pushed the Enabling Bill through which gave him as Chancellor great personal powers.

On our way from Berlin to Potsdam we pass through huge crowds of cheering people. Potsdam is smothered in flags and green garlands. Only with difficulty can the road be cleared for the Cabinet and the Members of Parliament to pass. We are nearly suffocated by the multitude. Hindenburg enters the Garrison Church (*Garnisonskirche*) together with the Leader. A deep silence reigns. Briefly and solemnly the President of the Reich reads his message to the Members of the Reichstag and the German people. His voice is clear and firm. In our midst stands a man who unites whole generations.

Then the Leader speaks. His tone is dominating and when he ends we are all greatly moved. I sit near Hindenburg and observe tears in his eyes. All rise from their seats and enthusiastically acclaim the ancient Field-Marshal, who shakes hands with the young Chancellor. . . .

He stands there at the salute; the whole scene is bathed in sunshine; the hand of God is held in invisible benediction over the grey town of Prussian grandeur and duty.[6]

During the ceremony Hitler and Goebbels very pointedly left the Church service in order to pay an official visit to the graves of men whom they wished to be regarded as Nazi martyrs.

The day ended with a performance of *Die Meistersinger*, and after that Goebbels gave a lavish party for the builders, bricklayers and decorators who had transformed his ministry in such record time, and helped him "play that trick on the bureaucrats".

Triumphal speaking tours of Germany were undertaken by Hitler and Goebbels (often together) both before and after the March election. Goebbels was determined that no one should be left out of the atmosphere of victory and rejoicing. Twice during this period of flushed celebration, in February and again in April, he revisited Rheydt where only a few months before he had been received with insults and violence. How different now. With Magda and his baby daughter in a basket, Goebbels arrived from Dortmund and surprised his mother. The following day the town seems to have become so excited by his presence as to be, he says, "in a state of incredible commotion". In April he revisited Rheydt officially as Minister;[7] there is a certain sinister quality amounting almost to vengefulness in the reason he gives for this:

I put up with being accorded a great reception in my native town in honour of my mother, who has been calumniated, slandered, belittled and persecuted in this place for years, and has suffered unspeakably from it. One knows what this sort of thing is like. To be a social outcast is to be mortally stricken. It is torture for an old woman to have heard nothing for years but remarks of pity, or indignation, on account of an unruly son who lives at daggers drawn with Church, State and Society....

That is why I have come to Rheydt to show her this day that all she has had to suffer for my sake, and for our cause, has not been in vain.[8]

Hitler and his colleagues were vigorously pressing forward with the policy of *Gleichschaltung*, which meant bringing everything into line with National Socialist ideas. With this in mind, Goebbels assembled representatives from the film industry and the film press in the Kaiserhof Hotel and spoke to them at length about the future of film production in Germany. He began by reassuring his audience about the stability of the new régime, and went on to explain how much both he and the Führer enjoyed films and how much they were prepared to do for the industry. Films in the new Germany were to have an important cultural and artistic mission. It all sounded very rosy, especially to those who had themselves used those very terms in the criticism of films that had been vulgarised by the box-office. Then Goebbels surprised everyone by giving a list of the films he considered the German film-makers should emulate. They were *Battleship Potemkin, The Nibelung Saga, Anna Karenina* and *The Rebel*—the first a famous production made in Soviet Russia and all of them films with which Jews had been prominently associated as producers or directors. This initial meeting with the film industry representatives put up the signpost, but Goebbels was too preoccupied to set up full-scale machinery to reorganise film production at this stage. It was not until

September that the Reich Film Chamber was created to control the activities of the industry.

The main channels for Nazi propaganda, however, were initially the press and the radio. With the press Goebbels had had long experience, and it was merely a matter of quickly silencing and eliminating hostile newspapers and journals. Broadcasting, on the other hand, in 1933 was still something relatively new in society, though Goebbels was already well prepared to take it over and develop it to the full.

The task was not difficult because the German radio was organised on a unified national basis not unlike, in some respects, broadcasting in Britain under the B.B.C. In 1928 the German Post Office obtained considerable powers over the ten provincial companies which provided the broadcasting service in various regions of the country, and it drew the licence fees paid by the public owning receiving sets. There was no commercial radio in operation. The Post Office also controlled the National Broadcasting Company, which owned the majority of the stock of the regional companies, and it both owned and operated the national transmitters responsible for putting out the companies' programmes.

As soon as his ministry was created, Goebbels took control of the machinery of broadcasting on behalf of the State, reconstituting the National Broadcasting Company and putting it under his ministry. Nazis were put in key positions. As soon as possible the transmitters were increased both in number and in power, and the radio manufacturers were vigorously pressed by the Ministry to make special very cheap 'people's' radio sets (*Volksempfänger*) on a vast scale. In the year 1933-34 German homes owning a radio set increased by over a million, making the total sets in use in excess of six million. By 1938 the figure was 9½ million, and after this even smaller and cheaper sets were made available for the workers so that radio would be virtually in every home. In addition, on every important occasion (such as a speech by Hitler) a special loud-speaker organisation was established to instal equipment in such places as schools, factories, offices, public halls and in the open air. By 1935 the Nazis could boast that when Hitler chose to broadcast he could have an audience of not less than 56 million Germans. Goebbels said: "With the radio we have destroyed the spirit of rebellion."[9] Or, as one of his assistants put it even more pungently: "Real broadcasting is true propaganda. Propaganda means fighting on all battlefields of the spirit, generating, multiplying, destroying, exterminating, building and undoing. Our propaganda is determined by what we call German race, blood and nation."[10]

Nor did Goebbels leave the habit of listening to chance. A system of local 'wireless wardens' was established to keep contact with the public, send in reports, and see that all important broadcasts were known of in advance and made available through the loud-speakers set up in public places.

In April, only a month after becoming a minister, Goebbels began his organised boycott of the German Jews. This was a deliberate act of blackmail. The Nazi leaders were alarmed at the vivid pictures of violence and oppression in Germany which filled the world press. Goebbels immediately attributed these reports to the Jewish exiles whom Nazi violence had driven from their homeland, and he seized the opportunity to punish the Jews who were still left in Germany. "Generosity does not impress the Jews," he wrote. "One has to show them one is equal in everything."[11] So the boycott was officially organised, though news of it only served to make the Nazis more than ever suspect abroad.

On 1st April, initially for one day only, all Jewish shops were closed by force, and Storm Troopers stationed in front of their entrances. It rested with the Jews left in Germany, Goebbels proclaimed, to persuade their kinsmen abroad to stop the talking. Otherwise the closure would be repeated, and in any case kept in the background, as he put it, in the form of a permanent threat. The following day the Nazi press, in calling off the boycott, boasted that the Jews had now learned their lesson.

One of the more astute decisions made by Goebbels at this time was to adopt 1st May, the traditional day of celebration for the Communists, as the day of national rejoicing for the Nazis. The Communists, faced with suppression, might have tried to exploit it as the occasion for a rally, but Goebbels was determined to take the day over in as large a way as possible. He makes this massive celebration the climax of his published diary. The festival, organised on a lavish scale, was planned on paper by 26th April, rehearsed on 28th April, and mounted in the grand manner he understood so well. It was above all to be a rally of the workers! Delegations were sent from every part of the Reich, and the day had naturally been proclaimed a public holiday by a special Act of the Reichstag put forward by Goebbels himself on 24th March.

The swastika flags and banners curled in the air and the children paraded. "I speak to them from the depth of my heart," writes Goebbels. "It is easy to speak to children if one understands their little souls."[12] Goebbels' stepson Harald presented a large bunch of roses to the ancient President Hindenburg as he sat side by side with Chancellor Hitler. Then the entourage moved to the Tempelhofer Feld where the great mass demonstration of the representatives of the German workers waited. Hitler and the President received the delegations that had come in by air, and the rest of the day was spent in eating and speech-making. At night Goebbels claims a million and a half people were assembled on the Tempelhofer Feld, while similar organised assemblies took place on varying scale throughout the country. Searchlights swung across the heads of the multitude. "One recognises nothing but a grey mass, shoulder to shoulder." A radio-link established exact synchronis-ation with all other assemblies throughout the nation when Goebbels proclaimed a minute's silence for a mining disaster which had most opportunely occurred that very day. Hitler then spoke in praise of the dignity of labour and of how the worker was to be the essential factor in the new Germany. A million and a half voices joined in singing the Horst Wessel anthem. Before presenting Hitler to his vast audience, Goebbels saw that the sun would soon break through the clouds. He timed his own speech so that the God-given light should stream down on Hitler as he took his place on the speaker's rostrum.[13]

The following day, 2nd May, the S.A. and S.S. took possession of trade union offices throughout Germany. Union officials were arrested, maltreated and imprisoned. A new German Labour Front was pro-claimed under Robert Ley. It was a *coup d'état*.

With so much success on his hands, Goebbels' next demonstration was a serious blunder he was never to live down. During 10th May, at his direct instigation, groups of Nazis in Berlin and in all other German university centres were formed into raiding-parties to break into libraries, both private and public, and seize there the books of proscribed authors. These books were flung out into the streets where they were collected by other gangs of Party thugs and taken, in the case of Berlin, to the Franz-Josephsplatz for the night's ceremony. By the time it was dark the volumes which Goebbels had chosen for this barbaric martyrdom were piled like the bricks of a crumbled building in a vast, disorderly heap. Load after load of books, tied into bundles, were delivered by the Party mobs who, as they arrived, shouted and yelled in the cause of Nazi *Kultur*. Books by Jews and Marxists lay scattered beside classics, and classics beside the works of modern authors who had inspired Goebbels' hatred. Then at dusk the students, urged on by Storm Troopers, arrived with their torches to set fire to the books and to dance like savages round the flames, chanting the slogans prepared for them: *Brenne, Heinrich Mann, Brenne, Stefan Zweig, Brenne, Erich Kästner, Brenne, Karl Marx, Brenne, Sigmund Freud, Brenne, Heinrich Heine* and so on, like some ritual death by fire. Perhaps no one knew that on one of the blackened, curling pages was a sentence written by Heine in 1823: "Wherever they burn books, sooner or later they will burn human beings also."

The flames lit up the Opera House on the one side and the University of Berlin on the other. Then a line of cars drew near bringing Goebbels to make a national broadcast from the scene of the giant bonfire. Goebbels stepped to the microphone and proclaimed the end of the age of "extreme Jewish intellectualism". "The evil spirit of the past" was rightly committed to the flames. This was "a strong, great and symbolic act", he went on. "Never, as today, have young men had the right to cry out; studies are thriving, spirits awakening. From these ashes there will arise the phoenix of a new spirit."[14]

But he must have had misgivings as he left the students and the Storm Troopers to their orgy. He ordered the ceremonies to be reported with restraint in the press, and even staunch supporters of the Nazis (such as Heinrich Hoffmann, Hitler's personal photographer) regarded the burning of the books as a grave error that would do the movement great harm in world opinion.[15] He was right.

The success of the régime from 1933 until the war is a model demonstration in the technique of calculated and wholly successful aggression.

The sheer ability of Hitler, coupled with his intuitive genius for smelling out the weakness of his opponents both at home and abroad, accelerated the pace of events until the spoils began to fall into the lap of Germany with the gathering speed of a landslide. Later Hitler was led by his vanity to rely more and more on his own individual intuition until he became deluded by the myth of his omnipotence, and forgot that he was human and fallible. He left behind him the men on whose help he had relied to achieve his initial successes, and he lived increasingly like a recluse absorbed in his personal divinity. Like Napoleon he came to trust in his star rather than in the advice of men such as Goebbels, who might have helped him secure the plunder his astuteness had won for him and would probably have kept him back from launching the European and later the world war which was to destroy them all. Had Hitler taken Goebbels' advice he might still be in power today and be the absolute master of the central parts of Europe, if no more.

Hitler adopted the policy of divide and rule. No one to whom he gave power was excluded from the effects of this soul-destroying policy, not even Goebbels who had come to regard Hitler as his personal friend.[16] But he, like the rest, was not exempt from the Führer's system of government which gradually made him the active source of all decisions, many of which were announced without prior consultation with his ministers. Departments of government such as Goebbels controlled were deliberately made to overlap with each other, and bitter rivalries were created among the ministers and their senior assistants; rumour was thus encouraged, and intrigue, both secret and open, inevitably developed among rival ministers to secure prior knowledge of Hitler's intentions and to be the first to take advantage of any changes in policy or administration that seemed likely to occur. Within the next ten years Goebbels was to learn to his cost how difficult it is to be the infallible prophet of a divine being who is inconsistent in his confidences. Such methods might pass in the hurly-burly of party struggle, but they could not be applied to the administration of a great State. The German tendency to over-organise and clog the machinery of government was accentuated by the Nazi leaders who could do little else but regard each other with suspicion, knowing by what unscrupulous means each one had achieved his authority. In trying to outwit and frustrate each other they merely impaired the functioning of the régime, though they spent much of their time boasting of its efficiency.

To begin with, however, the ecstasy of the sudden possession of power seemed only a glorious extension to the old struggle. Opposition had to be made illegal, and this was great fun for those who had in the past suffered at the hands of the men who were now placed overnight at their mercy. Concentration camps (the invention of the British, said Göring to Sir Nevile Henderson,[17] with an ironic reference to the Boer War) were set up to cope with all those still spirited enough to oppose, but the majority of the German nation was either cowed into submission or persuaded that what was being done by Hitler would indeed make Germany a land fit for a master-race to live in after the humiliation of the past fifteen years. For those who did not agree, Hitler soon had at his disposal a network of camps and prisons as well as the handymen of the S.A., the S.S., and of the Gestapo (*Geheime Staatspolizei*) which had been created in 1933 immediately he had come to power. Heinrich Himmler, Supreme Commander of the S.S., who had once been the inefficient secretary whom Gregor Strasser had replaced by young Joseph Goebbels and whom Hitler had rediscovered in 1929 running a small poultry farm near Munich, was appointed head of the Prussian Gestapo in 1934. Now he could keep men instead of fowls behind his wire fences.

The immediate years saw the quick, careful creation of controls that made Germany secure for Hitler, side by side with the conduct of a foreign policy based initially on caution. The most dramatic event in the half-submerged process of forging these controls was the bloodbath of Saturday and Sunday 29th-30th June 1934 in which Goebbels played a prominent part. This was the "night of the long knives" which continued its massacre over two days and nights and involved many hundreds of men and women, how many hundreds will never now be known. Of Hitler's early opponents within the Nazi movement only Gregor Strasser and Ernst Röhm had emerged as potential leaders of subversion. Strasser, as we have already seen, had retired in disgust and anger a year before, but Hitler had not forgotten his dis-

loyalty and the dangerous temptations Strasser's comparative modera-
tion had represented to other prominent Nazis at a crucial moment in
the fight for power. Röhm, as leader of the S.A., was in an even more
powerful position than Strasser had been, so powerful indeed even
Goebbels himself was for a while in danger of drawing into association
with him.

To the S.A., the riff-raff who had learnt the taste of blood, the
establishment of their party in power meant the time had come
for the dividing of the spoils. Hitler, however, was still anxious to
seem respectable in the eyes of both Germany and the outside world,
and was fully prepared to go through the diplomatic routines of
morning-dress and top hat and face-saving constitutionalism for so
long as it seemed to him advantageous to do so. But the men of the
S.A., the fist behind the throne, were impatient for jobs and sinecures;
they wanted to set about expelling the fatted swine from the capitalist
front-office and take over the spoils for themselves. They were increasingly jealous, too, of the privileged position of the regular Army,
the *Reichswehr*, whose formality and professionalism they despised.
The S.A. was radical and revolutionary by origin, and it numbered
now between two and three million men. Goebbels, too, had always
been more radical in outlook than his master, who knew by instinct
the value to him of the industrialists and the generals. He needed
their support to help establish his régime. They had to serve their
turn.

Röhm became increasingly impatient with his position and concerned over the restiveness of his men, in spite of the fact that in
December 1933 he had been created, as Chief of Staff of the S.A., a
member of the Reich Cabinet. His was still the amateur army, though
pensions were granted in February 1934 to those who had suffered
bodily in the political fighting.

But what Röhm wanted was to become Minister of Defence, with
charge of all the armed forces. Hitler knew neither Hindenburg nor
the Army High Command would agree to make such an appointment.
Hindenburg, however, would soon be of no further use to Hitler. He
was dying, and the question of his successor was all the time in the mind
of Hitler, who was determined it should be himself, for he needed the

President's constitutional authority over the Army. He had gone so far as to agree to the reduction of the membership of the S.A. by two-thirds when Anthony Eden, Lord Privy Seal of Britain, had visited Berlin in February 1934 and discussed the status of the S.A. He had even agreed to reduce the offensive power of the remaining third. This apparent concession had suited his purpose. It not only set him in a good light with Britain, as a prominent power in Europe which had its eye on him, it gave him an excuse to reduce the influence of the Party's private army which he no longer wanted to keep at its original fighting strength. In April he held private conferences with the Minister of Defence and the Commanders-in-Chief of the Army and Navy during naval manœuvres off Kiel, during which he is thought to have come to terms with them.

How far Goebbels was in sympathy with Röhm cannot now be precisely determined.[18] His radical leanings and constant association with the S.A., who had supported him on innumerable difficult occasions in the past, must certainly have coloured his views. Also he was to some extent a personal friend of Röhm—in fact the only friend Röhm now had among the leaders of the Party. Up to within about a fortnight of Röhm's death Goebbels was in active contact with him, and then suddenly he decided to betray him as he had betrayed Strasser in 1926. Goebbels, it must always be remembered, was loyal first of all to power. He was close enough to Röhm to know what was within the bounds of possibility. Had Röhm displaced Hitler, Goebbels would naturally want to keep his high position in the State, if not better it. However, as the point of no return was reached, he decided once more for Hitler. When the time for the assassinations came, Goebbels, aware of what suspicion might do for him while vengeance ran riot, stayed close by Hitler, the only place where he knew he would be safe. Otto Strasser claims that he has documentary proof of the fact that Goebbels, as late as the third week in June, had long and secret meetings with Röhm in the Bratwurst-Gloeckle, Röhm's favourite tavern in Munich. Both the owner and the head-waiter of the tavern were among those murdered during the week-end purge, though neither of them was involved politically. But they were, says Strasser, witnesses of the meeting which Goebbels had at all costs to keep hidden.[19]

Hitler was ready for a show-down, and the technique he used was substantially the same as that employed against the Communists in the case of the Reichstag fire. He invented a plot and then set about destroying those he claimed were involved in it before it had materialised. The situation was further aggravated by a violent attack on the régime, its methods and its propaganda made with great courage by von Papen, Vice-Chancellor of Germany and the favourite of Hindenburg, at the University of Marburg on 17th June. Goebbels at once suppressed reports of this speech, which had in fact been written for von Papen by Edgar Jung, a prominent right-wing intellectual, but copies were smuggled abroad; Goebbels himself had been attacking the aristocratic and bureaucratic class to which von Papen belonged and he continued to attack it with renewed venom. Once again it became clear to Hitler that the time was ripe to put the house in order, in spite of his personal regard for Röhm, the only one among the Nazi leaders who had been in the position to address him with the intimate form of '*du*'.

Hitler was later to give his own account to the Reichstag of what happened during the crucial month of June. He made great play with the appeals he had made to his former friend to remain loyal to the Nazi cause. He admitted Röhm's notorious addiction to homosexual practices. Then he claimed that Röhm was conspiring to take over the Government from him by force in a putsch timed to take place at the end of June. What in fact happened was that Hitler's vengeance overtook Röhm and many others whom Hitler credited with disloyalty to himself before there was any question of an active plot against him. Among those who were to die in the purge were Gregor Strasser and the former German Chancellor von Schleicher.

The purge was arranged, with the Army's connivance, by Göring and Himmler. On 28th June Hitler went away to attend a wedding in Essen, while Göring and Himmler ordered the police and the S.S. to stand by for action. Röhm himself was away on sick leave, unarmed and unguarded by the banks of the Tegernsee some forty miles south of Munich, surrounded only by personable young men, and the whole of the S.A. were in fact on leave. On 29th June Hitler was in Godesberg on the Rhine, where he was joined by Goebbels who had brought him news that the Berlin S.A. had been ordered to report to their posts. This was, of course, a strategic lie. Hitler made his decision. On the night of the 29th he flew to Munich, and simultaneously the first wave of the purge began. Goebbels, mindful of his personal safety, kept close to Hitler. At dawn a fleet of cars took Hitler and others who had joined him, including Goebbels, out to the lakeside house where Röhm was staying. There Röhm was dragged from the bed he was sharing with a youth; he was pale from the night's excesses and even more so from horrified astonishment at this visitation as by a troop of avenging angels. Otto Dietrich, who was among those present, remembers Hitler pacing up and down before the Storm Troop leader "with huge strides, fiery as some higher being, the very personification of justice".[20] Röhm was taken forthwith to Munich and shot.

His mission accomplished, Hitler and his men flew at once to Berlin. Gisevius, the member of the German underground who gave evidence at the Nuremberg Trials, was among those at the airport who saw Hitler arrive out of a blood-red sky—"a piece of theatricality", as Gisevius observes, "that no one had staged". A guard of honour presented arms. Hitler stepped out of the plane. Gisevius observed that "he wore no hat; his face was pale, unshaven, sleepless, at once gaunt and puffed". There was silence as Hitler shook hands with Göring, Himmler, Frick and others waiting to receive him; during the ominous moments the only sign of activity was the "monotonous sound of clicking heels". The others had by now come out of the plane, and last of all "a diabolic, grinning caricature of a face appeared —Goebbels". Gisevius saw "a long, tattered list" in Himmler's hand, which Hitler took from him. There was incessant whispering as Hitler, Göring and Himmler went through it. Then Hitler tossed his head in anger, and went off to the line of cars waiting to take him from the airport.[21]

Gregor Strasser was kidnapped and shot in the Prinz Albrechtstrasse prison in Berlin—it was given out he had committed suicide, though he had in fact received a bullet in his main artery which in bursting gushed blood on to the cell wall and gave the S.S. a showpiece that lasted for weeks. Von Schleicher and his wife were surprised and shot in their flat one after the other in the presence of their maid, who escaped by a miracle to tell the story. Von Papen barely escaped with his life, and several of his staff were killed. Hitler admitted to fifty-eight executions that week-end, but the number of influential members of the S.A., the Catholic leaders and others against whom the Nazis had worked up a case amounted to not less than four hundred and was probably far more. Karl Ernst, and certain of the men who had assisted him with the Reichstag fire, were assassinated. Men were shot in their houses; others were killed and their bodies left in swamps and woodlands. Many were said to have committed suicide. Any official documents there were connected with the purge were ordered to be destroyed, and Goebbels prohibited the press from referring to any of those who had been executed or had disappeared. A few bare announcements were made on Hitler's authority. It was six weeks before Hitler himself came forward with his official account of the purge, by which time Germany was seething with rumour. Hitler declared: "Everyone must know for all future time that if he raises his hand to strike the State, then certain death is his lot."[22]

Less than three weeks later Hindenburg was dead; his death came on 2nd August 1934. Hitler immediately assumed the office of President whilst remaining Chancellor and so fulfilled the next stage in his ambition by becoming Commander-in-Chief of the Armed Forces of the Reich. The regular Army was paraded forthwith to take the oath of allegiance to Hitler's person. Goebbels in a suitably sad voice announced Hindenburg's death over the radio. This was followed by half an hour's silence. Then Goebbels spoke again announcing the unification of the offices of President and Chancellor under the title of Führer and Reich Chancellor.

In the following month, September, Goebbels paid his first visit to Switzerland as official representative from Germany to the League of Nations in Geneva, where the Disarmament Conference was in seemingly interminable session. Wherever Goebbels went, either sight-seeing or in conference, he took along a bodyguard of Storm Troopers whose presence created a bad impression. Hitler some months before had made a brilliant speech in the Reichstag in which he had expressed his dislike of war, but nevertheless had demanded for Germany equality in the right to bear arms since the other nations, and notably France, showed no willingness to disarm themselves. In October, after Goebbels' return from his brief visit to the Conference, Hitler used France's continued refusal to disarm as his excuse to withdraw (regretfully, of course) from the Disarmament Conference and also from the League of Nations itself. Germany became the lone wolf of Europe.

It was now simply a matter of timing the ascent to greater power and independence for himself and for Germany. The story is well known; it is written into many of our own lives. In July 1934 Hitler made a first trial of his strength in the abortive uprising in Austria which failed after the assassination of the Austrian Chancellor Dollfuss. In Germany Hitler instituted the system of organised plebiscites in order to demonstrate to the world the apparently unanimous backing of the German people for his party. In 1935 came victory in the Saar plebiscite, the re-adoption of conscription in Germany in defiance of the Versailles Treaty, and the enactment of anti-Jewish laws making the persecution of Jews legal. In 1936 came the re-occupation of the Rhineland in violation of the treaty of Locarno, and the start of the Spanish Civil War with the backing of both Germany and Italy. In 1938 the year began with a second purge, this time of the Army generals who were against Hitler's policy; this was followed by the occupation and annexation of Austria, and the organised intimidation of Czechoslovakia which led to the Munich agreement in October and the ceding of the Sudetenland to Germany. In 1939 followed the occupation of Czechoslovakia, the annexation of Memel, the campaign against Poland over Danzig, the occupation of Danzig by an influx of Storm Troopers disguised as tourists, the pact with Soviet Russia, the invasion of Poland, and the declaration of war on Germany by Britain and France.

These crowded years meant for Goebbels the stage management of Nazi public relations and propaganda as well as the establishment through his ministry of controls over all means of expression inside Germany. He also had to learn the attributes of power, and how to play the part of a Reich Minister in the particular circumstances created by Hitler which were never easy because, as we have seen, he permitted no one to share his full confidence; nor did anyone, including Goebbels, quite know where he stood either with Hitler or with the others who were more likely than not colleagues only in name. Goebbels was perhaps as secure as any of the Nazi leaders, but even he had periods when he was out of favour with Hitler and received his instructions at second hand.

The Ministry, however, was his pride, and he was determined to make it a model of efficiency staffed by able men devoted to the Nazi cause. At the same time he made his first attempts to deal personally with men of stature in the arts and in journalism and to bring them into the orbit of National Socialism. In this he was far less successful, for he had now for the first time to deal directly with men of the highest talent who knew that both Germany and the world were watching them to see what they would do to defend the basic rights of liberty of expression and freedom in the arts.

An example of this failure was his dealings with Fritz Lang, who was one of the most famous of the German film directors and Jewish on his mother's side. Lang has revealed how, immediately after the Nazis came to power, Goebbels summoned him to the new Ministry.[23] Lang had never met Goebbels before. "He told me," wrote Lang subsequently, "that, many years before, he and the Führer had seen my picture *Metropolis* in a small town, and Hitler had said at that time that he wanted me to make the Nazi pictures." He did not mention the fact, however, that he had just banned Lang's most recent film *Das Testament des Dr. Mabuse*, a horror-fantasy of a paranoiac who aspires to world domination which Lang later claimed to have some symbolic references to Hitler. In spite of this ban, which remained unmentioned, Goebbels exuded charm and offered him a prominent position in film production. Lang pointed out that he had Jewish blood in his veins. Goebbels said he was prepared to overlook this in view of Lang's distinguished service in the First World War. Lang could not understand why an exception was being made in his case; he knew of only too many Jews who were losing their jobs. He asked for twenty-four hours to think the matter over. He returned home, asked a friend to book him a sleeper on the night-train to Paris (but not, of course, in Lang's name), and fled the country, leaving his fine house and his art collection to be taken care of by the Nazis. An uncut French version of *The Testament of Dr. Mabuse*, made at the same time as the German original, was smuggled into France and edited there. Lang never returned to Germany under Hitler's rule.

Typical of Goebbels' consistently ruthless methods was his handling of Ehm Welk, editor of *Grüne Post*, the Ullsteins' most profitable weekly journal. Goebbels used a trivial incident to imprison the editor and to ban the paper indefinitely. The real reason behind this action was his desire to expropriate the Ullstein chain of publications and printing plants, which was the largest and wealthiest combine of its kind in Germany. This expropriation figure was fixed at twelve million marks, though the organisation was worth some hundreds of millions. Even the twelve million marks were finally confiscated when the Ullstein family was broken up and the older members forced to emigrate.[24]

Meanwhile those Jewish artists, writers and intellectuals who were able to do so were leaving Germany, taking with them what possessions they could or abandoning their property altogether in a precipitate rush to quit their country overnight in the face of real or imagined threats to their personal safety. The case of Fritz Lang was typical. Goebbels' ruthless anti-Semitism denuded Germany of much of her creative talent.

These individual torments were the direct result of Goebbels' ministry with its specialised departments created to supervise each branch of German art and culture and with its rules and orders and directives which gradually blocked up the loopholes of free expression and confined the spirit of Germany in a vacuum. The following departments of the Ministry were set up:

DIVISION I. Legislation and Legal Problems; Budget, Finances, and Accounting; Personnel Administration; Ministerial Library; National Chamber of Culture; Council of Commercial Advertising; Fairs and Exhibitions.

DIVISION II. Co-ordination of Propaganda and Public Enlightenment; Regional Agencies of the Ministry; German Academy (*Hochschule*) of Politics; Official Ceremonies and Demonstrations; National Emblems; Racial Questions; Treaty of Versailles; Youth Organisation; Business and Social Politics; Public Health and

Athletics; Eastern and Border Questions; National Travel Committee.

DIVISION III. Radio: National Broadcasting Company (*Reichsrundfunk-Gesellschaft m.b.H.*)

DIVISION IV. National and Foreign Press; Journalism; Press Archives; News Service; National Association of the German Press.

DIVISION V. Cinema; Moving Picture Industry; Cinema Censorship; Youth Literature Censorship.

DIVISION VI. Theatre, Music and Art; Theatre Management; Stage Direction; Design; Folk Art.

DIVISION VII. Protection against Counter-Propaganda at Home and Abroad.[25]

At the head of this initial system of departmental controls sat Goebbels, neatly dressed and meticulous, a martinet of the new bureaucracy. He hand-picked his relatively small staff, for he always claimed that he did not want to set up a large organisation. In fact, even as his ministry grew in later years, his headquarters staff is said never to have exceeded a thousand, though it probably did. He gave his departmental chiefs a fair degree of independence, and he expected them to show initiative of the right sort. He dispensed charm or rage as seemed to him most appropriate, disciplining his subordinates or encouraging in them the will to work his way.

In his office routine he became pedantically tidy. When he arrived in the morning he expected his desk to be laid out to perfection with its battery of coloured pencils placed at the ready for work. He reserved for himself the use of green ink or pencil, and he employed this colour to make his derogatory remarks on the work submitted to him for comment. In his personal working habits he showed an uncommon gift for concentrating on the particular job in hand. He would keep his secretaries busy while he rapidly dictated thousands of words. Then he might relax for the few minutes that remained free before moving off quickly to keep an appointment to speak before a large audience. His vanity demanded that he should always act his own undoubted efficiency in order to keep his staff in a state of perpetual admiration.

As the need arose, Goebbels issued decrees and orders to assist the work of his ministry. These were all of a kind calculated to seal the arteries of creative work in Germany, and there are only too many examples which may be quoted. In September 1933 Goebbels sponsored the Law which created a Reich Chamber of Culture to work alongside his ministry. He was President of this organisation and it was decreed that every worker in the cultural field had to belong to his appropriate section of it. There were seven of these sections, or sub-chambers; the Chambers of Broadcasting, Press, Literature, Fine Arts, Theatre, Music and Film. Membership included not only the creative cultural workers such as writers, broadcasters, actors and musicians, but also those whose function was to equip or to present the arts, such as publishers, radio manufacturers and musical instrument-makers. The Chamber also engulfed other cultural organisations—such as libraries, choirs, orchestras, and acting schools.

In the following month, October 1933, came the Journalists' Law, which made all journalists into State servants who had to be in possession of a licence issued by Goebbels. This followed the expropriation of the left-wing and Communist press—with its printing plants and capital assets—during the previous spring and summer. Jews were debarred (with certain rare exceptions) from any form of journalism, and only those who could prove they had pure Aryan descent (this had to go back to 1800) and had married a person of equal purity could own or be concerned in the ownership of a newspaper. In April 1934 Hess (not Goebbels in this instance) decreed that an Examining Committee for the Protection of National Socialist Literature should be established to censor books.

In January 1935 as we have already seen, the order appeared that artists and lecturers could not leave Germany to fulfil contracts without the authorisation of the President of the appropriate section of the Reich Chamber of Culture. In April 1935 the Chamber of Literature was empowered to draw up a black list of books considered to be hostile to Nazi policy. Publishers thereafter had to consult this list before reprinting any book as well as submitting any new work they wanted to publish to the Chamber of Literature. In the same month it was further decreed that independent newspapers could be abolished in favour of party newspapers if they offered unfair competition! In November 1936 Goebbels even went so far as to prohibit criticism of the arts.[26] Other decrees prohibited the publication of speeches made by Ministers, the quotation of early speeches by Hitler without prior approval, the acceptance by Germans of any Nobel Prize. This last (a decree by Hitler, not Goebbels) followed on the award of the Nobel Peace Prize to the German pacifist writer Carl von Ossietzky, who had been confined in a concentration camp since the night of the Reichstag fire. Goebbels was forced to release him when the Nobel limelight fell suddenly upon him in November 1936. In any case it scarcely mattered since he was a dying man. In 1937 Hitler instituted his own German National Prizes for Sciences, Art and Learning. It was difficult, however, to make German writers respond to the inspiration of Nazism on a level suitable to sustain the full national publicity involved in public awards. When, in 1935, the Schiller Prize for contemporary drama became due for award (it was founded originally in 1859 and was presented every six years) no one was thought by officialdom to be worthy of the prize.[27]

In the face of this flood of decrees, orders and rules few people dared to write, speak or publish without consulting the letter of the law and checking their position. Jokes could not even be made in cabarets traditionally dedicated to political irreverence, such as the Katacombe and Tingel-Tangel in Berlin. A press hand-out worded in the stiffest official language appeared during May 1935 in which these cabarets were condemned as the resorts of Jews or other elements hostile to the State. "An actress impersonating a prostitute," the statement says, "made light of the collections for the Winter Aid Fund, and agitation took place against collections in general; military and Party uniforms were calumniated, the organisation of the party made a laughing stock, and the conscript system slurred. A hundred per cent Jew, who as such enjoys only the rights of a guest in Germany, dared to make disparaging comments on political events in Germany." Arrests and questioning by the police followed. "When questioned, some participants in the cabaret's political performance proved to be partly very superficially, partly not at all informed about important establishments of the new State which they made the object of their sarcasm; they will have the opportunity to make up for this short-coming by decent and solid work in a camp."[28]

Not all cabaret artists were as easy to control as this. Werner Finck, for example, was a compère famous for his wit who, early in the régime, got into serious trouble for raising his right hand in the official salute and saying *"Die aufgehobene Rechte"*, which has the double meaning "raised right hand" and "suspended rights". Goebbels had Finck put in a concentration camp, but thought it politic to release him after a while because of his fame and influence as a wit.

Sir Nevile Henderson also refers to "one irrepressible but very popular comic artist in Munich who spent his time in and out of the Dachau concentration camp".[29] This was Karl Valentin; he used to tell the story of Dachau with its soldiers, its machine-guns, its dogs, and its successive barriers of wire fencing, some of which was electrified. But, he would add, all this was nothing to him. He could get in any time.

In 1937 Goebbels decided it was time to purge the museums and art galleries of the pictures he regarded as degenerate and he planned—again wrongly—to stage a special exhibition of Degenerate Art. The exhibition was a great success and Goebbels sent it on tour. But who was to say wherein the success lay? For many people this seemed to be their last chance to see pictures free from the swastika and uniform. Heinrich Hoffmann records that he prevailed on Hitler to get some of the paintings saved from the stigma of being included in the exhibition. According to Hoffmann Goebbels wanted to burn all pictures which were taken from the galleries as unacceptable to the National Socialist conception of art; among the works condemned were pictures by Renoir, Gauguin and Van Gogh. Hoffmann claims that he prevailed on Hitler to stop this vandalism.[30] Soon, indeed, Göring, Goebbels and Ribbentrop, like Hitler, became art collectors, bargaining against each other in the auctions until the time came when the pictures belonging to collections in foreign countries became the spoils of war.

Goebbels initiated regular conferences for those who had managed to stay employed in the creative professions. We have already referred to his speech at a conference of German film-makers convened very

shortly after the establishment of his Ministry. Soon a system of con-
gresses was initiated at which it was possible for the Government to
make clear to practitioners in such public arts as the film what it was
they should practise. In 1935, for example, Goebbels organised an
International Film Congress at which he personally put forward certain
principles for German film-making. They were not very original. He
emphasised that the film had its own technique distinct from that of the
theatre on which in the past it had been far too dependent. "More
than all other forms of art," he said, "the film must be popular in the
best sense of the word." Nor must it lose its strong inner connection
with the people. Films should be strictly contemporary in spirit even
when dealing with subjects set in the past; once they achieved this
quality they would bridge the nations and become the "spokesmen of
our age". Finally, he said, the State must be prepared to subsidise film
production as it subsidises the other arts.[31]

For Goebbels the development of the cinema became the most
absorbing of his duties. Both he and Hitler had always enjoyed films
as members of the cinema audience, and the glamour of film production and of the pretty women associated with it attracted him now that
he suddenly found himself in a position of authority over the industry.
Before long he was to come completely under the spell of the cinema,
seeing films privately night after night either at the Ministry or at one
or other of his luxurious homes which were all equipped for projection.

At the start he decided against outright nationalisation of the industry,
because of the complex organisation of the individual companies and
the important links that existed between them and the foreign distributors, which gave German production a valuable export market
for her films. The industry was dominated by certain large companies;
the most prominent of these was UFA, which had come under the
control of the industrialist Hugenberg, whose nationalist politics were
eventually to make him the ally of Hitler. Hugenberg had control
of the two most widely shown of the German newsreels, UFA and
Deulig. Though Hugenberg's prime concern was to make money
through UFA and its associated chain of cinemas, he saw to it that the
newsreels reflected his own standpoint and that certain of UFA's
feature films were nationalist in their subject and treatment. In 1937,

however, Hugenberg was bought out on Goebbels' own terms and UFA became state-controlled.

Goebbels, as we have seen, set up the Reich Film Chamber to control the industry. It was divided into ten sections to administer Production, Studios, Research and Technical Matters, Short and Propaganda Production, Home Distribution, Foreign Distribution, Cinemas, Non-commercial Exhibition, General Administration, and the Film Group, the last section concerned with registering all film workers as suitable persons to be employed in the industry from the point of view of the Party. The control of film scripts was exercised from the Film Department of the Ministry itself, and a Film Credit Bank was created to centralise the financing of production. In February 1934 a Reich Film Law was passed setting up a Censorship Committee under the control of Goebbels' Ministry to judge every film produced in Germany. Six grades of commendation were recognised. A film was either (1) particularly valuable politically and artistically, or (2) valuable politically and artistically, or (3) valuable politically, or (4) valuable artistically, or (5) valuable culturally, or, finally (6) of educational value. The greatest value was obviously political. Goebbels created an annual award for the best German film, and the first of these was given to a UFA production, *Refugees*, directed by Gustav Ucicky, who was famous for his nationalistic subjects. Among the early Nazi productions were *Bleeding Germany*, *Storm Trooper Brandt*, *Hitler Youth Quex*, celebrating the Hitler Youth movement, and *Hans Westmar*, a film based on the Horst Wessel story. Indeed, Goebbels was wise enough not to press the industry to make more than a few prestige feature films directly concerned with propaganda, nor did they attract the audiences which flocked to the normal kind of box-office musical, comedy or drama. The German film industry was denuded of much of its creative talent through the various purges that sent directors, writers, designers, cameramen and others to seek political asylum and work in the studios abroad. Although many films of merit were produced in spite of the circumstances imposed by Goebbels' Ministry, creative work in any full or true sense was almost impossible and German cinema sank into a moribund artistry dependent on escapism. Goebbels' dream of a major development in films inspired by the Nazi régime never suc-

Goebbels as a member of the Reichstag. *Left, above,* leaving his car outside the Reichstag, 1930. *Right, above,* entering the Reichstag, 1930. *Below,* in his car with Frick (extreme right), 1932.

Goebbels' marriage, 21 December 1931. Hitler acted as best man. *Above*, the wedding ceremony. *Below*, the procession after the ceremony.

ceeded. To this there was only one exception, the director Leni Riefenstahl whose personal belief in Nazism and personal devotion to Hitler were matched by a talent of unusual power. It is ironic that she worked as an individualist with the direct authority of Hitler and had as little to do with Goebbels as possible. The films she made for Hitler were masterpieces of propaganda—in particular *The Triumph of the Will* (1936), a pæan of praise derived from her cameramen's coverage of the Nuremberg Rally of 1934, and *The Olympiad* (1938), in which she used the occasion of the Olympic Games visiting Germany to turn the event into a glorification of Hitler.

Although Goebbels did not directly order the industry to make more than a handful of films during his twelve years as Minister, he never stopped interfering with what was being done. Klitzsch, the head of UFA, liked to be left alone to make harmless pictures with few political implications. But Goebbels could not leave him or anyone else alone. He soon learned how to throw his weight about over advance scripts and finished films alike, and it was here that his constant surveillance became irksome to the producers. He demanded cuts, he suggested additions, he exercised his authority to have productions shelved, he interfered with casting, and all the time he used his new social position as a Reich Minister to exact favours and to ingratiate himself with actresses.

On the other hand, certain of the artists of distinction whom he sought to exploit learnt how to handle and to some extent forestall his requirements. Emil Jannings, for example, who had returned to Germany from Hollywood before Hitler came to power, was not a Nazi and chose to appear in a succession of films which had no relation to current problems. Then followed a duel of wits between them.[32] Jannings in private called Goebbels '*Hinkefuss*' (the lame duck) and even imitated his limp in *Der Zerbrochene Krug* (*The Broken Jug*), a film which Goebbels ordered to be withdrawn and which Jannings managed to persuade Hitler to reinstate on the screen because of its popularity. For as long as he could Jannings used his powerful position as a great star to evade Goebbels' attempts to commit him to appearing in a Nazi prestige production. But eventually he was cornered and forced to play in the violently anti-British film *Ohm Krüger*, the script of which Goebbels supervised and, in part at least, wrote himself with Jannings particularly in mind.

The most tragic of Goebbels' interventions was his persecution of individual men and women in the film industry whose private lives offended the Nazis. Although he failed completely to break up the devotion of Hans Albers for Hansi Burg, a well-known Jewish actress in exile whom he supported while she was away from him and married only after the war, he so harried another popular actor, Joachim Gottschalk, because he would not divorce his Jewish wife that he drove them both to commit suicide; they killed their three-year-old child as well rather than leave it to be an orphan brought up in Nazi Germany. This suicide, which formed the basis for the story of the post-war film, *Ehe im Schatten*, shocked everyone. Goebbels, who was also shocked, though for different reasons, forbade people to attend the funeral, but a large gathering of men and women famous in the film and theatre refused to take notice of the ban and went to pay their respects to their colleagues who had died rather than be parted.

Goebbels previewed every issue of the newsreels that he could, and every major production of the feature studios. In addition to this, he viewed foreign films, particularly those which he had forbidden release in Germany. He saw every anti-Nazi film of which he could obtain a print. For example, he complained bitterly to an American correspondent, William Bayles, after seeing a Hollywood film *I Was a Nazi Spy*, in which the lavish good taste of the interior decoration of his office was travestied as a soulless building full of Nazi flags and emblems.[33] He looked at these films quite dispassionately and professionally as good or bad examples of propaganda. When the films were shown at his own home he would see them either alone or with a small circle of his immediate staff (his aides and secretaries) and house guests.

Acute as was Goebbels' insight into events and situations, his failing tended to lie in his understanding of people. Both men and women were elements in his life that he made use of. He had no capacity for real sympathy or for intimacy. He had charm; innumerable people testify to this. But the charm, like the venom that often lay beneath it, was a self-conscious exercise. It is difficult to find people who liked him.

The professional observers, the foreign correspondents, who had to deal with him are broadly-speaking of the same opinion about him. Edgar Mowrer, the American journalist, says he was "agreeable in manner, confident with a pen, middle-class in conviction, cynically adaptable in opinion, unusually intelligent . . . supreme in that insolence which goes so far to impress wavering votes".[34] William Shirer, another American correspondent, refers to his "evil but fertile brain";[35] he makes constant ironic reference to him as a liar and he even considers the much-praised voice "unpleasant". Lochner is content to say: "I loathed Dr. Goebbels."[36] Goebbels was equally unpopular with his colleagues. Dr. Schacht at the time he was President of the Reichsbank told Vernon McKenzie: "I would have hit Goebbels many a time if he hadn't been a cripple!"[37]—this because of his acid sarcasm which he did not hesitate to use in conversation. For von Hassell, the diplomat who was finally executed after the Generals' plot, Goebbels was "the most dangerous of the party leaders" and "a filthy dog".[38] The American Ambassador, William E. Dodd, characterised him in his diary as "far cleverer than Hitler" and "a past master" at oratory. "He makes a point of stirring animosities and hatreds," he added.[39]

A somewhat different approach to the character of Goebbels is made by Sir Nevile Henderson, the British Ambassador in Germany from 1931 to 1939. He wrote of him:

The 'little doctor' was probably the most intelligent, from a purely brain point of view, of all the Nazi leaders. He never speechified; he always saw and stuck to the point; he was an able debater and, in private conversation, astonishingly fair-minded and reasonable. Personally, whenever I had the chance, I found pleasure in talking to him. In appearance and in character he was a typical little Irish agitator. . . . When, however, he was on a public platform or had a pen in his hand no gall was too bitter and no lie too blatant for him.[40]

Goebbels, however, was prepared to face unpopularity. To him it was the price of power. He preferred to be feared rather than loved, and even went so far as to admit this later on in his career to one of his war-time secretaries, von Oven. There was only one person in his public life whom he had ever addressed by the intimate term '*du*'. This had been his early associate Karl Kaufmann.

One of the difficulties with which Goebbels had to cope was the handling of the foreign correspondents—men over whom it was difficult for him to exercise control and whom he knew in many cases were critical of him and his methods of handling the news that they were after. From 1934 he normally used the method of press conferences at the Ministry to announce new decrees or other more important changes to the foreign correspondents. William Shirer, the American correspondent, describes in his diary how on 16th March 1935 he was summoned with the others to the Ministry, and how Goebbels "limped in, looking very grave and important" before reading in a loud voice too fast for dictation the text of the new law introducing conscription in defiance of the Versailles Treaty. Then he left his officials to give guarded answers to the questions the correspondents began at once to shoot at them.[41]

During the first year of the Ministry Goebbels made the mistake of neglecting the foreign press, as Louis Lochner points out;[42] Lochner, an American journalist, was President of the Foreign Press Association at the time and was after the war to edit a section of Goebbels' war-time diaries. Later Goebbels gave tea-parties, receptions and *Bierabende* for the journalists who, after all, were the men that created the main picture of the new Germany for the public abroad. Even with them, however, the same kind of prevarication as that invented for the home press was thought sufficient to pass muster. In important press conferences he was quite prepared to give out patent lies as, for example, on the occasion described by Lochner when he claimed to the correspondents at a conference on 10th November 1938 that the accounts of the wanton destruction of Jewish property by Nazi hooligans the day before (events which the journalists had all witnessed for themselves) were "stinking lies" (*sind erstunken und erlogen*).[43] What possible good could such denials do, thought the astonished journalists as Goebbels went on vituperating in utter disregard for the obvious truth. Goebbels merely said what he wanted the correspondents to hear him say. He could then watch for their reports and take action if he found they went too far in their criticism. According to Vernon McKenzie, another American journalist, foreign correspondents in Germany, although not subject to direct censorship, were held responsible for what Goebbels regarded as the accuracy of their published reports, and formal expulsion orders could be and were issued if warning proved insufficient. McKenzie claims that some twenty-five expulsion orders were served on foreign correspondents in the six years prior to the war, and that others left 'voluntarily' when warned to do so since, to quote one of the Nazi formulas, their "safety could not be guaranteed". In all over fifty correspondents left Germany because, either directly or indirectly, they were ordered to go. Among those expelled were Dorothy Thompson, Edgar Mowrer, and one of the London *Times'* leading correspondents, Norman Ebbutt.[44]

Over and over again Goebbels showed his ignorance of the character of countries outside Germany, although he had the foreign press studied by his monitors. In the whole of his life he spent in all only a few weeks abroad on brief visits such as his few days in Geneva in 1933, his official visit to Greece in 1936, and an occasional visit to Italy. He tended to regard the rest of the world as if it were, from the point of view of propaganda, an unattached annexe to Germany which should be treated as far as possible in the same manner. He certainly did not understand world reaction to the Nazi persecution of the Jews. This reached its height in the appalling pogrom of November 1938, the facts of which, as we have seen, Goebbels tried to persuade the press to dismiss as the exaggeration of rumour. The old Party propaganda technique of the repetition of lies in a situation where the truth is totally withheld might on many occasions be made to work in the vacuum of Germany, but it was useless and at times farcical in a world which still had free access to the news. This is constantly borne out in the exasperated comments made by experienced foreign correspondents such as Shirer and Lochner.

He was not, however, content to leave the fate of world opinion of the régime to the representatives appointed by the foreign press. In the years before the war an elaborate system of public relations was built up abroad by the Germans themselves. In 1934 some 260 million marks were spent on propaganda outside Germany. Some 300 German-language newspapers were published abroad, and it has been estimated that the Nazis either owned or had financial interest in about 350 newspapers published in other languages.[45]

The German news agencies became highly efficient services. For example, Transocean, which operated for Goebbels in South America, was by 1939 sending out free news in excellent Spanish with free photographic illustration in matrix form for immediate use in the press. Sometimes as much as 20,000 words a day would be made available to the Latin American press. The tenor of this news was always anti-British. Transocean was careful to mix its doctored material with scrupulously accurate local news.[46]

In his initial efforts to gain ground in the United States, Goebbels went so far as to engage Ivy Lee, the American public relations pioneer and expert who had made his name through popularising John D. Rockefeller, reputed at the time to be the most unpopular man in the United States. Goebbels must have considered him to possess the necessary experience to popularise Hitler. He had, at any rate, the right references and, according to the American Ambassador, William E. Dodd, Goebbels paid Lee $33,000 a year.[47] The advice Lee gave was sound—get friendly with the correspondents. Goebbels responded by expelling the very ones best qualified to spread alarm and despondency about Germany in the eloquent articles and books they wrote when they reached home. The result was a series of anti-Nazi books which were widely read in every country in which they were published. On the other hand, as we have seen, Goebbels established a recognised system of press conferences in 1934, probably as a result of Lee's advice.

Propaganda attachés were posted to the German embassies abroad. Just as Goebbels constantly sent instructions to the German press (which on occasion fell into the more enlightened hands of the foreign correspondents, as Shirer reports),[48] so he sent out secret instructions on the propaganda line to his foreign agents. These dangerous documents again sometimes got into the wrong hands, and shed as true a light on Germany's policy as Hitler's *Mein Kampf* for those who were prepared to face its appalling literary style and prolix argument.

Goebbels' instructions to his agents when Germany left the League of Nations with a more-in-sorrow-than-in-anger pose revealed the face behind the mask, and they were published in *Le Petit Parisien* after a copy had been smuggled out of Germany. Goebbels was revealed to be writing in this vein:

To the outside world all our propaganda must underline impressively that Germany does not wish for anything but a peaceful settlement of all pending problems. . . . In a skilful way all those who have refused to accede to Germany's rightful demands must be blamed for the failure of a peaceful understanding. . . . This must be done unobtrusively and in a constantly varying manner. . . . We must persuade at least part of public opinion abroad that Germany has no other way than to take what is absolutely coming to her.[49]

Under the guise of business-men, journalists, press agents and tourists, the emissaries of the Nazis were sent abroad with instructions to do their best to spread the right ideas about the Third Reich. In 1938 there were as many as eighty-three accredited German journalists in London alone.[50] These agents acted as spies, sending in reports to their masters and making contact with elements which were thought to cause trouble in such countries as Egypt and Palestine. Reports which have come to light accuse the British of ruthless repression and atrocities in Palestine. German agents did all they could to aggravate the difficult situation in those countries before the war.

A large number of German international organisations, in addition to those associated with journalism, were created or adopted to help Nazism abroad. They included the Fichte League, the German Students' Foreign Service, the Anti-Jewish World League, the German Academy (for indoctrinating teachers and students going abroad), the People's League for Germanism Abroad, the League of German Business Employers, and so on. This miscellany of organisations was estimated by 1937 to be spending some £21 million a year on propaganda work outside Germany.[51] Every German authorised to travel abroad had a propaganda baton in his knapsack.

The following instructions issued to the representatives of the Fichte

League, an organisation dedicated to pan-Germanism and originally founded in 1914, shows how concentrated and purposeful the German penetration abroad endeavoured to be:

Experience shows that it is effective for our leaflets to be left lying about in factories, schools, banks, trains and cafés, quite casually. Mouth-to-mouth propaganda is also important.

Make lists of all important people, note their political views and supply them regularly with our pamphlets. Never give them more than one at a time, for this decreases their interest. If possible supply the press with our pamphlets so that it can give publicity to our views. If some papers persist in an anti-German tone, answer this immediately with letters to the editors. Our leaflets are gratis.[52]

By 1935 Goebbels' Ministry as a whole was using up enormous sums of money. Its domestic budget was over 130 million marks, its overseas budget (including the lavish grants to the Transocean News Agency) was over 120 million. A further 40 million was set aside for work in film and theatre. In addition, Goebbels was said to have at his disposal a fund amounting to another 45 million marks a year.[53] Ambassador Dodd reveals in his diary that Schacht was troubled at the amount of German currency that was circulating abroad illegally. His investigations during 1935 led him to mark some of the notes that were issued to Goebbels, and he soon discovered that certain of these were among the notes that were eventually to be found in circulation abroad. Schacht complained direct to Hitler, but his complaints only rebounded against himself.[54]

In spite of his efforts to bring all propaganda both at home and abroad under his single control, Goebbels did not finally have it entirely his own way. On his assumption of power he carefully acquired for his own ministry those departments in other ministries which had any concern with the press or with public relations in the broadest sense of the term. From the Ministry of the Interior he acquired control over the press and radio, the moral censorship of plays, books and films, and the regulation of public holidays. From the Ministry of Economics he took over supervision of State-controlled advertising and the promotion of industrial exhibitions and trade fairs. From the Post Office he acquired their tourist agencies for Lufthansa and the railways. Most important of all, he won the first round in the contest for German publicity and public relations abroad. This he acquired at the expense of the Ministry of Foreign Affairs, which was initially under the control of a minister who was not a Nazi, Baron von Neurath, whom Hitler was eventually to dismiss to make room for Ribbentrop.[55]

So, in 1938, Ribbentrop became the first Nazi Foreign Minister. Ribbentrop was as bitterly ambitious and unscrupulous in his methods of acquiring power as Goebbels himself, and they were never anything else but rivals. Ribbentrop insisted, however, in setting up his own propaganda organisation and holding press conferences of his own at his ministry for the foreign correspondents. Otto Dietrich, Hitler's Reich Press Chief, tells the story of this battle for control:

One day at Hitler's headquarters Ribbentrop persuaded the Führer to commit to him in writing the conduct of all propaganda intended for foreign consumption. Propaganda Minister Goebbels knew nothing at all about this. The morning of the following day movers, sent by the Foreign Office, appeared at Goebbels' various offices in Berlin to remove all the physical apparatus used for foreign propaganda. Goebbels' men barricaded themselves in their rooms, and the Propaganda Minister himself promptly telephoned to Hitler for help. Hitler, who had actually signed the order to Ribbentrop, ordered Goebbels to come at once by plane. When Goebbels arrived, he told him to sit down with Ribbentrop in a compartment of his special train and not to leave it until they had ironed out their dispute. Three hours later both men emerged red-faced and informed Hitler—as might have been expected—that they could not agree. Furious, Hitler withdrew and dictated a compromise which largely revoked his previous written order. In practice, however, Ribbentrop never adhered to this latter decision. Holding a facsimile of the first, rescinded order, down to the end of the war he continued to challenge the Propaganda Ministry's jurisdiction in all German missions abroad.[56]

So deep did the rift become that the two ministers set up their own rival press clubs to attract the foreign journalists on a social basis. Nor was the rivalry hidden, as a story told by Mackenzie shows.[57] On the important occasion of the announcement of the Soviet-German pact, Boemer, Ribbentrop's spokesman to the press, said: "Only eight persons in the world knew about the completion of our negotiations with Moscow before public announcement was made. And one of them was not Dr. Goebbels!"[58] What served to anger Goebbels in this rivalry merely amused the correspondents, who delighted in any of the jokes circulating round Berlin at Goebbels' or Ribbentrop's expense.

It was Goebbels' violent anti-Semitism which most seriously undermined his reputation in the eyes of the journalists. He was not content to publicise the decrees against the Jews initiated by others; he himself actively promoted the persecutions and pogroms. As we have seen, it was Goebbels who planned the blackmail of the Jews who had left Germany at the expense of those who remained, by ordering the closure of Jewish-owned shops in 1933. It was Goebbels who harried writers, artists and actors who had Jewish relations or connections, though he was prepared to endeavour to come to terms that seemed advantageous to the Nazis with certain Jews of exceptional talent, such as Fritz Lang.

But the most savage display of anti-Semitism in Germany before the war was the pogrom which followed the murder of von Rath, a member of the staff of the German Embassy in Paris, on 7th November 1938, a few weeks only after the completion of the Munich agreement which represented a further triumph for Hitler's policy of expansion. The assassin was a Polish Jew aged seventeen, Herschel Grynszpan, who may well have been the victim of a plot to provide the Nazis with an excuse to initiate a decisive campaign of persecution of the Jews which they could subsequently claim to be a spontaneous outburst by the German people. Grynszpan did not fall into Nazi hands until four years later, when Goebbels stopped the propaganda trial which had been planned and had the murderer executed. Now, however, his problem was the organisation of the pogrom.[59] As we have seen, he assembled the foreign press on 10th November and claimed that nothing was happening to harm the Jews—"*den Juden ist kein Haar gekrümmt worden*—not a hair of a Jewish head has been disturbed", is what he is reported as saying by Lochner, who was present.[60] Yet, as Sir Nevile Henderson describes it:

In revenge for the murder by a young unbalanced Jew of a German diplomatist in Paris, at the instigation of Dr. Goebbels' propaganda press, and with the connivance and actual participation of Himmler's secret police and extreme Nazis, squads of German hooligans reverted to the barbarism of the Middle Ages and indulged in an orgy of violent ill-treatment of the Jews such as even the Middle Ages could scarcely equal.[61]

Goebbels himself wrote on 11th November:

If I had organised the demonstrations, there would have been not a mere few thousand but four hundred thousand to seven hundred thousand people in the streets, and the result would have been quite different and more thorough.[62]

Meanwhile throughout Germany Jewish shops were broken into and robbed, Jewish property was sacked and burnt, synagogues everywhere were desecrated and set alight. Jews themselves were seized and beaten up, arrested and thrust into concentration camps. Here the world could see on no small scale what was to happen in the next eight years when Germany gained control over whole populations of Jews and laid them waste in grave-pits and mass incinerators. The violent world reaction against this November purge led to President Roosevelt recalling the American Ambassador and to universal condemnation, not least in the British press, of what had happened. But already Hitler and Goebbels were convinced that Britain had become the centre of anti-German feeling as the result of Munich, and had started a counter-offensive in the German press which was to be fomented until the declaration of war made it obligatory.

There survive some verbatim notes of a Cabinet meeting held on 12th November at which Göring and Goebbels discussed the whole question of the segregation of the Jews in Germany. These notes

reappeared at the Nuremberg Trials. Nothing could be more revealing than the casual inhumanity of these remarks, which were supposed
at Nuremberg to whitewash Göring at Goebbels' expense.

Goebbels: . . . Furthermore, I consider it necessary to eliminate Jews
completely from appearing in public, particularly whenever such
appearance might have a provocative effect. Do you realise that even
today it is quite possible for a Jew to share a compartment in a sleeper
with a German? I think the Reich Minister for Transport should issue
an edict whereby there would have to be special compartments for
Jews, stipulating further that when that particular compartment happens
to be filled up, no Jew would be entitled to claim any other seat; that
Jews must not under any circumstances mix with the Germans in the
train, in fact they should not have the right to be seated at all unless
every German in the train has seating accommodation; and rather than
have a Jew sitting in one compartment filled or half-filled by Germans,
I would have him stand outside in the corridor.
Göring: Wouldn't it be simpler and more reasonable just to give them
compartments of their own?
Goebbels: Maybe, but certainly not when the train is crowded.
Göring: Well, what of it? There would have to be just one Jewish
coach in each train, and when that one is occupied other Jews will
jolly well have to stay behind.
Goebbels: Very well, but then suppose there aren't that many Jews
who, shall we say, want to use the Berlin-Munich express? Suppose
there are only two Jews in their coach or compartment, whereas all the
other coaches and compartments are overcrowded? In that case those
two Jews would be sort of specially privileged. Hence the ruling
should be, Jews may only claim a seat when all Germans are properly
seated.
Göring: I don't think it is necessary to put all this into an edict. Suppose
that sort of situation arose—a Jew or two seated in an empty compartment of an otherwise crowded train—well, what the hell! They
would just be kicked out, wouldn't they, even if they had to sit in the
lavatory for the rest of the journey. We don't need any legislation for
that, do we?

Goebbels: ... There is another point that requires some consideration. Would it not be opportune to stop Jews altogether from entering German woods and forests. Nowadays Jews still run around the *Grunewald* in droves. I would say that that is provocative and incidents may, and indeed, do happen.

Göring: Very well, then, let's give the Jews a certain part of certain woods of their own, and Alpers can see to it that certain animals are settled there too—I mean animals who look like Jews, I am thinking of elks who have that sort of a hooked nose, haven't they?[63]

Later in the same Cabinet meeting it was decided to make the Jews pay for the damage done to their property—which was already regarded as belonging to the State. A collective fine of a thousand million marks was imposed on the Jewish community as a whole, and a time-limit set for its delivery.

As the Chief of Propaganda in Germany, Goebbels reserved the right to himself to be the spokesman on the platform or over the air on every important occasion in these historic years for Germany. It was he who announced the death of Hindenburg and then, after a suitable interval of silence, the combination of the offices of President and Chancellor in the person of the Führer. (The French Ambassador and others believed that Goebbels had re-drafted the late President's testament, which was not published for several days and contained much uncharacteristic phrasing in a style more suitable to an experienced Nazi writer.) It was Goebbels who on 13th March 1939 made the official broadcast announcement of the annexation of Austria and launched the campaign that "Hitler wants peace". And it was Goebbels who made two fighting speeches in Danzig in June 1939 claiming, as usual, that German nationals were being persecuted and that the Free City should come back to Germany.

Goebbels himself wrote constantly, directing various campaigns of propaganda against those who opposed the current development of the Reich. He initiated successive campaigns against Austria, Czechoslovakia, Poland and Britain. His articles had all the old, fighting virulence of the days when he was campaigning for the Reichstag elections or shouting down the Communists in Red Berlin.

The whole social pattern of life for Goebbels changed when he became Reich Minister. In the first place he became a relatively wealthy man. Among the papers that survived the holocaust of Berlin was a mass of documents relating to Goebbels' private accounts. These reveal that only a month before Hitler became Chancellor Goebbels owed an embarrassing amount of income tax. A handwritten record of his normal income from 1933 to 1937 also survives, and is listed as follows:

1933	34,376 marks	1935	62,190 marks
1934	134,423 marks	1936	63,654 marks
	1937	66,905 marks[64]	

These figures, however, do not seem to take any account of his income from the Eher Verlag, the Central Publishing Company of the National Socialist Party, except possibly those for 1934. Between December 1935 and December 1936 he drew advances of 290,000 marks on account of future royalties, whereas the actual earnings of his books during that year were 63,416 marks.

Goebbels was meticulous over money, carefully compiling his expense accounts even at the height of his power. He demanded the same punctiliousness in his staff, while many other Nazi leaders gloried in their extravagance. In spite of his radicalism he must have shared his father's desire to make good in the most bourgeois sense of the term, and in any case his highly developed æsthetic sense demanded lavish interior decoration and furnishings once he had the means to acquire them. Nevertheless, he had to watch his reputation with the working classes of Germany. Once he made the mistake of letting a newsreel about his family be released in which his young children were shown with their ponies and grooms. Conscious that both his new position and his personal taste demanded an entirely new standard of living, he tried to cover up any suspicion that he really liked luxury. At a press reception Louis Lochner heard one of Goebbels' representatives explaining carefully to a group of German provincial newsmen that the Reich Minister was really an extremely modest man who put up with the inconvenience of living on a grand scale because of the needs of his official position. This turned out to be 'inspired', for other ministry officials were saying precisely the same thing to other provincial newsmen![65]

Apart from his official residence in Berlin, Goebbels acquired two fine properties for himself—Schwanenwerder on an island in the Wannsee and Lanke on the Bogensee, both estates on lakes a short distance from the capital. Schwanenwerder had belonged to a Jewish millionaire who had been expropriated, and Goebbels bought it relatively cheaply. Documents survive to show that he raised a mortgage of 100,000 marks towards its cost.[66] The price of this property, which he acquired around 1934, was 350,000 marks, or about £17,500. Goebbels subsequently told one of his war-time secretaries, von Oven, how he had just received 100,000 marks from the Nazi Publishing House as an advance on his diary *Vom Kaiserhof zur Reichskanzlei*. Even with the help of the mortgage and his own savings, Goebbels was still some 70,000 marks short of the price. When Hitler heard of this he said he would make his minister a present of the money out of the royalties he had just drawn from the sales of *Mein Kampf*. A day or two later Hitler asked Goebbels to wait a moment after a meeting. He then reappeared carrying two parcels, which turned out to contain 70,000 marks made up in fifty-mark notes. This, Hitler explained, was in order to keep the amount from being entered in the books![67]

Lanke was an even more beautiful lakeside estate which lay some forty miles east of Berlin, and Goebbels first sought to acquire it about 1939. But he miscalculated the cost of his substantial building projects; his original estimate of half a million marks fell short of the real cost, which reached some two million. He landed himself into serious financial difficulties, and in the end he had to appeal to Dr. Winckler, the Nazis' financial adviser and negotiator, to get him out of them.[68] Winckler supplied a little money unofficially, but this was useless, and the President of the Deutsche Bank himself intervened. Winckler, most unhappy at being involved, was again summoned by Goebbels who was in a desperate position by now. Winckler suggested Hitler might help. Goebbels rejected this at once; Hitler had already rebuked him for extravagance. Winckler then suggested Göring; this was also impossible, since Göring and Goebbels were scarcely on speaking terms.

Eventually, however, Goebbels consented to let the matter be put to Göring. Winckler with some difficulty managed to persuade Göring to let the property be considered an official residence to be paid for by the film industry and "on loan" to Goebbels for the period he was in charge of the German cinema. Winckler came back in triumph; Goebbels' original 500,000 went back into his pocket, while Winckler himself took over the management of the property on the Reich Minister's behalf.

Goebbels placed a very high value on his literary work. He exacted 4,000 marks from *Das Reich* for each of his regular weekly articles, and later on, during the war, he refused an offer from the Party Press of three million marks for the right to publish all his diaries after the war should be over.[69] He looked on these records of his as the only authentic and properly maintained account there was of the history of Nazi Germany, and he felt they were worth far more than the sum offered.

Lavish though he was in matters of property and clothes (he possessed an enormous wardrobe which grew to some hundreds of suits), he was frugality itself at table. His guests always came away complaining of their hunger. He frequently invited people from the film world to lunch or dine with him, and it became customary for those who knew how little was in store for them to go to a restaurant independently before or after visiting the Reich Minister. When full-scale rationing was introduced in war-time, Goebbels insisted that his guests brought their ration books with them, and a silver salver was passed round the table for the coupons.

Goebbels opposed the lavish meals in which the other Nazi leaders indulged, more especially Göring, whose famous parties he refused to publicise. He deliberately played down the gala reception at the Opera which Göring staged in April 1935 when he married the actress, Emmy Sonnemann. When Göring held a luxurious ball in January the following year, Goebbels censored the pictures and refused to pass for publication those of which he disapproved. On very rare occasions, however, he was capable of giving parties on the grand scale. In July 1936 he sponsored a 'Venetian night' on an island in the Wannsee for three thousand guests with a sumptuous dinner and a vast bar. There was dancing in the open air and the performances of a ballet. This was an international occasion, however, for the delegates attending the International Chamber of Commerce. But he also saw to it that little enough got into the press. Another magnificent occasion the same year was Goebbels' garden party on his new estate at Schwanenwerder to celebrate the Olympic Games which were being held that year in Germany. This party, at which certain guests got drunk and misbehaved with some young actresses from the film studios, became a minor scandal which had to be hushed up. Soon after Göring gave a huge party, a *Bierabend*, which was a model of respectability by way of studied contrast. But the fact remains that Goebbels cared little, if anything, for either food or drink and was determined to make a virtue out of this Lenten attitude in order to repress other more hungry people than himself.

Otto Dietrich has given an extraordinary description of Hitler's social life before the war, a life in which both Goebbels and his wife were continually involved. Hitler's glaring prominence in world politics could have made him host to innumerable people of importance from many countries who, whether they admired him or not, would have welcomed the chance to meet and talk with him. But Hitler, who could not brook either argument about his opinions or any form of challenge to them, preferred to spend his leisure time with the same small, commonplace circle of admiring friends that included the wives of certain of his ministers and always involved his favourite, Magda Goebbels. Hitler's intimate friends had to be prepared for the constant summons which at the shortest notice would require their presence at his table either in Berlin or Berchtesgaden; after a meal they would listen to his endless reminiscences that usually lasted until the small hours, because the Führer could not bear to be left alone. At the more formal luncheons and dinner parties at the Chancellery when distinguished guests had to be entertained, Goebbels did his best to lighten the atmosphere when the visitors fell silent, turned into glum auditors because of Hitler's endless monologues. Dietrich, who was often present on these occasions, describes Goebbels' assiduous social efforts:

The visitors let Hitler talk; they themselves contributed nothing. The exception was Goebbels . . . he would toss cues to Hitler during the conversation, would take up Hitler's ideas, carry them still further, and take advantage of the opportunity to obtain oral decisions from Hitler on the most diverse matters. If Hitler did not speak and Goebbels did not put in his oar, there were often prolonged, embarrassed silences which the host expected to be broken by the interjection of jokes. . . . Goebbels would repeat the latest political witticisms in Berlin jargon —though he made a point of picking only the innocuous stories and those that were about Göring and not himself.[70]

Hitler greatly enjoyed the company of actresses, and Goebbels was always prepared to introduce them to the Führer.

The need in Goebbels for both the company and the sexual intimacy of women was very great indeed. His vanity demanded that he should be loved and courted by women, and the incessant irritation caused him by the physical inferiority of his stature and by his limp was compensated as far as ever possible by the satisfactions of his bed. He needed a succession of love affairs to guarantee his superiority as a man of artistry and culture, and he took care to see that no one, not even his wife, deprived him of this right. It was early in September 1938 that Schacht spoke of the matter to von Hassell, who recorded it in his diary:

He also told me that Goebbels was pretty much in disfavour because of his affairs with actresses and other women who are dependent upon the Propaganda Ministry for jobs. This was getting to be too much of a scandal. Hitler was in a rage, also, because he wanted to divorce his wife. Goebbels, knowing the mood of the people, was opposed to the rash war policy.[71]

There was always a spoilt and frustrated child dodging in the shadows of Goebbels' nature with its greedy hands held out for the sweetmeats. The devouring of women was part of his childish passion for repletion and the mastery of sex. Goebbels, however, was intelligent and tasteful enough to realise that women should be wooed and flattered even if they offered themselves readily to his advances. He knew how to talk to women, how to kiss their hands, how to send flowers and give little presents, how to prepare a rendezvous in the night, and how to use gentleness and good manners in bed. When he wanted to impress a woman he gave her little personal gifts and nose-gays of flowers which she knew he had selected himself and not ordered by telephone through a secretary. Above all, he gave her his time; the minute by minute rush of the day was abandoned for the timeless concentration of eroticism. Certain women, proud that they had been among those who had attracted these attentions from a man in Goebbels' privileged position and with his great taste in matters of love, have admitted privately their enjoyment of their passing relations with him.

On his marriage to Magda he found himself very much in love with his beautiful wife. They were the kind of newly-wedded people who enjoyed exchanging little endearments in public to impress those who were watching. All they caused was amusement. Magda was not strait-laced. She had been brought up in the same period of easy morals as her new husband and had herself taken some advantage of this. Magda was used to luxury, and what for a year or two she lost in money (when her former husband's generous allowance ceased) she gained by making her flat the social centre of the Nazi hierarchy and basking in the sunshine of the Leader's friendship. There is no doubt that Hitler held her in high regard and paid her a great deal of attention socially, while she worshipped him in return.

Goebbels, however, insisted that his wife, like a good Nazi, should be fruitful and multiply. He treated his stepson Harald with affection, but both his male pride and his patriotic duty demanded the almost annual production of children of his own. On 1st September 1932 came his daughter Helga; then on 13th April 1934 Hilde; on 21st October 1935 Helmuth; on 9th February 1937 Holde; on 5th May 1938 Hedda; and in October 1940 Heide. The alliteration in the names was the result of some whim of Goebbels and his wife. There are many witnesses to the correctness of Goebbels' behaviour to his children. He gave them due measure of his time, playing with them and being a good father, proud of his increasing flock.

Magda's constant pregnancies, and her tendency to ill health, to some extent released Goebbels' energies at a time when his increasing contacts with the pretty women of the theatre and the film studios excited his susceptible passions. Magda was apparently prepared for him to have occasional affaires with actresses and society women. At Schwanenwerder, in any case, he had the advantage of guest-houses and pavilions set out in the grounds where he could arrange to meet whomever he liked and remain with her undisturbed. Young actresses, young secretaries, girls prepared to offer themselves to him in a daze of admiration, seemed to be his favourites.

It was in 1936 that Goebbels met for the first time the young Czech actress Lida Baarova, who was working at the time in Germany. Although she was barely twenty years old, she had already begun to make successful appearances in German films. In private life her name was closely linked with that of the famous star Gustav Fröhlich, with whom she was living at his luxurious residence on the island of Schwanenwerder, near Goebbels' own estate. Goebbels had, of course, seen her frequently at the innumerable film parties and receptions which he attended as Minister, but like everyone else he regarded her as in love with Fröhlich and likely any time to become his wife. They met also at Schwanenwerder, and it was Magda who had first invited Baarova to come to her house and have tea. The invitation was accepted; and as these private social occasions grew in number she began to sense the Herr Minister's personal interest in her. She was barely half his age, but she was already tiring of her relationship with Fröhlich. The mature charm of Goebbels increasingly impressed her. She was falling in love with him.

This was the position in 1936 when, with many other stage and film personalities, she attended the Nuremberg Congress; there she met Hitler in the presence of Goebbels. Hitler began by apologising that an error had been made in not sending her flowers. "But why, my Führer?" she asked. "Because you have got married," said Hitler. "No, my Führer," she replied. "To Herr Fröhlich," persisted Hitler. "No, my Führer," she answered. "What, not married?" growled Hitler. "No, my Führer." Then it was Goebbels' turn to make her confirm that she was still free. He asked her, too, in a softer voice whether she and Fröhlich were indeed not married or about to marry. "No, Herr Reichsminister," she said yet again.

Baarova's next encounter with Goebbels was at a reception a day or so later. There were large numbers of people present, but she found herself sitting next to the Minister. She was well aware of the touch of intimacy he was seeking to establish with her in the dense crowd. The orchestra near-by was playing the lilting music of the song 'Eleanor', and a singer was returning every so often to the insistent, recurrent refrain: "*Ich liebe dich; Ich liebe dich.*" With the throng pressing all round them, Goebbels leaned towards her and whispered with a smile: "*Ich dich auch*; I too." This was his first declaration of love to her.

Later in the Congress she attended another reception where Goebbels singled her out about half an hour before he was due to address his vast audience. He invited her to leave the reception-room and go with him to another room where, he said, they could speak in private about her career. She was surprised, and could not help expressing her astonishment at the time he had chosen to take her aside. "But, Herr Reichsminister, your speech . . . ?" "That doesn't matter," replied Goebbels. "I'm used to that sort of thing. What matters now is that I must have a few words with you in private." Still most surprised, Baarova withdrew to another room with him. The moment they were in private, Goebbels once more declared his love for her.

Baarova did not know what it was right for her to say. She could only feel anxiety that within a few minutes this man beside her would be on the rostrum in front of the microphones and she would be just one of the audience filling the massive auditorium. She was about to protest when he kissed her on the mouth. She felt her lipstick print itself on him, and she was quite desperate what to do next. But all she saw then was Goebbels grinning at her and wiping his face with a handkerchief. "Listen," he said. "I must go now. But don't forget; I shall speak for you only." Trembling she left him and took her place in the audience. Goebbels knew where she was sitting. At one moment when he paused in his speech, he looked directly towards her, smiled, and drawing his handkerchief from his pocket, wiped his mouth where her lipstick had been. They shared this secret moment while ten thousand people watched knowing nothing.

Goebbels had an exquisite sense of occasion with women. He knew how to establish the charms of intimacy. He knew that what a woman really enjoys is not watching the man she loves expending his talent in public or in the skilful conduct of his business affairs; what she values is his ability to show even on public occasions that he can turn aside from his business and devote the whole of his attention to her and her alone. Goebbels' reputation as a man who worked day and night stood him in good stead where women were concerned, because he knew how to pay them the supreme compliment of a busy man and give them his time without once seeming to care that he might be needed elsewhere. "But, Herr Reichsminister," they would say before they really knew him, "what about your conference, your broadcast, your speech . . . ?" "These things can wait," Goebbels would say. "After all, I am with you."

With the pressure of Goebbels' kiss in her memory, Baarova waited anxiously for her next private meeting with him. During the following two years, Goebbels gave what seemed unlimited time to her. They met at all hours of the day and night. He loved talking to her about herself; he helped her with her problems, however small or great they might be. She lived now in a small apartment in Berlin, but mostly they spent their interludes of love in Goebbels' private pavilions at either Lanke or Schwanenwerder. Although Baarova's success as a film-star meant that she was comparatively well off, she insisted on using a diminutive Czech car which puttered along noisily and even drew the attention of Hitler to its absence of star quality. "Why can't Baarova afford to get a proper car?" grumbled Hitler. Goebbels forthwith offered to give her one, but she refused. She preferred her old Czech vehicle. Normally Goebbels did not attempt to give her expensive presents, only well-chosen gifts which she knew he had taken great care to select because he knew that they would please her.

It became evident to more people than themselves that they were deeply in love. Baarova's high cheek-bones, characteristic of Slav beauty, fascinated him; so did her accent, with its slow Czech enunciation in her rich, sensual voice. She was no taller than Goebbels, and they looked well together. Her distinctive femininity, her strong passions, her sweetness which was the sweetness now of a growing maturity and not of youthful innocence, made him happier and easier in love than he had ever been before. Never once in the whole two years they were together did they find occasion to quarrel. There was no need now for the posturing and the play-acting which had characterised Goebbels' youthful attitude to love. They were happy together without strain or tension. They did not care that the gossip of Berlin was beginning to centre round them. They did not care, but Magda did.

She asked Baarova to tea. This seemed to the young girl a formidable invitation to receive. Magda was, after all, one of the leading society women in Germany. She was almost twenty years older than Baarova. She had powerful friends, not least, of course, Hitler himself. And she was the wife of the man Baarova loved. Goebbels' mistress became very nervous, but she felt she must accept the invitation and find out what was behind it.

The meeting was very different from what she had expected. Magda embarrassed her by becoming highly emotional. She began by saying that she knew all about Joseph's love for her, and that if he needed Baarova's love then the situation must be accepted. Then she poured out her heart to the girl. Because of this they must be like sisters to each other, she said. They must call each other by the intimate term of '*du*'. They must kiss. Baarova was both frightened and revolted by the self-abasement of this woman who could have been her mother. All she could say was: "*Ich kann nicht.*" Magda continued to press her, but added very seriously when they parted: "However much you love Joseph, you must never, never bear him a child." This, at any rate, Baarova was readily able to agree, and so she tore herself away. Magda, she realised, had to be the official wife and child-bearer. Baarova must remain the mistress like the rest of Goebbels' women.

But in spite of this assurance, Magda remained unsatisfied. Whether she was heart-broken or not—and both Naumann and von Wedel deny the many stories that she was not herself entirely faithful to her husband—she knew that pride alone demanded some action from her to put a stop to a love affair which was increasingly becoming a public scandal. Goebbels took no notice of her protests, and eventually she set about preparing for divorce. To help in the collection of evidence, she employed Goebbels' Under-Secretaries at the Ministry, Karl

Hanke, who was devoted to her and ready to take the risk of spying on the Minister. Between them they set about gathering the evidence necessary for divorce proceedings. Meanwhile, Magda refused to let her husband enter the house at Schwanenwerder, and once more new fuel was added to the fire of Berlin gossip. Hanke documented Goebbels' liaisons with the assiduity of a private detective.

When Hitler heard that the separation of Magda and her husband was leading to a divorce, he was horrified. He decided that he must deal with the matter himself. Magda had told Göring of her intentions, and Göring had told Hitler. The Führer summoned her to Berchtesgaden, only to learn from her own lips that she refused now to have anything more to do with her husband. Hitler prepared next to see Goebbels. He returned to Berlin and sent for him. Goebbels then told him the solemn truth about himself and Baarova, and he is alleged to have declared he was ready to resign at once from his Ministry and be posted abroad in the foreign service rather than give up the woman he loved. Hitler is said to have become very angry and made it abundantly clear to Goebbels that he was in no position to indulge in a private scandal. He was a prominent and indispensable servant of state. He ordered him not to see Baarova again. This, he said, was a *Führerbefehl*, a command that could not be disobeyed.

There seems no doubt at all that Goebbels was completely sincere in his love for Baarova and in his readiness to sacrifice his position as Minister if this might enable him to maintain his association with her and perhaps eventually, when he was free to do so, to make her his wife. Baarova herself claims that she never wanted him to take the ultimate step of resigning his Ministry. They had certainly talked together of marriage once Magda's intentions were known to them; Goebbels had even discussed persuading the Führer to send him abroad where he might take her with him. But Goebbels was not in the habit of discussing political affairs with her, and when Hitler finally took matters into his own hands and ordered Goebbels to sever the relationship forthwith, the news came as a cruel and wholly unexpected blow. She was abruptly summoned to Count Helldorf's office and told of the Führer's command.

Helldorf was chosen by Hitler to deal with the matter because he was at this time Chief of Police. Baarova, sensing there was to be trouble, took with her to the interview an intimate friend, Hilde Körber. Helldorf began by telling her that it was Hitler's orders that she and Goebbels must not see each other again for at least six months. If by then their love was still uncured, the matter of the divorce might be reconsidered. As he spoke, Baarova fainted. Hilde Körber, who was herself by now approaching hysterics at this dire news and its effect upon her friend, sprang to her help and cried out for eau-de-Cologne. Helldorf, alarmed at the violence of the reaction he had caused in the two women, hurried to the wash-room adjoining his office and snatched at the nearest bottle. By a macabre touch of comedy, he grasped in his agitation a bottle of hair tonic in mistake for eau-de-Cologne. The error was not discovered until Baarova's face was already bathed in the liquid. Perhaps the fact that the moment she recovered she had some difficulty in cleaning her face was of greater help to her than the eau-de-Cologne would have been. With Hilde trembling beside her, they tried to put her face to rights. Helldorf dropped his official manner and spoke to Baarova earnestly as a friend. He told her as gently as he could that if her love affair were not terminated once and for all, it would not be a matter of preserving her career, but of preserving her life. She must leave Germany as soon as possible. On hearing this, Baarova collapsed into hysterics. She threatened immediate suicide unless she could talk to Goebbels within the hour. Life had no more meaning for her. She screamed and raved until eventually Helldorf undertook to telephone Hitler straight away in order to see what might be done. Twice he retired to another room and spoke to the Führer. At length he obtained the necessary permission. Then Hilde took the sobbing woman back to her apartment. There Baarova waited for the sound of Goebbels' voice.

Eventually the phone rang and she heard him speaking to her. His voice was calm. The first thing he said was: "I am speaking from my friend Hermann Göring's house." Hitler had forbidden him to speak to her without a witness standing by the telephone. He called her Liduschka as he had always done, and she wept bitterly. Goebbels tried to calm her. He spoke of their duty and their need to be brave.

Then he said good-bye to her, and added enigmatically and finally: "*Bleib wie du bist*; stay as you are."

Goebbels retired alone to Lanke for a day or two to recover his self-control. Baarova was left to weep, and only Goebbels' words prevented her from carrying out her threatened suicide. Her films were removed from the screen and her contracts cancelled. She herself lay in bed, ill and hysterical. Goebbels never made any direct contact with her again; yet she stayed a while in Berlin, hoping to reach him. She did in fact see him once more before she left Berlin. Rach was driving Goebbels down the Kurfürstendamm when they saw Baarova driving her small car quite close to the Mercedes. For a while the two cars kept pace with each other, and Baarova could not prevent herself following Goebbels into the back entrance of the Ministry where she guessed he was going. The cars came to a halt. She and Goebbels looked at each other. His face betrayed no feeling, but she knew he had wanted this long, last, solemn look at her. It endured maybe barely a minute, but her memory of the moment remains undimmed by time. Then Goebbels motioned to Rach; the car slowly pulled away, and that was the end.

Hitler was, in fact, determined to keep for himself the man who was so useful to him, and he was resolved to bring Goebbels and his wife together once more. Magda at first refused to be reconciled to her husband. She still pressed for a divorce. But Hitler, who was the Führer, saw to it that the reconciliation he wanted finally took place. He summoned them both to Berchtesgaden and re-made the marriage with his own hands. A celebrated photograph on the front page of the *Berliner Illustrirte Zeitung* shows the three of them together. Only Hitler is smiling. As a symbol of the reconciliation the last daughter, Heide, was conceived soon after the war had begun. She was called the *Versöhnungskind*—the reconciliation child. Goebbels by then had resumed the full flood of his work and the occasional pursuit of less harmful mistresses. Von Hassell records at the end of January 1939 that "Goebbels' period of disgrace with Hitler seems now to be over".[72]

When the time came towards the end of the war at which Goebbels thought fit to burn his private papers, his aide von Oven remembers the Minister looking through a collection of old photographs. Suddenly he stopped and showed the young man a large portrait of a woman. "Now," he said, "there's a beautiful woman." Von Oven looked at the photograph. It was of Lida Baarova. Goebbels stared at her face for a moment, then tore the picture across. "Into the fire with it," he said.[73]

CHAPTER SIX

"These Years of Triumph"

THERE SEEMS little doubt that Goebbels in spite of his venomous speeches and articles would have preferred there to be no war. He had had experience of what propaganda, backed by the parade of force and private tyranny, could effect without the dislocation of national life occasioned by the open waging of war with armies. He realised better than Hitler himself that to fight wars by means of armies meant putting the conduct of the Nazi campaign for power into the hands of professional soldiers, who would immediately be given an opportunity to attempt the frustration of Hitler's ambitions by the demands of military tactics.

However, Hitler's luck stayed with him as, one by one, he plucked the easier fruits that open warfare now permitted. The new German Empire, having already taken in Austria, Czechoslovakia and Memel (which bordered East Prussia and Lithuania) extended its range to Danzig and western Poland in 1939 and to Denmark, Norway, Holland, Belgium, Luxembourg and France in the spring of 1940. Later in the year Italy, which had entered the war just in time to be party to the collapse of France, invaded Greece using her bases in occupied Albania to help her. At the same time Hungary and Rumania became subservient to Germany. All these territories, whether fully occupied or not, had to be guarded and policed. They also had to be supplied with Nazi propaganda originating in the first place through Goebbels' and Ribbentrop's agents. Goebbels endeavoured to make himself aware of the state of morale in all the territories under German dominion and to devise the right variants of his basic propaganda to suit their different needs.

Hitler had become very sure of himself and the ripe, quick victories only confirmed him in his sense that his intuitive analysis of every situation went beyond the vision of the men who surrounded him. As early as 10th October 1939 he said this emphatically to his Commanding Officers in remarks such as these which occurred in a statement he made to them: "As the last factor I must in all modesty name my own person: irreplaceable . . . I am convinced of my powers of intellect and decision . . . I shall shrink from nothing and shall destroy everyone who is opposed to me. . . . In the last years I have experienced many examples of intuition. Even in the present development I see the prophecy."[1] It was obligatory for Goebbels to support this self-assessment by the Führer, and whatever occasional qualms he might have had about Hitler's judgment, especially during the long intervals of the war when he was comparatively inaccessible, he never really doubted Hitler's genius. At the worst he regarded him as over-tired, misguided and ill-advised.

Hitler's desire for open war had grown as his mood had hardened, especially against Britain which he came to regard as the prime opposer of his will. He welcomed the war in the way his Staff Officers, the professional soldiers, did not. As the war progressed he approached it more and more like some avenging angel, while they saw it with the often jaundiced eyes of men concerned with practical strategy.

Even during the first two years of the war—"these years of triumph" as Goebbels called them—there were certain frustrating difficulties for a man of Hitler's intractable temperament, in particular the High Command's aversion to the invasion of Britain, Mussolini's opposition to many of Hitler's actions (especially his occupation of Rumania in October 1940) and his own basic distrust (in spite of Ribbentrop's sanguine view) of the pact with Russia, whose actions in the Baltic, when Stalin ordered the occupation of Estonia, Latvia and Lithuania in June 1940 plainly showed that she put no trust in Germany. The Russians followed this immediately by threatening Hitler's interests in Rumania, more specially the oilfields; it was this that led subsequently to the German occupation of that country. In addition, Hitler completely failed to bring Franco into the war.

After the collapse of France, Hitler was disappointed in his hopes of a British capitulation. "I feel it to be my duty before my own conscience," he said in a speech before the Reichstag on 19th July 1940, "to appeal once more to reason and common sense in Great Britain.... I can see no reason why this war must go on."[2] But if Britain became the first major stumbling-block in Hitler's war (seeing that he neglected to invade and conquer her through Operation Sea-Lion), the second was undoubtedly his own overweening ambition. No sooner had he reluctantly been persuaded to postpone the invasion of England than he set the German Army the task of Operation Barbarossa—the invasion of Soviet Russia. He was also forced almost simultaneously to provide German troops to invade the Balkans because of Mussolini's surprise attack on Greece, which had not been timed in co-operation with Hitler and which he bitterly resented. Hitler found that he had to provide the stiffening necessary to keep Mussolini's armies in the field not only in Greece but also in North Africa, where the Allies achieved their first notable victory by routing Graziani's forces at Sidi Barrani in December 1940. But even while he was arranging to salvage Italian honour, he was laying the foundations for the invasion of Russia. He was also urging Japan to attack Britain in the Far East, but Japan in the end evolved her own policy and precipitated America into the war when she attacked Pearl Harbour on 7th December 1941. Once more Hitler was completely taken by surprise.

Meanwhile Hitler found that Yugoslavia, which lay in his path to Greece, dared to put up a resistance. German bombers were sent to destroy the capital, Belgrade, and in three days killed over 17,000 people. Goebbels was at his desk at six in the morning on the first day of Operation Punishment, as this avenging flight was called.[3] In the same month, April 1941, Yugoslavia capitulated and the British evacuated Greece. Mussolini's honour was for the moment salvaged. To reinforce his supremacy, Hitler sent a virtually unknown General to take command in North Africa—Erwin Rommel. British hopes of an easy victory in North Africa faded, and Hitler once more turned his attention to Eastern Europe. In a series of conferences with the High Command Hitler laid down his plans for the rapid conquest of Russia, which was to be a massive source for the supply of food for Hitler's armies. They would then be free to turn and pulverise Britain. None the less Rudolf Hess, believing he was interpreting

Hitler's dearest wish, made one last sensational attempt to win a peace settlement out of Britain when he flew on his fantastic mission by Messerschmidt on 10th May 1941. Hitler, who appeared to be as amazed as Churchill at what had happened, went on with the organisation of Operation Barbarossa. The German armies crossed the Russian frontier at dawn on 22nd June. Within a few days they had driven deep into Soviet territory and within three weeks reached Smolensk, some 200 miles from Moscow.

Tactical divergencies between Hitler and the High Command then began to emerge; while the professional soldiers wanted to make for Moscow, Hitler coveted the granaries of the Ukraine. He and he alone was in a position to overrule them, and in doing so he turned what might have been a major defeat for the Russians into that phase of the struggle which was to be the turning-point of the Nazi fortunes. The Germans drove on to Kiev, and Hitler himself became confused in his selection of objectives to be reached as the autumn rains came in to prepare the ground for the snows of winter. He wanted Leningrad, he wanted Moscow (and he was only eighty miles from it in October), and he wanted the Black Sea coast and the Caucasus. The battle front stretched a thousand miles, and there were well over a million Russian prisoners to control. Göring, talking to Ciano after the November meeting with the Italian Fascists in Berlin to found the New Order for Europe, boasted that between twenty and thirty million people would starve to death in Russia during the year, and that the Russian prisoners had begun to eat each other. Hitler believed Russia to be all but defeated and forced his frozen armies to press on their campaign in appalling conditions of cold. The day before Hitler heard to his amazement of Japan's attack on Pearl Harbour, the Russians also surprised him with a massive counter-offensive designed to relieve the threat to Moscow. Nevertheless, Hitler formally declared war on the United States without any thought that the Americans might ever threaten him in Europe. Roosevelt, he declared, was the tool of the Jews.

Hitler managed to stem the Russian offensive and save his troops from a Napoleonic retreat in the depths of winter. He made himself Commander-in-Chief of the German Army; he deprived generals of their commands and, in some cases, of their rank. He let it be known that he blamed the High Command for the failure to subdue Russia. He ordered a state of no retreat, whatever the cost in lives. Inadequately clothed to resist the acid cold, his men died by tens of thousands from freezing without the need of death from the Soviet guns. At a terrible cost the Russians were held until the spring of 1942 came and Hitler was able to bring his army up to strength again, supplemented by Finnish, Rumanian, Hungarian and Italian troops which he valued only statistically. "We all feel at this moment the grandeur of the times in which we live," he said in a public speech in March. "A world is being forged anew."[4] He then set about reaching Stalingrad on the Volga and the Caucasian oil-fields. By September Stalingrad was becoming the turning-point of the Russian campaign, and a second winter had to be faced with an enormously elongated front. Hitler refused to see the grave dangers to which he was laying himself wide open. Goebbels was horrified by the stories his aide Rudolf Semmler told him after a period of service on the Eastern Front which culminated in Stalingrad itself.

Earlier, at the end of May, the R.A.F. made the first of its thousand-bomber raids on the German war industry. Now the Germans at home as well as the Germans on the dreaded Eastern Front knew to their bitter cost the price of Hitler's ambition.

Such is the broad picture of the first three years of the war; the hundred and fifty weeks that saw the maximum of victory for Hitler before his fortunes began to recede. It was a period of intense work, interest and difficulty for Goebbels, who had perpetually to keep the limelight focused on the right news at the right time and in the right place for the right audience.

The war for Goebbels, of course, was war ceaselessly waged through propaganda. The most intimate records that survive from this period are sections of Goebbels' own official typewritten diaries (beginning at 21st January 1942) and a diary of his experiences with the Reich Minister kept by Rudolf Semmler, a member of Goebbels' staff who was promoted to serve in his more intimate circle at the end of 1940. Frau Semmler held her husband's diary after the war, and selections from it have been published. Goebbels' massive typescripts (some 7,000 sheets in all, singed and smoke-scented) narrowly escaped burning

The Nazi leaders pose after Hitler's appointment as Chancellor, 30
January 1933. In the centre, left to right: Goebbels, Hitler, Roehm,
Goering; Himmler and Hess, extreme right.

Goebbels at his desk in the Ministry (*left*); and, *right*, on the rostrum of the
Tennishallen, 1933.

Goebbels as political orator and showman. *Right, above*, inciting a crowd against the Jews, 2 April 1933. *Left, above*, the resulting pogrom against Jewish-owned shops. *Below*, the burning of the books, May 1933.

by Russian soldiers in the courtyard of the Propaganda Ministry; they were involuntarily saved by a junk-dealer in search of salvage. The task of editing a generous selection of them for publication was undertaken by Louis P. Lochner during 1947-48.

From the first Goebbels seems to have realised that the war would be long and arduous. Hans Fritzsche, who at the time the war started was Head of Goebbels' Press Division, recalled what the Minister had said to him:

What the bourgeois calls the temper or the mood of the people is not a decisive factor in war-time. Enthusiasm is only like a straw bonfire, which is of no use to us, and there's no point in stoking it. After all, how long does it last? Let's have no illusions about it: this will be a long and tough war. For this war a firm determination which manifests itself in the daily fulfilment of duties is more necessary than the noisy celebration of victories.[5]

Certain American journalists, such as Shirer, stayed in war-time Germany to report events, and to give an occasional first-hand picture of Goebbels at work. On 22nd August, a few days only before the war was declared, Shirer was amazed to open Goebbels' paper *Der Angriff* and read:

The world stands before a towering fact: two peoples have placed themselves on the basis of a common foreign policy which during a long and traditional friendship has produced a foundation for a common understanding.[6]

This, from the conqueror of Red Berlin, was astonishing. But Goebbels' purpose was to express what must be expressed, not what he might wish to express. He had not been let into the secret of the German-Soviet pact in advance, and so had no time to prepare himself. All he could do was follow the *volte-face* of the day.

Goebbels turned his mind to many events out of which advantage might be gained. On 3rd September the *Athenia*, a British liner filled mostly with women and children on their way to America, was sunk by torpedo; Goebbels announced the news in a form of his own devising. He claimed that Winston Churchill, the First Lord of the Admiralty, had personally ordered the destruction of the *Athenia* in order to be able to accuse the Germans of sinking her! On another occasion he adopted the method of surprise attack; he summoned the foreign journalists to a special press conference of apparent importance on 24th September only to stalk in "snorting like a bull" (says Shirer) and deny a story published by an American journalist, Hubert R. Knickerbocker, that the top Nazi leaders had deposited gold abroad in case they lost the war!

If these were examples of misjudgment, Goebbels also had his successes. When the French capitulated it was Goebbels' idea that the *wagon-lit* coach to which the Germans had been summoned by Foch in 1918 to sign the terms of armistice, should be hauled out of its special museum in Paris and brought back to the original spot in the Forest of Compiègne so that the formal admission of the defeat of France could be staged in exactly similar circumstances. It stood there, isolated in a clearing beneath the trees, pathetic as a discarded piece of rolling-stock, and into its cramped and faded saloon the representatives of the defeated nation edged their way to face the Führer, who sat in the same seat that Foch had occupied twenty-two years before. Hitler could scarcely hide the tremors of his triumphant sensations beneath the stern expression he assumed for the cameras.

Whatever the problems or opportunities which occurred as a result of the unforeseen events of the war, Goebbels' primary duty was to supervise the behaviour of the great interlocking propaganda machine he had built up during the past ten years and expanded to meet the needs of the war. This machine was designed to interlock as between the Party and the State and as between the propandist and his public in every department of expression at every level throughout the nation.

The main instruments of power were on the one hand the Party Propaganda Department and on the other the Ministry and the Reich Chamber of Culture. At the head of each of these—as Director, Minister and President respectively—was one man, Goebbels himself.

The Propaganda Department was a section of the National Socialist Party and therefore was directly linked to the Party political movement as a whole. In addition to Goebbels' Propaganda Department the

Party had a press division under the control of Otto Dietrich and a section dealing with the business management of the press headed by Max Amann, a rapacious drunkard who amassed untold wealth and whose official duties were carried out by his tireless and efficient deputy, Fritz Reinhardt.

The Propaganda Department employed full-time paid and part-time unpaid officials whose responsibility it was to see that every aspect of propaganda worked effectively in a hundred different ways from the public use of loud-speakers and leaflets to the collection of money for this or that official fund. These officials for example and their voluntary helpers were the Party's publicists and promoters, and the highest store of all was set by the development of orators and agitators in special training centres set up in every *Gau* or Party District, of which there were forty-three in Germany. There was even a Party Speaker's Certificate available to be won by ambitious agitators. According to their skill and effectiveness speakers were graded as Reich Speakers, that is, well-known national orators, Squad Speakers good for intensive drives, and District Speakers, confined to local work. Detailed instructions as to what they must say were constantly issued to them by the Party and the Ministry. By 1940, 140 full-time officials were occupied solely in routing and scheduling speakers for the Party. Other sections of the Propaganda Department were concerned with the staging of demonstrations and rallies (with their attendant publicity), the promotion of political broadcasts and the organisation of their reception nationally and locally through the system of voluntary 'wireless wardens', the production of short propaganda films and their exhibition by means of some 1,500 mobile film vans, and the organisation of local 'propaganda wardens' to provide liaison between the Party and every element in the community. The propaganda wardens were particularly important in youth work and they were, among other activities, responsible for conducting Hitler Youth religious ceremonies which were Nazi adaptations from Church services complete with Gospel readings from *Mein Kampf* and the Hitler Creed.[7]

From Goebbels' point of view it was unfortunate that Hitler let the veteran Nazi Max Amann remain in charge of the whole business side of the Party's publications. As head of the centralised printing and publishing house of the Party, the Eher Verlag, the total publishing enterprise of the Party—books, journals, pamphlets, posters as well as a vast network of Party-owned newspapers—came under his control. Similarly, Otto Dietrich, another of Hitler's friends and early associates, had control of the policy of the Party newspapers throughout the country and of the regional 'press wardens', the voluntary political liaison officers between the local community and the press. No fresh 'independent' newspapers could originate without the consent of both Amann and Dietrich. Although their departments were separate from that of Goebbels within the Party, they were supposed to co-operate closely with him in his other capacity as Minister for Propaganda. However, Dietrich had autonomy in putting out press statements, and relations were frequently strained between him and Goebbels on this account.[8] From their chief offices in Berlin and Munich, Amann and Dietrich kept a highly organised supervision over every Nazi-controlled newspaper and every German journalist both at home and abroad. They also organised the selection and training of young Party members who aspired to become journalists. Every *Gau* had its Party press office to deal with the Party's press relations at the regional level and under these came some 840 local press offices responsible among other duties for the proper distribution and sale of the Party's many newspapers.

As Minister of Propaganda Goebbels had seen to it that there was no such division of power as remained between himself and Dietrich in the Party propaganda machine. That he was not wholly successful in bringing every aspect of propaganda under his direct supervision we have already observed; when Ribbentrop came to power at the German Foreign Office he succeeded in regaining control of German propaganda abroad and set up rival press conferences for the foreign journalists. Both Goebbels and Ribbentrop established their own press clubs, but Goebbels went one better and secured heavy labourers' rations for the correspondents in September 1939. Shirer claimed that Goebbels thought the way to a journalist's heart was through his stomach; the concession meant that they got double rations of meat, bread and butter.[9] The food cards were distributed fortnightly after the regular press conferences. Correspondents were also encouraged to import food parcels from Denmark. Ribbentrop and Goebbels vied with each other in impressing those foreign journalists whose expense-accounts were less generous than the payments made to their more fortunate colleagues, and the bribery even extended to other pleasures than those of food and drink.

Very broadly speaking, while the Party propaganda machine was an executive organisation to see that the Party's policy and directives were effectively carried out, the Propaganda Ministry had a creative function. It organised and co-ordinated the Government's public relations. But Goebbels knew only too well the dangers of over-lapping and did his best to interlock the two machines so that they would feed rather than frustrate each other. It also gave him the chance he wanted to tie in the 'independents', Amann and Dietrich. Dietrich became one of Goebbels' Under-Secretaries of State with special responsibility for the Ministry's home and foreign press divisions; Amann was one of the Vice-Presidents under Goebbels of the Reich Chamber of Culture, with special responsibility for the Press Chamber.

The Ministry itself had been enlarged to fifteen divisions; to these must be added the seven Chambers of Culture which were in turn co-ordinated with the appropriate divisions in the Ministry. One of these divisions was concerned solely with this problem of co-ordination. As in an advertising agency, it was of the greatest importance to see that every campaign was a total effort, using all the resources of each division. This Division of Co-ordination was also a planning depart-ment, staffed by experts who were authorities on all possible aspects of life and activity in Germany and abroad. For example it organised special travelling exhibitions, such as the ironic 'Soviet Paradise' exhibi-tion of 1941-42, and an anti-Jewish congress in 1940 for which carefully chosen documents and pictures were assembled to expose "the rapacity, the uncontrolled sexuality and the parasitic nature of the Jews".[10]

Apart from the personnel and administrative divisions which super-vised the Ministry itself, there were divisions to deal with the main forms of expression (film, theatre, music, fine arts and literature), with the press, broadcasting, traffic and tourism and with the entertainment of the fighting forces. In addition another division was concerned with propaganda abroad, working as closely as disharmony permitted with Ribbentrop's Ministry, or with Bohle, the head of the special department controlling Germans abroad. There was, for example, often considerable difference of opinion between certain ambassadors in neutral countries and the press attachés on their staffs, who were nominated by Goebbels. But, as we have seen, every German permitted to go abroad was expected to do what was required of him in the way of propaganda for his country, or he would be unlikely to get an exit permit, especially in war-time. The German-controlled news agencies continued their work on an increased scale in those areas where they remained free to operate, such as Latin America, Sweden, Switzerland and Portugal.

At home Amann and the Nazi's financial adviser, Max Winckler, had acquired as many newspapers as they could for the Party's press organisation. Having made conditions impossible for the press through various decrees (such as that of April 1935 which in order to ensure "the independence of the newspaper publishing industry"[11] forbade any transfer of ownership without express permission, or the subsidising of any newspapers by organisations like religious bodies), Winckler had been instructed to move in and offer a nominal price for any publication put in difficulty. Gradually the Party acquired the greater proportion of the newspapers of Germany at comparatively little cost, and sometimes at no cost at all except some tricked-up form of compensation payable at a later date. By 1941 the circulation of German newspapers (24,600,000) represented largely that of the Party-owned press, and included sales in the occupied countries.[12]

Conferences were held daily at the Ministry to give guidance and control to the press representatives and written directives (handed only to certain accredited delegates from each paper) gave the editors their instructions. It was Mussolini who first used the term the "orchestration of the press"; in doing so he revealed precisely what Goebbels aimed at achieving through his press conferences. "Although the German news policy still serves informational purposes, its principal design is to instruct and direct public opinion," wrote Goebbels in an internal memorandum sent to his district offices at the beginning of the war.[13]

Radio, as we have seen already, had been brought under the control of Goebbels' Ministry at the earliest opportunity in 1933, and a special division was created to supervise broadcasting in Germany. The system of voluntary local watchdogs on behalf of the Party—the wireless wardens—had been organised the same year, while the Reich Chamber of Broadcasting looked after the political purity of those responsible for every aspect of broadcasting. In war-time the position as regards listening to news or programmes transmitted by foreign stations became extremely complex when Germany had overrun Europe. In 1942 Germans might listen to any station in Belgium, Holland, Occupied France, Poland, Norway, Yugoslavia and Occupied Russia. On the other hand it was a crime to listen to Denmark because she was, nominally, still independent from the political point of view and therefore free to quote news or statements from Allied sources; it was also a crime to listen to broadcasts from Germany's allies—Italy, Hungary, Rumania. There was, however, a rigorously controlled system of listening permits for Government officials and others, the nature of whose duties required them to keep in touch with what the enemy was saying. These permits were often limited to particular kinds of programme and strictly confined to the periods of duty. A radio monitor, for example, whose work consisted in transcribing B.B.C. news and talks, would be a criminal if he went on listening to the B.B.C. when he was off duty, and it was a crime for him to speak to the uncontaminated about what he had heard. To be discovered in the act of clandestine listening to forbidden broadcasts meant imprisonment and the concentration camp. But curiosity about foreign radio was naturally intense. Goebbels in his war-time diary is constantly complaining about the outlandish excuses people trumped up to get a foreign listening permit out of his Ministry.

The Propaganda Ministry devised an ingenious system for taking over the broadcasting facilities of other countries the moment they were overrun by the German Army. The following account of the 'occupation' of the Hilversum transmitter in Holland was given to Charles Rollo by one of the station's announcers, who subsequently escaped to Britain:

Berlin radio reporters arrived at Hilversum, thirty strong, the day after the Dutch Army had surrendered. They came prepared to replace any equipment that might have been smashed, and if necessary, even to install new transmitters. With them were enough transcribed programmes in Dutch to last two weeks, and printed programme schedules ready for distribution. After some thought, however, they decided to let the Hilversum announcers carry on as usual, except that all music by British, French or Jewish composers was banned and for a few days all news broadcasts were suspended. When news was resumed, the Dutch announcers were told they might say anything they pleased; guards with loaded revolvers in their hands sat around to discourage untoward comments. This was a brilliantly clever policy. The Dutch people, recognising the familiar voices of the old announcers, were greatly reassured, and many concluded that things were not going to be so bad after all—until Nazi brutality shattered this comforting illusion. Incidentally, among the trucks of the German radio unit was one which is still waiting to be unloaded. It contained two months of recorded programmes labelled—'For England'.[14]

Goebbels laid down a careful policy for approach to be made by Germany to the foreign listener before conquest. The first stage was to establish a friendly atmosphere—Germany the neighbour. The second stage involved criticism developing into open attack on the country and the policy of its leaders. The third stage involved the threats of violence to come and the need for the people to get rid of their leaders and capitulate. The last stage was the interim period of deliberate confusion before the Germans themselves took control of the nation's broadcasting from the home stations.

The R.R.G., the German Broadcasting Company owned by the Ministry, remained responsible for the whole of the German radio, which in war-time became a continuous round of two main elements —distraction and instruction. The instruction—news, political talks, propaganda—was devised in close consultation with the Broadcasting Division of the Ministry; the Head of the Home Press Division, Hans Fritzsche (later to be among the accused at the Nuremberg Trials and to be acquitted), was himself the most prominent war-time radio personality, and Goebbels' most carefully considered war-time articles, those contributed weekly to *Das Reich*, were regularly read to the listeners to give them intensive coverage.

As far as distraction went, Goebbels himself initiated what he called "merrier and brighter" programmes in 1941 because of the urgent need for relaxation mostly in the Armed Forces.[15] In an article published on 1st March 1941 in the *Völkischer Beobachter*, he wrote defending his relaxation of the rules that had hitherto strictly forbidden the broadcasting of jazz on the grounds that it reflected either a Jewish or a Negroid spirit, according to whichever seemed appropriate at the moment of speaking:

Our experience with the problems of broadcasting has taught us that the organisation of programmes on the radio has to depend not so much on theory as on practice. Soldiers at the front after a hard battle appreciate what they called "decent music", which means light music, in their cold and inhospitable quarters. People are in general too strained to absorb more than two hours of an exacting programme. If a man who has worked hard for twelve or fourteen hours wants to hear music at all, it must be music which makes no demands on him. After much preparatory work two programmes are now again to be broadcast during the main transmission hours: one on the Deutschlandsender for serious and classical music, another on the Reichssender for light entertainment music, especially during the evening. . . . It is important to secure good humour at home and at the front.[16]

He was even prepared to permit jazz for the Forces:

We should like to speak quite freely about whether the German radio ought to broadcast the so-called 'jazz'. If 'jazz' means music which completely disregards or even makes fun of melody, and in which rhythm mainly shows itself in an ugly squeaking of instruments offensive to our ears, we can only answer in the negative. . . . On the other hand, it should not be claimed that the waltzes of our grandmothers and grandfathers must be the end of musical evolution and that everything that goes beyond them is evil. . . . We are not living in the Biedermeier epoch but in a century whose melody is determined by the hum of machines and the roar of motors. . . . The radio must pay due attention to this fact, if it does not want to run the risk of "sticking to the frock-coat" . . . We feel bound to consider the just demands of our fighting and working people.[17]

Goebbels then announced through this article that there was to be a Forces Programme organised by Reich Cultural Warden Hans Hinkel concentrating on popular music of all kinds. Hinkel was also head of the Troops Entertainment Division of the Propaganda Ministry.

The German Home Service, as distinct from the Forces Programme, consisted of little but long stretches of music (mostly of high quality) punctuated with news bulletins, talks, interviews, eye-witness reporting and outside broadcasts connected with the war. The great personalities on the air were Goebbels and Fritzsche—apart, that is, from Hitler, whose voice was heard less and less often as the war progressed and his public appearances diminished almost to vanishing point. Goebbels spoke in the relaxed, easy manner of the trained professional, his beautiful voice pronouncing with assurance every word and phrase of his carefully composed script. Fritzsche attracted attention by developing an ironic style with the heavy, underlined humour appreciated by the great lower-middle-class public for which his star broadcasts were intended. His prime function was to score off the unheard enemy—his news, his views, the statements of the Allied leaders.

The German European Service, the propaganda radio in foreign languages, had by 1942 extended (mainly in the form of news and talks) to twenty-seven languages. Countries completely occupied found their stations taken over and German-inspired radio coming through their loud-speakers, but countries retaining some measure of independence, such as Denmark, kept a corresponding independence in broadcasting. But as Germany took over the radio-stations of other countries, wavelengths were re-allocated to permit broadcasts to be directed in the appropriate languages to countries which were outside Germany's direct control—either as allies, neutrals or enemies. Broadcasts had to be graded accordingly—whether they were, for example, in Byelorussian, English, Gaelic, Hungarian, Swedish, Turkish or Italian, each of them among the languages in which there were regular services. The German armies of occupation also had to be supplied with German-language programmes.

Short-wave transmitters permitted German propaganda to reach out internationally—to America, the British Dominions and Colonies, the Far East, the Moslem world, Africa and Latin America. This multi-language service extended over the whole twenty-four hours, and included German-language programmes addressed to Germans and German-speaking people all over the world. In the English-language services the technique of heavy humour and loaded irony was obviously considered appropriate as so many broadcasters adopted it—"that liar Winston Churchill, First Lord of the Sea Bottom. Ha! Ha! Ha!" It reached a certain degree of finesse in the initial style of Lord Haw-Haw's propaganda talks to Britain; William Joyce caught on to the dissatisfaction which made the British feel uneasy before Winston Churchill became war leader. Naumann claims that Goebbels liked Joyce and thought highly of him even after he had ceased to be so effective on the radio.

Another division of the Ministry was concerned with the instruction and entertainment of the Forces. The 'Strength through Joy' organisations supervised touring concert parties; musicians, actors and other artists were sent to entertain the German Army wherever it might be. The development at home and abroad of Army Welfare Centres, where concerts, film-shows, theatrical entertainments and indoor sports could be organised, came under Goebbels' Ministry, as did the publication of Army newspapers and magazines such as *Oase*, the journal of the Afrika Korps printed in Tripoli. By the end of 1941 there were 60,000 Front libraries in circulation, stocked by means of nation-wide book collections of approved reading. The Party Propaganda Office saw to it that the works of Dr. Goebbels were included in these libraries.

A further piece of organisation to meet war conditions was undertaken by the Propaganda Ministry; this was the formation of the Propaganda Companies to serve the press, newsreels and radio from the battlefronts. Film cameramen, reporters and commentators were mobilised into a general pool under military discipline and sent to complete coverages either singly or in groups, and they were also required to engage in active service in addition to their professional work. There was therefore no segregation for the war reporters; their life in fact was harder than that of the fighting man and their casualties were heavy. Goebbels' own aide and press officer, Rudolf Semmler, had to serve the best part of a year on the Eastern Front before being allowed to return to his privileged place alongside the Reich Minister, whom (as we have said) he surprised by his account of the fighting in Stalingrad.

The theatre was kept alive in war-time Germany; it was claimed in the 1940-41 season that 355 State theatres, 175 independent theatres and 142 open-air theatres were operating—an incredibly large number even for the country which supported the largest number of theatres in Europe.[18] Many plays were written of a nationalist or National Socialist character, though the absence of quality in contemporary work led to a revival in Germany's numerous local theatres of the production of the classics. The eternal flow of plays on Frederick the Great (Goebbels' ideal German monarch) gave the dramatists, like the film-makers, a staple theme to which they could return again and again.

After radio, however, it was upon the film that Goebbels relied for his most effective propaganda. Not that he expected all German films to contain propaganda, far from it. But he realised how important it was to develop a strong newsreel, documentary and instructional film service as well as to encourage the production from time to time of feature films inspired by his Ministry and on certain occasions by himself personally. He spent a great deal of time, for example, on the script and the editing of *Ohm Krüger*, the violently anti-British film of the Boer War released in 1941.

As we have seen already, the German film industry was not formally nationalised; Goebbels preferred to control it through the Reich Film Chamber and the Films Division of his Ministry. In any case, his nominees were in charge of each of the production companies. But by 1937 the largest of these companies, UFA, had become *reichseigen* (that is, State-owned) and the dominant factor in the German film world, extending its power into Austria and the Czech Protectorate. This centralisation took place in order to prepare the industry for its assault on the cinemas of occupied Europe, and special distribution companies were set up in the conquered territories to reopen the cinemas for the exhibition of German films. Prints of American and British films held by local distributors were of course destroyed or taken for use as raw material. The German film agencies in Allied and neutral countries were well organised to secure the maximum distribution for those German films considered suitable for exhibition in these territories. In addition to normal distribution through the theatres, films were shown in the occupied countries by means of mobile film vans, and special units were formed to produce short films for this specialised kind of exhibition.

Propaganda began in the newsreels, was developed in special documentaries, many of which were feature-length, and appeared again in those fictional or dramatic films that were inspired by Goebbels. In a speech delivered at the UFA Palace Cinema in Berlin in October 1941 Goebbels said:

The National Socialist State considers it a first duty to infuse into art new impulses which shall deepen public understanding of the greatness of the time. In the domain of the film the directive is the most important encouragement and stimulus to creation. . . . Among recent films *Request Concert, Bismarck, Jew Süss, Ohm Krüger, J'Accuse* and *Homecoming* were made on official orders, and I must pay German film artistes the compliment of saying that they tackled these jobs with the greatest enthusiasm.[19]

Request Concert was a romantic film of a young German soldier reunited with his sweetheart during a radio request concert. *Jew Süss* was anti-Jewish, *Homecoming* was anti-Polish (with a scene of some Polish Jews trying to rape Paula Wessely, who played a German school-teacher), and *Ohm Krüger* was anti-British. *J'Accuse* was a sinister film advocating the mercy-killing of people who were physically incapacitated, and was designed to fit in with a special Gestapo campaign, and *Bismarck* returned once more to the theme of the united

Reich. Most German feature films, however, were of an escapist nature, and productions averaged a hundred titles a year.

Newsreels were inflated in length to some forty-five minutes. It was claimed by the Ministry that by 1942 2,400 prints were made of each weekly newsreel. Certain of the feature-length documentaries were films of marked power and virulence. Such films were *Baptism of Fire* on the conquest of Poland, *Victory in the West* on the war in France and *The Eternal Jew*, a violent and at times obscene attack on the Jews. The last film, produced in 1940, was described in the *Deutsche Allgemeine Zeitung* as follows:

There are revealing scenes in the Polish ghettoes—scenes in the synagogues where Jews are doing business, filth in the synagogues, close-ups of Jewish faces. Then the film shows by trick photography the spreading of the Jews all over the world in the form of rat migrations —assimilated Jews are shown—statistics of the number of Jews in the different professions—photographs of Rathenau, Vice-Police-President Weiss, Tauber, Lubitsch, Reinhardt, Chaplin and so on. A skilful selection of photographs of Jewish films and revues is given. The most frightful chapter comes at the end: the cruel, inhuman, barbarous slaughter of animals.[20]

Baptism of Fire and *Victory in the West* used the method of building up shots of conquest and destruction to pæans of Wagnerian music and sardonic commentary. One almost endless series of shots in *Baptism of Fire* shows the roofless shells of Warsaw's buildings as they looked from a low-flying aircraft, while the commentary mocks at Chamberlain for the futility of his decision to support the Poles in their struggle by going to war with Germany. Films such as *Baptism of Fire* were given prestige screenings at the German embassies in those countries which Germany hoped to bring under her power, and so helped to make real Goebbels' belief that propaganda rightly used was an important part of warfare. The aim of these films was to impress rather than to inform, in fact to blackmail the audience into a bloodless surrender. This sensational dramatisation of German power must have seemed a terrifying spectacle to those immediately responsible for their country's future relations with Hitler. Nor were the showings of these films confined to the nations that were occupied or soon to be occupied. German agents, wherever they could, pressed them into distribution in the neutral countries, and it has been claimed that Goebbels had at his disposal some £30 million a year to spend on film distribution outside Germany.[21] The latest newsreels and other films were flown from their source of production to the laboratories, and within a very short while all the edited material was ready for dispatch to each European centre or sent by air, for example, to Latin America for immediate release to neutral cinemas. The stark realism of the newsreel material from the battlefronts and its immediacy in date were both essential points in the policy of the Films Division of the Ministry.

The Germans also used silent films for training and propaganda for the Forces and in schools. These films were made by UFA and by a certain limited number of independent producers working in close association with the Ministry.

Work on the preparation for such an important propaganda film as *Ohm Krüger* represented for Goebbels a genuine creative participation in production. The film had always been a medium that attracted him, and his position as Minister gave him the right not only to suggest subjects to the industry but to indicate how they might be treated. On no individual film did Goebbels work more closely than on *Ohm Krüger*, which Veit Harlan directed and which featured Emil Jannings as Krüger. The subject of the struggle between the Boers and the British had always appealed to the Germans since before the days of the First World War, and national prejudice favoured the defeated Boers. Many lines of the script of this film seem to come from Goebbels' pen—as, for example, when Krüger says to his nurse: "If one repeats a lie often enough it is believed," or: "One must be a dreamer to become a ruler."

At one end of the film Krüger declaims against Britain: "That's how England subjected our people. We were a small nation. Great and powerful nations will rise to beat England to pulp. Then the world will be free for a better life."

The creative hand of Goebbels is everywhere apparent. With a matchless effrontery he depicts the Nazis' own methods in their con-centration camps in order to blacken the reputation of Britain, and he identifies the father-figure of Krüger with Hitler. The film is constantly influenced by the technique of Eisenstein in *Battleship Potemkin*, as if Goebbels were consciously endeavouring to equal the film he regarded as a masterpiece of propaganda. Finally, his malicious humour is introduced in the witch-like characterisation he imposes on Queen Victoria and in making the youthful Winston Churchill into a villainous Commandant of the concentration camp!

An intimate picture of Goebbels at this time has been created by Rudolf Semmler who, in January 1941 at the age of twenty-seven, became nominally a press officer but actually an aide living in Goebbels' immediate circle. He approached his new job, a promotion from another position in the Ministry, with some trepidation—"I have heard stories of his violent temper"—and he knew that his predecessors had been numerous and had, most of them, been sent away in disgrace by their "temperamental boss". However, at their first formal meeting he found Goebbels to be quite charming. He soon learnt, though, that he would have to accept his position in the household as Goebbels saw it to be; apart from the valuable privilege of being able to listen to his very frank, if calculated, conversation, Goebbels' aides were often treated as superior lackeys who were required to look after the Reich Minister's affairs for him and speed him on his way. He also learnt Goebbels' attitude to all his staff.

Goebbels wants no real personal contact with his staff. He prefers them to be working machines, without personality, which can be switched on and off as he pleases. Frowein says he thinks of his fellow men and staff as he thinks of his fountain-pen or his wrist-watch—useful articles which have to be changed or repaired from time to time.[22]

Like others before him he soon found he would be half-starved at Goebbels' table, although the butler regularly demanded food coupons from him. He had to dress meticulously; one of his predecessors had been dismissed for allowing his trousers to become uncreased and wearing his cuffs frayed. Semmler's description of Goebbels, relaxed in conversation, is a very revealing one:

Goebbels' moods vary: either he is talkative or he broods silently. He will describe experiences, thoughts and impressions of the morning or of the day in an easy chatty tone, talking more to himself than to his guests or companions. If he is working on a speech or writing an article he sketches out his thoughts aloud. This is partly to see what impression his words make, partly to hit on new ideas and turns of phrase by the way. He likes telling stories of his life, and hands out praise and criticism of his fellow ministers and Party members in the most outspoken manner, the Führer himself not escaping. I can see that criticism is the salt of life to him.

Two hours ago one could hear him booming away at the daily propaganda conference, passionately defending one point or sarcastically refuting another. At table now he is more restrained and objective. Then we see another Goebbels, a sympathetic and attractive character.[23]

Semmler, observant and resourceful, noted Goebbels' hatred of Ciano ("an ill-licked cub") and of Ribbentrop ("his name he bought, his money he married, and his job he got by intrigue"); he seems, however, to have been an admirer of Winston Churchill, at least in private conversation. Semmler remarks on this in January 1941 which is all the more interesting because this was the period when Goebbels' public attacks on the British Prime Minister reached their height in his weekly articles—"those ice-cold eyes betray a man without feelings. To satisfy his blind and ruthless vanity he will walk over dead bodies. . . . He does not seduce children but nations. . . . Let Churchill gamble and England will pay," he wrote in the fulfilment of his campaign.[24] But the man he really hated was Ribbentrop; as Semmler put it: "Whenever talk comes on to Ribbentrop Goebbels always starts talking admiringly of Churchill."[25]

Göring he seemed now (in 1941) merely to despise. Goebbels regarded his own tendency to distrust others as a sign of wisdom, even of greatness.

Goebbels is full of distrust of the men around him, even of those closely connected with him. He maintains that this puts him in good company with Frederick the Great, Bismarck and Hitler himself, all classic examples of the suspicious nature of great men. Hitler, for example, always believed that he was being deceived, put no faith in his staff and colleagues, and could never shake off the feeling that important matters were concealed from him. And Goebbels himself watches the scene around him like a watchman on a tower with his telescope, always suspecting that somewhere intrigues are going on which may threaten his position. Goebbels secretly distrusts all his staff. He sees the worst side of every human being and admits frankly that he has become an uncompromising misanthropist.[26]

Semmler noticed how anxious Goebbels became if he were not constantly receiving messages and urgent phone calls or called upon to make some rapid decision. His state of mind in this respect seems to have been almost pathological; his restless nature needed the preoccupations of incessant activity. This was the sign that he was in demand and that he was not being by-passed by others in the circle of power round Hitler. His self-confidence depended on his being always at the centre of affairs, and it became part of the dance of attendance required by him of his staff that they should see to it that he was kept on the go.

It is to Semmler's personal credit that he seems to have retained a balanced judgment in the difficult task of pleasing Goebbels; though he admired him, his was by no means an uncritical admiration.[27] What is more important, he won Goebbels' confidence and was therefore able to record some very frank expressions of opinion from him.

Although Goebbels' position with Hitler was as secure as anyone's in the topsy-turvy world of Nazi hierarchy, it is plain that he was worried that the Führer was being ill-advised and that he himself had insufficient access to him; that the Nazi policy of propaganda was not wholly concentrated in his hands and that bad mistakes were being made—in particular by Otto Dietrich, the head of the Party Press Department, who was ultimately responsible to Hess (and later to Hess's successor, Martin Bormann) and not to Goebbels. This division of authority and consequent creation of rivalries never failed to enrage Goebbels, though such divisions were, as we have seen, part of the system Hitler had devised before the Party came to power. Dietrich's biggest gaffe was to announce at a press conference held at the Propaganda Ministry in October 1941 that the Soviet armies had been destroyed and that the Russian campaign was virtually at an end. This according to Semmler made Goebbels foam with rage because of its "unbelievable irresponsibility". Nor could Goebbels stop Hitler's own propaganda ideas; when the Russian campaign had started Hitler himself composed twelve solemn *Sondermeldungen* or special radio announcements which were intended to be impressive interruptions of the normal programmes with news of some new triumph of German arms. They were introduced by fanfares and followed by Wagnerian music. But what might have been a stirring piece of showmanship soon degenerated into a cliché as the supposedly hot news was taken out of the file time and time again to Hitler's orders. The special communiqué ceased to be special, and the fanfares began to cause amusement. To the master-showman Goebbels this was an intolerable misuse of a good trick.

When Hess flew to Britain alone in a Messerschmidt fighter plane on the evening of 10th May 1941 and landed near Glasgow by parachute, Goebbels was on tenterhooks as to the use to which the British would put what he regarded as a god-send from the point of view of their propaganda. He refused for once to give any directive; he was too angry. Fritzsche has admitted that Goebbels was completely at a loss what to do or say, and that he retired to bed in a sulk.[28] It was therefore left to Dietrich, as Head of the Press Division, to devise what statement he could. Dietrich blundered again, implying that Hitler's deputy had been known to be suffering from delusions! Everything possible was done by Goebbels during the next few days to distract the curiosity of the German public by playing up the military news—even according to Semmler elaborating on murders and traffic accidents. But time went by and Britain made no comment beyond the fact of Hess's identification and interrogation. However, on 13th May Goebbels went to see Hitler in Berchtesgaden, and found him in tears and looking ten years older.

Goebbels then began the process of the plausible breakdown of Hess's reputation. In conversation he joked about Hess's inability to overcome his impotence, and how he and his wife had had to resort to astrology and magic potions before a child was somehow or other conceived. When every *Gau* in Germany was required to send a parcel of earth to be spread symbolically under the child's cradle, Goebbels as Gauleiter of Berlin—an office he never relinquished—thought better of sending a paving-stone and despatched some manure from the garden instead.[29]

Though the exercise of his skill as a propagandist satisfied Goebbels deeply, he felt throughout the war that his knowledge of affairs and his abilities were alike neglected by Hitler. For him the practice of propaganda implied an active participation in shaping policy. For Hitler the war meant military strategy alone, and the advanced ideas which Goebbels imagined the Führer had learned in the magic days of the election campaigns that they had shared together only ten years previously seemed forgotten. Occasionally he was allowed to use his old tricks; in June 1941 it was arranged that he should seem to be in trouble for revealing in an article that Germany was soon to invade England. The article appeared in the *Völkischer Beobachter* and the edition was withdrawn as soon as the foreign correspondents had noted the article which it was hoped would distract attention from preparations for the invasion of Russia. Goebbels was put into artificial disgrace, and was delighted at his cleverness.[30]

But Hitler was shut away with his military maps, absorbed in the statistics of armies and weapons, embattled with his recalcitrant generals. Goebbels' world of words seemed specialised and remote, though Hitler admitted him on occasion to a conference, and listened to his tireless but vain attempts to be brought into a closer partnership on the level where policy was being devised. But the policy, he found, was that there was no policy but barefaced conquest in the East, and he had no friends to support him among Hitler's new entourage, in which Martin Bormann was the rising star. Goebbels was left to languish in the illusion of his own self-importance which he fed with his ceaseless round of activities. Yet while Hitler's sense of perspective diminished under the weight and worry of the Russian campaign, Goebbels' grasp of the essentials of the situation grew. It was he who realised that there should be an imaginative propaganda policy for Russia with the German armies represented as liberators bringing self-government to territories such as the Ukraine where there was a genuine desire for freedom from Communism. It was Goebbels who realised that what Germany herself needed was organisation for total war, and not false statements implying that the campaign was all but over as the winter set in. Had Goebbels managed at this stage to regain his lost influence with Hitler, he would undoubtedly have done anything he could to save the Führer from the catastrophe which was inevitable once the blind ambition possessed him to spread his armies over the face of Russia.

So Goebbels agitated on the touch-line, trying to intervene in the game. As soon as it was clear at the end of the summer of 1941 that, though deeply penetrated, the Eastern territories were by no means conquered, Goebbels prepared a memorandum to Hitler on the political handling of Russia. He despaired when he saw the Baltic German Alfred Rosenberg—a failure at every previous administrative job he had been given—appointed Minister for the East. The memorandum advocated the proclamation by Germany of a plan which would excite the active participation of the Russians and lead to widespread desertions from the Red Army. The memorandum was sent to Hitler and pigeon-holed. Rosenberg merely complained at Goebbels' interference, and the Russians learned from direct and bitter experience what Nazi liberation meant. Had Hitler adopted Goebbels' plan a form of victory might have been achieved in place of the holocaust of Stalingrad and the mass retreat of 1943.

To hear Goebbels talking at home, however, you might have been excused for thinking you were in the presence of the second man in Germany. He opened the heart of his ambitions to Semmler and to those in his circle of friends whom he trusted in what must have been conversations which unconsciously compensated for his neglect by Hitler. Goebbels saw himself first of all as the future historian of Germany; no other Nazi leader kept a diary, and Semmler soon noted down the facts after his appointment to the household.

For twenty years Goebbels has regularly and painstakingly kept a diary. Every day he spends an hour on this task. So far he has written twenty-three thick volumes in minute handwriting. Goebbels believes that one day this diary, read with the official archives, will provide one of the richest sources for the history of the National Socialist Party and for Hitler's years of power. He keeps this diary strictly secret and, so far as I know, no one is allowed to see it. The volumes are kept locked up in a steel cupboard, the key of which he always carries with him.[31]

Semmler confirms that Goebbels refused the Eher Verlag's offer of three million marks for the future publication rights of the diary; Goebbels preferred to regard these volumes as a legacy for his children and their descendants. He believed them to be historical documents of the first importance. Although the diaries were handwritten at this stage, they were soon to be dictated and specially typed by his confidential secretary Otte.

Goebbels often used to say how he dreamed of the time he could retire from politics, become a private citizen free to roam about, and dedicate his working life to his books. He could use his diaries, he said, as source material for a monumental life of Hitler, of which two volumes already existed in privately printed copies, but had "met with the Führer's disapproval". Then he planned to write a history of Germany from 1900 to the present day, a book on Christianity "of real political importance", and a treatise on films which would become a standard work for the cinema equal in importance to Lessing's book on the art and theory of the drama. In the book on Christianity "he would dispose of old-fashioned theories of Christianity, and lead from this criticism to an ethical system for the twentieth-century man".[32] He also hoped to launch now and then from some forest retreat the occasional scathing article on contemporary personalities and affairs in case anyone should think that the old dog had lost his bite. On another occasion he told Semmler that he would do all he could to keep his son Helmuth out of the "despicable occupation" of politics.

"Politics," he said to his young adjutant, "ruin the character; they develop the worst and meanest qualities by forcing into the front of men's minds their ambition, their vanity, their competitive spirit and their passion for influence and cheap popularity. The cause they are serving is pushed into the background. To many of them politics are only a means to eliminate competitors, to conduct vulgar intrigues and to attain personal power."[33]

Semmler also heard him declare his passionate love of political life. But there it was; he often noted how Goebbels contradicted himself, and liked to use his skill to build up an argument one day which he would as carefully destroy the next.

Yet he was proud of what he held to be his great contribution to the political life of Germany. Though he enjoyed the day-dreaming of himself as the great German historian writing his monographs and memories in the leisure of an honoured retirement, he claimed that without him National Socialism in Germany would have had a totally different character. One evening in December 1941 Goebbels told Semmler exactly what he thought this personal contribution of his had been. In four decisive ways, he said, he had vitally strengthened the movement:

1. National Socialism in South Germany had been a purely middle-class affair. The Socialist element had been at first entirely absent. As leader of the Rhineland National Socialists he had been the first to bring the Socialist ideas of the workers of the Rhine-Westphalia districts into the Munich programme. At first the Munich line had been very unpopular in the Rhineland, because it was little different from that of the German Nationalist Party and held no special appeal for the working class. He claimed he was the first to make the movement into a Socialist working-class party.

2. He had won Berlin and thereby prepared the way for seizing power in the Reich. Without control of Berlin the Party would have remained a provincial movement.

3. He had worked out the style and technique of the Party's public ceremonies. The ceremonial of the mass demonstrations, the marches with standards, and the ritual of the great Party occasions were the results of his experiments and of his achievements in Berlin. Anyone could see the difference he had made by comparing the beer-cellar gatherings in Munich with one of the giant demonstrations in the Berlin Sports Palace. The annual gatherings in Munich on 8th November, with their beer-drinking and waitresses moving up and down the room, always reminded him of skittle club meetings.

4. His fourth contribution had been his creation of the Führer myth.

Hitler had been given the halo of infallibility, with the result that many people who looked askance at the Party after 1933 had complete confidence in Hitler. That was why even now millions of Germans drew a distinction between the Führer and the Party, refusing to support the latter while believing in Hitler.[34]

Of these four points the last, perhaps, is the most interesting of all, though the boastfulness of the first claim is very much in character when one knows the facts. It will always be debated how far Hitler was a man whose stature was great even though his nature was evil, and no one can say how much he owed to the genius of Goebbels in helping him achieve public acceptance as Führer. The debt was obviously great; it might easily have been decisive. However that might be, once Hitler had achieved political and military power over Germany he had, or thought he had, less immediate need of Goebbels.

Goebbels had his own conception of his task at this present juncture of the war; he told Semmler: "I can play a political rôle as spiritual physician to the nation."[35] He felt responsible for morale not merely among the civilian population but among the armed forces as well. Yet his own morale suffered because he was left so much to his own devices. He was for most of the time cut off from Hitler, the only source of his inspiration, and he was avoided by the rest of those who were already in positions of influence with the Führer or in process of arriving there. This was particularly true in the case of Bormann.

In what time he had left over for domestic life, Goebbels made a study of his children. Again it is Semmler who depicts this particular domestic relationship with a revealing observation: Goebbels' children only seemed to be attractive to him on his own terms.

The more I see of this man from close to, the more puzzling (but also fascinating) I find him. For example, does he love his children? Certainly not in the way that most fathers love their children. I have never noticed on his part the least sign of affectionate behaviour towards one of the children. Yet they are very attached to him, but they mostly only see him at the week-end and then generally to get chocolate.

He will only find it interesting to give attention to his children when their minds begin to react to his intellectual ways. He never gets down on the floor, like any ordinary father, to play trains with Helmuth, but he already conducts with his daughters Helga and Hilde, eight and six and a half years old, conversations which must test their brains severely. With these two, who are in fact precociously intelligent, he likes to play intellectually. The other children will only hold his attention when they come to the same stage.[36]

In January 1942 this particular source of information about Goebbels ceases; Semmler was sent as a war reporter to gain experience at the fighting front. He ended up, as we have seen, in Stalingrad itself, though he was to return the following December to resume his previous work with Goebbels. However, substantial sections of Goebbels' own diaries are available from 21st January 1942 and extend to the end of the succeeding year, when Germany's fortunes had begun seriously to decline. The lengthy fragments of these diaries cover in all some eight months only of the two-year period. Their character is totally different from that of the private diary of 1925-26, which was highly personal, or the diary edited for publication by Goebbels as the book *Vom Kaiserhof zur Reichskanzlei* (English translation entitled *My Part in Germany's Fight*). This diary was Goebbels' own day-to-day record of events as he experienced them in his official capacity. It is private only in so far as he expresses his thoughts, judgments and prejudices on life in Germany, on the way the war was going and on the personalities with whom he came in contact including, of course, Hitler himself. Nothing appears in this later diary that he could not quite properly dictate to his confidential secretaries, the chief of whom was Otte, reputed the fastest shorthand-writer in Germany, and at present Chief of the Shorthand Bureau in the Bonn Parliament. Goebbels poured out his thoughts and reactions for an hour a day writing in long-hand. As soon as he discovered Otte, however, and the incredible speed at which he could record Goebbels' most rapid speech, he took to dictating the diaries.

Otte, appointed by Goebbels a Regierungsrat, a senior grade of civil servant, could take down 350 syllables a minute, and so the diary could become much fuller and longer than was possible when Goebbels had to write it by hand. He would ring up Otte at all hours of the night to complete the last twenty-four hours' stint, dictating to him at a running pace over the telephone until both of them were exhausted. Otte would sit up in bed with blankets wrapped round him against the bitter cold of winter writing away until Goebbels had talked himself out.[37]

It is always interesting to measure a person's view of his importance in public life against the facts. The diary presents the picture of a man who has come to regard himself as responsible for the conduct of Germany while Hitler is responsible for the conduct of the war. He never forgot that he was Gauleiter for Berlin as well as Minister for Propaganda; he took this other duty seriously because it gave him the powers over the capital city which he had always wanted for the country as a whole. Propaganda for Goebbels was never limited to control of the arts and the information services; it was control over a way of life, a New Order of living. During the middle years of the war he was really campaigning to get himself made Minister for the Interior or some war-time office which would put him in charge of the social life of Germany. Though he naturally had views about Hitler's conduct of the war and expressed them, he wrote only as a commentator. But in the domestic affairs of Germany he was always urging Hitler to be more ruthless with the bourgeois bureaucrats and to give him power which would enable him to take action against them and ensure that Nazi principles were put into practice in every phase of German life. Hitler always agreed with him, but his mind was on the war and Goebbels left their meetings (which seemed to average one a month, at any rate during the earlier part of 1942) without the necessary executive power having been granted to him. But he was building up his case on sound lines and he was eventually, in July 1944 when it was almost too late, to gain what he wanted from Hitler's waning authority. The only exception to this occurred in March 1942, when the Ministry of the Interior, headed by Dr. Wilhelm Frick, whom Goebbels despised, failed to take adequate measures to deal with the effects of the Allied bombing. Hitler then transferred the care of bomb-damaged areas to Goebbels' Ministry.

Meanwhile Goebbels liked to regard himself as Hitler's deputy in Germany, and was constantly making proposals to him to tighten up controls in the national life:

I proposed passing a law that whoever violates the commonly-known principles of National Socialistic leadership should be punished with imprisonment or in very serious cases with death. Such a law would enable us to put our domestic war effort on an entirely new basis and especially to lay hands on those who have hitherto eluded us. Schlegelberger, the Under-Secretary in the Ministry of Justice who since Gürtner's death has headed the German judiciary, always refuses my requests on the grounds that there is no legal basis for action. The proposed law would create that basis. Moreover, the failure of justice is really a question of personalities rather than of any lack of laws. . . . Justice must not become the mistress of the State, but must be the servant of State policy.[38]

Goebbels constantly worked himself up into a passion over the lax behaviour in war-time of his colleagues and of German officials, civil servants and professional men in general, especially those engaged in the law. He could not bear the sight of the luxury in which other Nazi leaders such as Göring and Frick continued to live. On one occasion he personally remonstrated at a Berlin railway station with some wealthy passengers who refused to sacrifice their amenities for servicemen who were travelling in discomfort. His old radicalism burned hot within him, and he longed for the Führer to assume the legal powers himself or create them for his Minister so that such people could be threatened with the concentration camps. He told Hitler of this incident and a hundred others. The result was always the same:

The Führer was in a frame of mind to agree completely with all my proposals for a more drastically all-out war effort. I needed merely to touch lightly on a theme and I had at once gained my point. Everything I proposed was accepted item by item and without objection by the Führer.[39]

But as soon as Goebbels left him, Hitler turned back to the conduct of the war and the drastic changes in internal administration were postponed. But Goebbels was nothing if not persistent at these meetings— "Unfortunately I had to complain about Dr. Ley . . . I told him of cases where justice had miscarried . . ." and so on.

Goebbels fed his vanity, which was wounded at the lack of executive power given him outside the propaganda field, by exploiting to the full his capacities as speaker, broadcaster and writer. Again and again he reports his success in glowing terms—"I have written an article about increased production and courtesy which undoubtedly will prove a major sensation on publication"; "In a few monumental sentences I gave a picture of the present situation which drew storms of applause"; "My definition of grumbling as 'the soul moving its bowels' . . . has already become a household word throughout the nation". Nor are the plaudits limited to Germany. King Boris of Bulgaria told him his articles in *Das Reich* were "part of his everyday reading. Indeed, he even told me that he uses the arguments advanced in these articles in all his diplomatic negotiations." Even the Allies, Goebbels notes with approval, follow his statements carefully. Goebbels prided himself on his frankness; their non-diplomatic quality, he thinks, is so rare that it makes his work valued abroad as it is at home. "They want to know exactly what's what and what is likely to happen. That's the main reason why my articles are as fascinating to Germans as they are for foreign readers. They state bluntly what we mean and talk a language which is otherwise rare in political circles."[40]

With Goebbels' frankness, as he called it, also went his ruthlessness. He was revolted by the enemies of the State being let off. He had no use for preserving the lives or liberties of backsliders at home or saboteurs in the occupied territories abroad. He had no interest in the minorities that came under the German 'protection'. The only thing that matters is the propagation of the gospel of National Socialism. Of the aspiration of the minorities in the Baltic States, for example, he writes:

National Socialism is much more cold-blooded and realistic in all these questions. It does only what is useful for its own people. In this instance our people's interest undoubtedly lies in establishing rigorous German order without paying any attention to the claims, whether justified or otherwise, of the small nationalities living there.[41]

A year later, in May 1943, he quotes with approval Hitler's statement that "all the rubbish of small nations (*Kleinstaatengerümpel*) still existing in Europe must be liquidated as fast as possible. The aim of our struggle must be to create a unified Europe. The Germans alone can organise Europe properly." Of German behaviour in France he can only say: "We Germans are too good-natured in every respect. We don't yet know how to behave like a victorious people."

Worst of all is the revelation of his desire to exterminate the Jews in Europe. His statements here make it plain that he was fully aware of the atrocities that were being carried out in Germany and the occupied territories where the extermination camps existed. Goebbels never wrote more callously and brutally than in these constant passages in his diary when he comments on the progress the Nazis were making in the destruction of the race they had chosen above all others to eliminate from Europe.

The Führer once more expressed his determination to clean up the Jews in Europe pitilessly. There must be no squeamish sentimentalism about it. The Jews have deserved the catastrophe that has now overtaken them. Their destruction will go hand in hand with the destruction of our enemies. We must hasten this process with cold ruthlessness. We shall thereby render an inestimable service to a humanity tormented for thousands of years by the Jews. This uncompromising anti-Semitic attitude must prevail among our own people despite all objectors.

(14th February 1942)

The Jewish question must be solved within a pan-European frame. There are 11,000,000 Jews still in Europe. To begin with, they will have to be concentrated in the East; possibly an island, such as Madagascar, can be assigned to them after the war. In any case there can be no peace in Europe until every Jew has been eliminated from the continent.

(7th March 1942)

Finally we talked about the Jewish question. Here the Führer is as uncompromising as ever. The Jews must be got out of Europe, if necessary by applying most brutal methods.

(20th March 1942)

Beginning with Lublin, the Jews under the General Government are now being evacuated eastward. The procedure is pretty barbaric and is not to be described here more definitely. Not much will remain of the Jews. About 60 per cent of them will have to be liquidated; only about 40 per cent can be used for forced labour. The former Gauleiter of Vienna, who is to carry out this measure, is doing it with considerable circumspection and in a way that does not attract too much attention. . . . One must not be sentimental in these matters. If we did not fight the Jews, they would destroy us. It's a life-and-death struggle between the Aryan race and the Jewish bacillus. No other government and no other régime would have the strength for such a global solution as this.

(27th March 1942)

Had Goebbels lived to stand trial at Nuremberg these and other passages in his diaries would have been sufficient to condemn him.

Goebbels' admiration for Hitler remained absolute. He did not always agree with the Führer's decisions, but he was always able to blame these divergences on the ill-considered advice Hitler received from his generals, ministers and favourites. After Hitler had addressed a mass meeting in the Sportpalast on 30th January 1942 Goebbels wrote:

The Führer has charged the entire nation as though it were a storage battery. . . . As long as he lives and is among us in good health, as long as he can give us the strength of his spirit and the power of his manliness, no evil can touch us. The entire people became convinced of this anew today.[42]

What Goebbels took most pride in were his personal contacts with Hitler, reduced as these were now to the occasional private meetings at which they seemed to discuss everything with great earnestness from the war to vegetarianism. Goebbels was worried by the appalling strain to which Hitler had subjected himself, and marvelled at his strength.

The Führer, thank God, appears to be in good health. He has been through exceedingly difficult days, and his whole bearing shows it. The Führer is really to be pitied. He must take the entire burden of the war on his own shoulders, and no one can relieve him of responsibility for all the decisions that must be made.[43]

It is not difficult for me to gather from this whole presentation of the situation that the Führer alone saved the Eastern Front this winter. His determination and firmness have put everything back in shape again. If today he is a sick and ailing man, that was a high price to pay, but it is worth it.

My work meets with the Führer's highest approval and gives him great satisfaction. It is wonderful for me to be able to talk over all sorts of personal things at length with the Führer. He has the effect of a dynamo. After spending an afternoon with him, one feels like a storage battery that has just been recharged.[44]

After this meeting, which took place in March 1942, Goebbels noted that "the Führer was very much touched when I took my leave. He wishes me to visit him again soon. I am almost benumbed at having to leave him."

Goebbels was delighted at the intimacy of the occasion and the sight of a dog playing at the Führer's feet.

A little dog which he has been given now plays about in his room. His whole heart belongs to that little dog. It can do anything it wants in his bunker. At present it is nearer the Führer's heart than anything else.[45]

Goebbels then stayed to dinner.

At subsequent meetings he continued to press Hitler to take more drastic measures to ensure the total compliance of the State with the principles of National Socialism, and drafted on his behalf a special message to the German people for 1st May 1942.

The Führer has approved my draft for his telegram to the German people for 1st May. It is an exceptionally compelling and far-reaching declaration in favour of a people's social State and will be excellent for our propaganda at home. For the first time we can record the fact that the Führer is committing himself so completely about the future aims of the National Socialist State.[46]

This message followed immediately upon a speech given by Hitler to the Reichstag on 26th April at which he had revealed the gravity of the situation on the Eastern Front and represented his own assumption of the powers of Commander-in-Chief as the reason for the salvation of the German armies. He then made a formal demand to the Reichstag for plenary powers on the home front along the lines that Goebbels had pressed him to do. This was, of course, granted him with all the necessary enthusiasm required of such a body as the Reichstag under National Socialism. The new law stated:

The Führer must have all the rights demanded by him to achieve victory. Therefore—without being bound by existing legal regulations —in his capacity as Leader of the Nation, Supreme Commander of the Armed Forces, Head of the Government, Supreme Justice and Leader of the Party, the Führer must be in a position to force, with all the means at his disposal, every German, if necessary, whether he be common soldier or officer, low or high official or judge, leading or subordinate official of the Party, worker or employer, to fulfil his duties. In case of violation of these duties the Führer is entitled, regardless of rights, to mete out punishment and remove the offender from his post, rank and position without introducing prescribed procedures.[47]

This meant that the existing laws of Germany could be short-circuited at any time by any minister in the name of Hitler. The lawyers and the bureaucrats could be disregarded. They were, after all, bourgeois in origin, and therefore "out of touch with the people", as Goebbels always put it. "Experts," he wrote, "are always handicapped in their relation to the common people. They lack the necessary instinct for realising what the people are thinking."[48] He

Goebbels entering the Tennishallen with his usual bodyguard of Storm-Troopers, April 1933.

The gestures of the Orator.

The Sportpalast: *left*, a Nazi rally seen from the platform end of the hall; *right*, the rostrum and banners.

always boasted that he preferred the judgment of his mother. Writing on 29th January 1942 he recorded:

In the evening I had a long talk with my mother who, to me, always represents the voice of the people. She knows the sentiments of the people better than most experts who judge from the ivory tower of scientific inquiry, as in her case the voice of the people itself speaks. Again I learned a lot; especially that the rank and file are usually much more primitive than we imagine. Propaganda must therefore always be essentially simple and repetitive. In the long run basic results in influencing public opinion will be achieved only by the man who is able to reduce problems to the simplest terms and who has the courage to keep for ever repeating them in this simplified form, despite the objections of the intellectuals.[49]

This special form of radicalism left Goebbels free to declaim against any traditional form of power that he happened to dislike on the grounds that it was negative, reactionary and out to frustrate the New Order which National Socialism represented in Europe. Diplomats, lawyers, generals—all in turn came under his lash.

The weakness of diplomacy lies in its social ties. These can never be quite overcome, and one must therefore be conscious of this weakness when determining one's policies. One must not stick to old methods that have long been outmoded but must conduct politics and war with modern methods.[50]

It really makes one despair to see how the bureaucracy of the civil service tries again and again to cramp the style of those who favour a radical conduct of the war and to create one difficulty after another for them. This bureaucracy always rests its case on so-called common sense and the wisdom of experience. Now the point is that our great successes in the past were achieved thanks to neither of these qualities. They were the result of clever psychology and a pronounced ability to sense the thinking processes of the broad masses of the population.[51]

Goebbels was also much concerned about the place of the Church in the National Socialist State. He resented the hold religion had on the German people, but regarded the whole problem as one which could not be faced until after the war. The best thing, he felt, was not openly to antagonise the Churches at this stage. In fact he admitted to von Oven, his aide, as late as April 1944, that neither he nor Hitler had ever discontinued payment of the normal Church taxes, which, according to the custom, everyone had to pay to his acknowledged denomination. Goebbels appreciated the irony of the situation, since the bulk of his income came from books that contained statements against the Church. Nevertheless, he was angry, for example, when the Party removed crucifixes from schools and hospitals.

It can't be denied that certain of the Party's measures, especially the decree about crucifixes, have made it altogether too easy for the bishops to rant against the State. Göring, too, is very much put out about it. His whole attitude towards the Christian denominations is quite open and aboveboard. He sees through them, and has no intention whatever of taking them under his protection. On the other hand, he agrees with me completely that it won't do to get involved now, in war-time, in such a difficult and far-reaching problem. The Führer has expressed that viewpoint to Göring as he often has to me. In this connection the Führer declared that if his mother were still alive, she would undoubtedly be going to church today, and he could not and would not hinder her.[52]

On the other hand, he resented an article published in Italy by Vito Mussolini, a nephew of the dictator, which stressed the need for Europe to retain the Christian leadership of the world. Goebbels' observations are significant:

It is obvious that the Italians are trying to lay claim to the spiritual leadership of Europe, since leadership in military affairs and in power-politics has slipped completely from their hands. I am ignoring this article in our commentary. There is no point in replying to such provocations now, as we are not yet in a position to publish all our arguments. We shall have to await a more favourable opportunity.

We shall probably not be able to tackle the Church question bluntly until after the war.[53]

Goebbels knew from personal experience the nature of the hold that both the Catholic and Protestant Churches had on large numbers of the German people. He was shrewd enough to realise that the inevitable trial of strength that must eventually take place between National Socialism and the religious conscience of millions of the German people had at all costs to be postponed until after the war was won and the greatness of the Nazis' own faith in themselves and their Leader vindicated before the world. Christianity in Goebbels' view was at one with the bourgeois values he detested because they were impervious to his propaganda and could only ultimately be answered by the extreme measures of the concentration camp to which recalcitrant priests had to be sent and where so many of them displayed a notable courage and great powers of resistance.

It is plain from the way this statement is worded that Goebbels realised the great problem the National Socialists would have to face when conflict with the Churches was finally brought into the open. He even doubts whether it is wise to bring to public trial a group of clergy who had been arrested for listening to broadcasts from Britain, and brought the matter to Hitler's personal notice so that the possible repercussions of the trial could be studied. It is even probable that religion still had some unconscious hold on Goebbels; this might account for his plan, outlined to Semmler, one day to write a book on Christianity.

His dislike of bourgeois values extended to sexual morality. In April 1942 he makes the following observations on his own district of Berlin:

Prostitution in Berlin is causing us trouble these days. During a raid we found that 15 per cent of all the women arrested had V.D. and most of these syphilis. We must certainly do something about it at once. In the long run we cannot possibly avoid setting up a "red-light district" in the Reich capital like those in Hamburg, Nuremberg, and other large cities. You simply cannot organise and administer a city of four millions in accordance with the conceptions of bourgeois morality.[54]

Goebbels' observations on Germany's principal antagonists, Britain, the United States and Russia, are of considerable interest. The opinions expressed in his official, personal diary should represent his true feelings; but if they do, it is strange to find such an outlandish mixture of shrewdness and sheer ignorance in a man of his intelligence who had had access for about ten years to confidential reports from German agents and embassies. In fact, his lack of knowledge of foreign peoples was one of his great weaknesses.

Of the Russians he writes:

They are not a people but a conglomeration of animals. The greatest danger threatening us in the East is the stolid dullness of this mass. That applies both to the civilian population and to the soldiers. The soldiers won't surrender, as is the fashion in western Europe, when completely surrounded, but continue to fight until they are beaten to death. Bolshevism has merely accentuated this racial propensity of the Russian people. In other words, we are facing an adversary about whom we must be careful. The human mind cannot possibly imagine what it would be like if this opponent were to pour into western Europe like a flood.[55]

He accepted the veracity of reports from the occupied territories in the East that starving Russians were prepared to eat human flesh, but was, however, a supporter of a policy which attempted to win the support of those Russians who were antagonistic to the Communist régime by setting up some semblance of free institutions under the German rule. In a thoroughly Machiavellian passage in his diary for 22nd May 1942 he writes:

We could reduce danger from the Partisans considerably if we succeeded in at least winning some of these people's confidence. A clear peasant and Church policy would work wonders in this respect. It might also be useful to set up sham governments in the various sectors

214

which would then have to be responsible for unpleasant and unpopular measures. Undoubtedly it would be easy to set such governments up and we would then have a façade behind which to camouflage our policies. I shall talk to the Führer about this problem in the near future. I consider it one of the most vital in the present situation in the East.[56]

His views on America are equally devastating:

A report on the interrogations of American prisoners is really gruesome. These American soldiers are human material which can in no way stand comparison with our own people. One has the impression one is dealing with a herd of savages. The Americans are coming to Europe with a spiritual emptiness that really makes you shake your head. They are uneducated and know nothing. For instance, they ask whether Bavaria belongs to Germany and similar things. One can imagine what would happen to Europe if this dilettantism were to spread unchallenged. But we, as it happens, shall have something to say about that![57]

I have received statistics about the number of Jews in the American radio, film and press industries. The percentage is truly terrifying. Jews are 100 per cent in control of films, and 90 to 95 per cent of the press and radio.[58]

About the British he is scarcely more complimentary, though he has during this period a great deal more to say about them:

One really wonders on what grounds the English had the insolence to declare war on the Axis powers. Either they did not know our superiority and their inferiority, or else—and this seems more plausible —they intended from the very beginning to have other countries and peoples do their fighting for them. At any rate, that's where I attack the English vigorously in the German press and also in our foreign-language broadcasts.[59]

That's the way English gentlemen are: they are nonchalant and polite as long as everything is well with them, but they cast off their masks and reveal themselves as brutal world oppressors the moment one trespasses on their preserves or a man appears on the scene with whom they must reckon.[60]

After the House of Commons had observed a minute's silence in December 1942 in memory of the Jews murdered in Poland, Goebbels wrote:

That was quite appropriate for the British House of Commons, which is really a sort of Jewish exchange. The English, anyway, are the Jews among the Aryans.[61]

Goebbels is, however, prepared at times to extend a grudging admiration to Germany's oldest opponent:

Although England is fighting at present against tremendous obstacles it cannot be said that morale among the common people is low. The English people are used to hard blows and to a certain extent the way they take it compels admiration.[62]

If Goebbels had, for the most part, a poor opinion of his enemies, we may comfort ourselves that he had a scarcely better one of his allies. He despised the Italians and, for that matter, the Fascist movement as a whole as contrasted with National Socialism.

The Italians are not only doing nothing about the war effort, but they are hardly producing anything worth while in the realm of the arts. One might almost say that Fascism has reacted upon the creative life of the Italian people rather like sterilisation. It is, after all, nothing like National Socialism. While the latter goes deep down to the roots, Fascism is only superficial.[63]

Goebbels touched now and then on one of the trickiest problems that faced him in assessing the value of the Axis partners to Germany— his inner conviction of their racial inferiority to the Germans. This obviously had to be kept very much in the background.

The Italians fight tooth and nail against being regarded as racially inferior to, or even different from, ourselves.[64]

With the Japanese this problem was equally difficult. Goebbels was second to none in admiring their military qualities—though he came eventually to distrust their news reports as much as the Allies distrusted his. But the race of these partners in the Axis presented other factors which embarrassed him as a representative of the German *Herrenvolk*.

The United States is trying desperately to drag us into a discussion of racial questions, especially with regard to Japan. . . . I have forbidden the German news services even to mention these somewhat ticklish and delicate problems, as I am convinced we can't win any laurels here. As a matter of fact our position with Japan and the problems of eastern Asia is rather precarious, since we are uncompromising in our racial views. It is best to overcome this difficulty by silence.[65]

Goebbels' views on the development of war-time propaganda were naturally coloured by his attitude to the people, whether German or foreign, to whom his ideas were addressed. He professed his belief in the fundamental importance of news, but it was news designed to serve political ends. "News policy is a sovereign function of the State which the State can never renounce," he wrote in February 1942.[66] "News policy is a cardinal political affair." He was against the Party (that is, Dietrich) having control over news; only the Government (that is, himself) should exercise this function. "During a war," he wrote on another occasion, "news should be given out for instruction rather than for information."[67] That was the essence of the matter. News put ideas into people's minds, and the ideas must be the right ones. In a significant passage, with certain important subconscious implications, he remarks:

In war-time one should not speak of assassination either in a negative or an affirmative sense. There are certain words from which we should shrink as the Devil does from holy water; among these are, for instance, the words 'sabotage' and 'assassination'. One must not permit such terms to become part and parcel of everyday usage.[68]

Even words isolated from the context of a sentence might prove dangerous. In February 1942 he planned the revision of the German-language dictionaries required in the occupied territories.

> I have given instructions for our ministry to prepare dictionaries for the occupied areas in which the German language is to be taught. They are, above all, to use a terminology that conforms to our modern conception of the State. Especially those expressions are to be translated that stem from our political ideology. That is an important form of propaganda from which I expect rather good results in the long run.[69]

Goebbels' broadcasts to Britain provide a most interesting case of his attempts to apply his special principles of propaganda to a voluntary audience in a State free from control by the Nazis. His biggest single triumph was the use of Lord Haw-Haw during the earlier period of the war.[70] His broadcasts began from Hamburg on 10th April 1939. William Joyce was a British citizen born in New York of Irish parents. He was a graduate of London University and had been an enthusiastic member of Mosley's Blackshirts, for whom he became Director of Propaganda. In Britain he had been violently anti-Semitic. Having broken with Mosley, he eventually left England in 1939 for Germany where he became known as Herr Fröhlich (Mr. Joyous!) and worked in Fritzsche's department in the Ministry. As soon as he began broadcasting in his dry, sly manner he intrigued the British public on the level of a music-hall joke. He was christened Lord Haw-Haw in the *Daily Express*. This kind of reception was exactly what Goebbels wanted—at first. Once his success was established he branched off into skits lampooning the British upper class with Orpington and Orpington (who met in their club to grumble about the war), Sir Izzy Ungeheimer, who avoided his taxes, Bumbleby Mannering, the parson who made money out of munitions, and Sir Jasper Murgatroyd, who gave away Britain's guilty secrets. His attitude was radical, and his concern was gradually to expose Britain to the British as a corrupt and hypocritical nation. For a year at least he was an unquestionable success, and Goebbels used him also for broadcasts to the United States. As soon, however, as Winston Churchill became Prime Minister, Haw-

Haw's manner hardened to match the new spirit in Britain. The fun was over and he lost his hold on the public. Shirer, who knew him in Berlin and found him "an amusing and even intelligent fellow",[71] states that by September 1940 Joyce claimed he had become a German citizen and that he considered National Socialism to be the radical movement to which he had always belonged in spirit. He also reveals that at first the Ministry thought his nasal voice quite unsuitable for broadcasting. Goebbels' own attitude to his manner on the air by 1942 was significant:

Our broadcasts in English are, after all, very effective, as I have been able to determine from a dependable source. However, an aggressive, superior, and insulting tone gets us nowhere. I have often said so to our various departments and shall now insist that this nonsense be eliminated immediately. At present you can only get anywhere with the English by talking to them in a friendly and modest way. The English speaker, Lord Haw-Haw, is especially good at biting criticism, but in my opinion the time for spicy debate is past. During the third year of a war one must wage it quite differently from the first year. During the first year of the war people still listen to the delivery; they admire the wit and the spiritual qualities of the presentation. Today they want nothing but facts. The more cleverly, therefore, the facts are put together and the more psychologically and sensitively they are brought before the listening public, the stronger is the effect.[72]

News, properly presented, was to become the staple form of propaganda to Britain.

A curious slant to Goebbels' propaganda is his use of the astrological, which is mentioned on a number of occasions in the 1942 section of the diary.

In the United States, astrologers are at work prophesying an early end for the Führer. We know that type of work as we have often done it ourselves. We shall take up our astrological propaganda again as soon as possible. I expect quite a lot to result from it, especially in the United States and England.[73]

Berndt has drawn up a plan demonstrating how we could enlist the aid of the occult in our propaganda. We are really getting somewhere. The Americans and English fall easily for that type of thing. We are therefore pressing into our service all the experts we can find on occult prophecies, etc. Nostradamus must once again submit to being quoted.[74]

As for films, Goebbels' favourite medium, the diary is filled with references to the progress of the industry in its penetration of the occupied countries and its success under ministry guidance and control. Goebbels also reports on various captured films he has seen privately and admired—including the Soviet *General Suvorov* and the American *Swanee River*. His observations on this Hollywood musical are of particular interest:

All the film producers have been visiting me. In the evening we saw an American Technicolor picture, *Swanee River*, which gave me an opportunity to make a number of observations on the creation of a new German film based on folksongs. The fact of the matter is that the Americans know how to take their relatively small stock of culture, and, by up-to-date treatment, to make of it something which is very *à propos* for the present time. We are loaded down far too heavily with tradition and piety. We hesitate to modernise our cultural heritage. It therefore remains purely a matter of history or for the museums, and is at best understood by groups within the Party, the Hitler Youth, or the Labour Service. The cultural heritage of our past can only be made fruitful for the present if we present it with modern technique. We shall have to do something about it. The Americans have only a few Negro songs, but they present them so topically that they conquer large parts of the modern world which is, of course, much attracted by such melodies. We have a much greater fund of cultural assets, but we have neither the artistry nor the mind to modernise them. That must be changed.[75]

The production of films continued in France under the eye of the Germans. The high quality of certain French films excited Goebbels' attention:

I took a look at another French film, *Annette et la Dame Blonde*. It is as witty and elegant as the Darrieux movie, *Caprices*. We shall have to be careful to prevent the French building up a new reputation for artistic films under our leadership that will give us too serious competition in the European market. I shall see that the most talented French film actors are gradually engaged for German pictures.[76]

Goebbels' official diary makes little mention of his domestic life. There are occasional references to his wife and children. In May 1942 he notes that Magda was due to speak to an audience of women on Mothers' Day and was "scared out of her wits". The following month he writes as if his wife had been ill again during the winter but mentions that she had recovered and was well enough to agree with him uncompromisingly "on the question of total war" which was by then uppermost in his mind after the fall of Stalingrad. The previous December he says how much he regrets the little time he can spare to be with his children.

Perhaps this reference to his children was all the more poignant for him because during that same month an attempt was made on his life. The discussion of such things was taboo according to Goebbels' code and no mention of the matter appeared in the press; there is, indeed, only the briefest reference in Goebbels' own diary to the trial before a People's Court of "the traitor who planned an attempt on my life and was condemned to death".[77] There is, however, a further reference in Semmler's diary. He gives the man's name as Kumerow and states that he was a wireless engineer. The plot had been to blow up the bridge leading across the water to Goebbels' Schwanenwerder property on Wannsee; Kumerow, posing as a fisherman, had intended to do this as Goebbels' car was crossing the bridge. He was arrested, according to Semmler, as he was placing the charge in position. After this, security precautions at the Ministry were tightened and Goebbels' offices were sealed off and placed under armed guard.

Hitler was horrified when he heard the news. Immediately additional guards were placed wherever Goebbels was in residence. On Christmas Eve a huge, elegant Mercedes arrived; it was bullet-proof and mine-proof with eight millimetres of armour-plate in its bodywork. The glass was three centimetres thick. It was Hitler's Christmas present, and it came with the Führer's best wishes and orders that Goebbels was in future to use no other car.

CHAPTER SEVEN

Total War

THE FINAL SURRENDER of the German armies at Stalingrad on 31st January 1943 is commonly regarded as the turning-point of Hitler's fortunes in Europe. Any celebration of the tenth anniversary of Hitler's rise to power on 30th January 1933 had to be forgotten. Goebbels did not hesitate to make the flesh of Germany creep at this dire news; muffled drums preceded the announcements on the radio and the newspapers the following day were edged with the black bands of mourning. In the same month of January British and American forces occupied French North Africa and General Montgomery completed his break-through of Rommel's lines at El Alamein. Hitler had ordered both Rommel and von Paulus to hold their ground to the last man. Neither succeeded; von Paulus became a prisoner of war and Rommel was eventually recalled home. After the Generals' plot of July 1944 Rommel was to be told to commit secret suicide because Hitler did not want to acknowledge in public that the most popular General in Germany had been among the traitors; he did so and was then accorded a State funeral in place of the firing squad.

The years 1943 and 1944, the years of total war, are also the years of Hitler's moral bankruptcy. Five million slave-workers from Russia, Poland, France, Holland, Yugoslavia and, eventually, Italy were press-ganged for sweated labour in Germany, which meant as often as not death from privation. The meaning of rule by the S.S. and the Gestapo needs no description here. The results shame our civilisation. The concentration camps and the extermination camps worked night and day in the fulfilment of the systematic policy ordained by Hitler and approved by Goebbels of destroying the Jewish race in Europe. So great were the numbers killed that the records became saturated and unable to keep count of the millions involved. Himmler, who was proud to be in charge of this operation, himself believed that more than six million Jews were slaughtered, gassed, starved or tortured to death. The Commandant of Auschwitz in Poland claimed that three million died at his camp alone, where the gas-chambers were specially designed to accommodate at a single time two thousand victims, who took from three to fifteen minutes to die "according to climatic conditions".[1]

In spite of Stalingrad, the Germans managed to hold on to their main positions in Russia through the summer, but in North Africa Hitler lost a quarter of a million men when his army was finally defeated in May 1943. In Italy Mussolini's régime was on the point of collapse, though Hitler twice summoned the Duce to conferences at which he tried to inspire him with the will to fight in the cause of history. But Mussolini said nothing. He went home for the last time as a free man and was placed under arrest on 25th July.

The Allies had landed in Sicily on 10th July. Though Marshal Badoglio, the head of the new Italian Government, claimed that he would maintain Italy's partnership with the Axis, Hitler knew instinctively that Italian capitulation to the Allies was only a matter of time. He hurried every man he could spare down into the Italian peninsula. He intended to take the leaders of the new régime and members of the Royal Family prisoner; he even planned to invade the Vatican. Goebbels was among those who dissuaded him from violating the Papal territory. But the first thing he needed to do was rescue Mussolini from captivity so that he might exploit him as a figurehead to justify his actions in Italy. He used to the full the six weeks that passed between the fall of Mussolini in July and the announcement in September of an armistice between the Allies and Badoglio to build up his strength in Italy.

The Allies landed successfully on the Italian mainland south of Naples. Hitler was concerned to hold central and northern Italy, and he succeeded for virtually a year. On 12th September Mussolini was rescued by a special squad of German commandos, accompanied by a film cameraman, to record the event, but he was by now an old and broken man clinging to his mistress and no longer able to sustain the rôle for which Hitler had cast him; nevertheless his restoration as Duce was publicised as a matter of form. The Fascist puppet government became a hotbed of petty intrigue, and eventually Hitler had Ciano killed. When the Italians at last recaptured the Duce and his mistress they shot them both and left their bodies hanging head downwards on barbaric display in the Piazzale Loreto in Milan. But by that time Hitler was confined to his Bunker.

Meanwhile the German forces were being slowly but inflexibly pressed back. Although they managed to hold the Allies in Italy during the hideous winter of 1943-44, they were not so successful in Russia where Hitler's policy of stand and fight to the death only led to unnecessarily heavy losses of men as well as of territory. Hitler refused all advice which implied a strategic withdrawal of his forces in any sector. He preferred them to die, or be taken prisoner. During 1943 in Germany itself the Allied bombardment of the industrial centres was massive, incessant and crippling; the Luftwaffe was chased out of the skies. In the same year the U-boat menace in the Atlantic was conquered.

Hitler himself, who was now fifty-five, became more and more the isolated, ageing figure, savagely berating his commanders for their incompetence. He was a sick man, suffering from partial paralysis, stomach-cramp and fits of giddiness. He was also kept constantly under the influence of drugs of many different kinds by his quack physician, Professor Morell, in whose hands he placed himself unreservedly and also those intimately connected with him, including Goebbels, who was not infrequently unwell. Unlike Goebbels, who was always out and about, Hitler almost entirely withdrew from public life and did nothing to comfort the hard-pressed German people by making his presence felt. Only rarely could he even be persuaded to make a speech or broadcast. This was left to Goebbels, who became a constant visitor to the devastated areas, where he did his best to hearten those who had suffered in the raids. Hitler remained hidden away most of the time at his Command headquarters which were remotely situated in East Prussia. After the fall of Stalingrad Hitler made only two public speeches of any importance and five broadcasts before his death. He withdrew himself into his dreams of conquest.

1944 was the year in which the fantasy of ultimate victory finally overcame his judgment. He dreamed that he would defeat the West by means of his secret weapons and the East through the overwhelming strength of the German Army guided by his intuitive strategy. Gradually his obsessions drove his ministers and commanders from him; Göring absented himself, living a life of luxury, while Ribbentrop no longer enjoyed Hitler's confidence. In the last year of his life those who managed to exercise spasmodic influence over him were reduced to Himmler, Bormann, Speer, Doenitz and Goebbels himself. Himmler's powers were spread wide through the S.S., the Army and the Intelligence Service; Bormann, Hess's successor, became Hitler's personal assistant, constant adviser and jealous watchdog; Speer was in charge of Germany's industrial war effort until he turned eventually against Hitler in 1945. Doenitz was to become Hitler's choice to head the Government which should follow on his death, with Goebbels as Reich Chancellor.

The many plots to kill Hitler—there are records of seven of them in 1943—all failed for one reason or another. Himmler was well aware that a large network of conspiracy was being created in Germany with the sole purpose of ridding the country of the Führer. Arrests were constantly made as suspicion centred round now one name, now another, but the fires of assassination could not be stamped out. Politicians, diplomats, generals, members of the German underground for political, religious or intellectual reasons formed conspiracies which waxed, waned and wavered in their endeavours to bring about the Führer's death. The plot which came nearest to success was that of 20th July 1944. Goebbels, as we shall see, played a decisive part in the frustration of the attempted *coup d'état* which followed. Hitler, shaken and still further deranged, survived to continue his grand strategy.

By this time the Russians had all but pressed the German armies out of Soviet territory, while the Allies had taken Rome in June. In the same month British and American forces had landed in Normandy; as usual Hitler blamed the incompetence of his generals and departed for Berchtesgaden with his drugs. He divided his time now between Berchtesgaden and his military headquarters in East Prussia. It was here, at Rastenburg, during one of his military conferences that the bomb placed under his table just failed to kill him on 20th July. Hitler's revenge on the conspirators was widespread and thorough, and Goebbels was at last given the internal powers in Germany for which he had been asking the Führer since 1943. His propaganda for total war now had teeth behind it.

The surviving fragments of Goebbels' diary give his comments on events occurring during certain weeks and odd days between March and December 1943. They are significant because they show the development of his thinking against the background of this adverse period in German history. Goebbels remained completely self-sufficient, his satisfaction with his own achievements in writing and speaking unimpaired. As he says: "One must have absolute self-assurance, as it is the only thing which can radiate assurance to others."[2] But what pleased him most of all was the praise he is able to record from the lips of the Führer, with whom he was in frequent contact.

The Führer became exceptionally open-hearted and personal at the end of our discussion. He hides absolutely nothing from me. Intimate talks like that really strengthen one's heart. The Führer assured me again and again that he was not only extremely satisfied with my work, but that he had the greatest admiration for it. German war propaganda was a masterpiece from beginning to end. I can therefore feel very proud of the recognition given me.[3]

The Führer spoke to Speer in terms of the highest praise for my articles in *Das Reich*. He told him he read them every time and had not once discovered a psychological error in them. He regards them as the best political prose now being written in Germany.[4]

In a curious passage he accepts what he readily interprets as praise from an enemy source at the same time as he reveals that the German people were not quite unanimous in their appreciation of him—partly, no doubt, because of the growing ruthlessness of his radicalism.

A number of English papers and periodicals have been laid before me which give evidence of great respect for my person and my work. The *News Chronicle* calls me the most dangerous member of the Nazi gang. I can feel very proud of this praise. If the English continue to respect my work so much, I believe I shall gradually also win the approval of the German people.[5]

Nevertheless, he seldom stopped impressing upon Hitler what were his own ambitions. First of all he wanted to gather every branch of propaganda into his own hands.

I developed my ideas to the Führer about the nature of propaganda. I believe that when a propaganda ministry is created, all matters affecting propaganda, news and culture within the Reich and within the occupied areas must be subordinated to it. I emphasised that I insist on totalitarianism in carrying out the propaganda and news policies of the Reich. He agreed with me absolutely and unreservedly.[6]

Then, secondly, he wanted Hitler to extend his powers as Gauleiter of Berlin to the whole of Germany. His pride in the control he possessed over the internal affairs of the capital is always evident, and he was particularly proud of the way in which he handled the aftermath of the bombing; this was something he continually brought to Hitler's notice.

He confirmed once more that in situations like that I am the supreme and sole commander of the capital. The ministries, too, are to obey my orders. The entire public life is subordinated to me. In times of catastrophe only one person can give orders.[7]

But, argued Goebbels to himself, if Hitler granted his effectiveness as Gauleiter of Berlin, why did he not give him similar powers for Germany as a whole?

Our propaganda within the Reich also doesn't seem to have the right spark to it, as I gather from a number of reports from Gauleiters. Here again the sad fact is that we are without a governing hand at home. I should be quite willing to undertake to solve all these problems, provided I were given the necessary plenary powers.[8]

For Goebbels there could be no hard line of demarcation between the actual administration of a country and the propaganda associated with it. Propaganda isolated from power was useless—"a sharp sword must always stand behind propaganda if it is to be effective".[9] Not only personal ambition but the sheer logical necessities of his work as he understood it demanded that he be given these plenary powers and so become the ruler of Germany while Hitler controlled the war. This would be a partnership in which there was no room for other ministers or commanders except in relatively subordinate positions.

Consequently, Goebbels now began to impress upon Hitler the need for the civilian population to be made to participate in the demands of total war as he conceived them.

Total war is giving me a lot of work to do, but matters are progressing according to rule and programme. . . . The people identify the idea and conception of total war with me personally. I am therefore in a certain sense publicly responsible for the continuation of total war.[10]

Goebbels' sense of power was always affronted when he contemplated immunity from the effects of war still enjoyed by many of the more privileged people in Germany, including some of the Nazi leaders.

I made complaint about a number of Reichsleiters and Gauleiters whose standard of living is very much out of tune with the times. The Führer had heard about this, too. He is going to forbid hunting for the duration of the war and the use of alcohol at any events sponsored by the Party. In principle only a one-course meal is to be served.[11]

It won't do for total war to be interpreted in a lax manner in one province and very strictly in another. The fact that hair-dyeing is forbidden to ladies in some provinces, but permitted in others, has resulted in the better-class ladies travelling from one *Gau* to another for their beauty treatments. That, of course, is not what is meant by total war.[12]

Von Oven records a similar aversion—on this occasion to the time-servers in the film industry, who, said Goebbels, curried favour with the Nazis now, but, "if ever we should have to go, they would be the first to curry favour with their new masters, telling them they have always been good anti-Fascists and that they were forced to accept all that money and all those honours from us".[13] Goebbels proved a sound prophet. He ached to bring such people as these to heel, to make them experience the lash of his authority—the authority Hitler still delayed giving him. Nevertheless, he credited himself with succeeding in becoming the internal ruler of Germany *ex officio*.

It is characteristic that during the war the Ministry of the Interior has done practically nothing about domestic politics. Whatever there is in Germany in the way of domestic policy stems from me. Naturally I can be very well satisfied about this development. If a strong man were in Frick's place, he would be in a position to cause me much trouble; as things are, I have been able to have my way in domestic politics. According to an old principle of mine, I never give up what I have once taken into my hands.[14]

Later, in 1943, and still without the executive power he wanted, he would grumble to von Oven about the inefficiency of other Party leaders. He said to him: "If only the Führer had made me Vice-Chancellor on the first day of the war, I would have seen to it that there was more decency about. The trouble is that the Führer has too soft a spot for the old Party members. True enough, those who were with him in the early days were tough and courageous men and they earned a proper reward once we got to power. But so many of them were put in jobs far too big for them to cope with, to say nothing of the corrupting temptations of power which, after all, one has to be a personality and a character not to succumb to."[15]

As the war slowly turned against the Nazis, Goebbels' ardent radicalism, lurking just below the surface, erupted volcanically.

National Socialism must undergo a renovation. We must link ourselves more socialistically with the people than before. The people must always know that we are their just and generous guardians. The

National Socialist leadership must have no ties whatsoever with the aristocracy or with so-called society.[16]

At the same time the leadership pointed forward under Hitler to the control of Europe and, through Europe, the world. To this over-riding purpose every other moral consideration was, in Hitler's view, and in Goebbels', completely subordinate.

The Führer gave expression to his unshakable conviction that the Reich will be the master of all Europe. We shall yet have to engage in many fights, but these will undoubtedly lead to magnificent victories. There-after the way to world domination is practically certain. To dominate Europe will be to assume the leadership of the world.

In this connection we naturally cannot accept questions of right and wrong even as a basis of discussion. The loss of this war would con-stitute the greatest wrong to the German people; victory would give us the greatest right. After all, it will be only the victor who can prove to the world the moral justification for this struggle.[17]

In these surviving fragments of his diary for 1943, Goebbels records no less than nine meetings with the Führer, most of them in private. In spite of the intolerable burden of his responsibilities, or perhaps because of them, Hitler seemed to welcome these prolonged conversa-tions in which every aspect of the war and the future greatness of Germany seems to have been discussed, never without thought of ultimate victory. Even allowing for Goebbels' need to parade Hitler's affection for him in the presence of his stenographers, it is evident that the two men had grown closer together and that Goebbels could to some extent meet Hitler's need in his isolated and artificial way of life for human companionship, encouragement and enthusiastic loyalty. By now there was no one but he in a position to give the Führer quite so much in the way of friendship combined with acumen.

The Führer was extremely nice and obliging. . . . At our parting he was exceptionally friendly and charming to me. I believe I can be a very strong support for him in these critical times. . . . All his wishes

—in my case he will not speak of orders—are to be made known to me through the channels with which I am familiar. If anybody else should claim that he is speaking with the authority of the Führer's G.H.Q. I can be sure it is not true.[18]

In spite of this growing intimacy with Hitler, Goebbels felt the need during 1943 to attempt to create certain safeguards by bringing Göring back into the Führer's favour. In so far as the Minister for Propaganda could trust anyone, he chose the men he knew well who had survived from the old days, preferring to deal with them rather than with the upstarts in Hitler's immediate circle, such as Bormann. Hitler retained a certain affectionate regard for Göring, although his failure to make the Luftwaffe impregnable had seriously discredited him and led to his semi-retirement in a life of luxury and ease. In 1941 Semmler gathered from his conversations with Goebbels that his Minister despised Göring. In December 1942 he noted down some gossip from Frau Goebbels to the effect that Göring had been for some years a cocaine addict. In 1943 Goebbels attempted to close down Horcher, the luxury restaurant in Berlin which secretly supplied Göring with forbidden food, and he deeply resented the way in which Göring managed to load Karinhall, his great residence in the country, with famous works of art looted from the museums or private collections of occupied Europe. Goebbels used to tell von Oven stories of Göring's unbelievable greed; of how for example during the days of poverty in the Party he had been offended by Göring eating all night in the sleeping compartment they had sometimes to share on their journeys to meetings and conferences. By the beginning of 1945 he wanted to have Göring tried by the People's Court for refusal to join in the total war effort.

But in 1943 it suited Goebbels' policy to attempt the rehabilitation of Göring in order to make him into an ally. He first approached him as early as March 1942.

In the afternoon I had a talk, lasting more than three hours, with Göring, in an atmosphere of the greatest friendliness and cordiality. I was happy we could be so frank. We surveyed the general situation, and I was gratified to find that we agree entirely on all important problems. Without having consulted each other we have arrived at almost exactly the same appraisal of the situation.

Göring is in exceptionally good condition physically. He works hard, achieves enormous successes, and brings sound common sense, without much theorising, to bear on his problem.[19]

A year later, with the help of Speer, Goebbels attempted to win Göring over to support his campaign for total war. All their previous causes of dissension were put aside when Goebbels visited the Reich Marshal in his alpine house in Berchtesgaden.

His house is high up on the mountain in almost wintry quiet. Göring received me most charmingly and is very open-hearted. His dress is somewhat baroque and would, if one did not know him, strike one as almost laughable. But that's the way he is, and one must put up with his idiosyncrasies; they sometimes even have a charm about them.[20]

They found a common interest in worrying together about Hitler's state of mind and body.

Göring evinced the greatest concern about the Führer. He, too, feels that he has aged fifteen years during three and a half years of war. It is tragic that the Führer has become such a recluse and leads such an unhealthy life. He never gets out into the fresh air. He does not relax. He sits in the bunker, worries and broods. If one could only transfer him to other surroundings! But he has made up his mind to conduct this war in his own Spartan manner, and I suppose nothing can be done about it.[21]

They found themselves in agreement in their criticism of almost everyone, including Rommel, von Paulus, Rosenberg, Ribbentrop and more especially "the three wise men" (as Göring nicknamed them) who were really the root cause of this unexpected *rapprochement* between Goebbels and Göring—Lammers, Bormann and Keitel, the men known now as the Committee of Three who were taking charge of Hitler and making life more difficult for Goebbels. Among their allies they counted on Speer, Himmler, Funk and Ley. At a joint meeting held a few days later, Goebbels records Göring's view of the matter.

So far as their authority and power are concerned, their relative importance is first Bormann, then Lammers, with Keitel an absolute zero. He is a locomotive that has run out of fuel, puffs out its last steam, and then suddenly stands still. Unquestionably these three intend to establish a sort of kitchen cabinet and to erect a wall between the Führer and his ministers. The Committee of Three is to be the instrument for putting this scheme into effect. This is simply intolerable.[22]

Hitler's own reaction to the proposal that Göring should be rehabilitated with the German public was not exactly enthusiastic, and by May Goebbels himself seems to be in doubt whether Göring can be of much further use. The German public were against him for his failure to protect them from the Allied bombing, and his way of life, which had previously entertained them, was now the source of bitter criticism. His failure to appear in public became the subject of rumour. It was even thought that he might have committed suicide.

Goebbels' attitude to handling news of the destruction in Germany had changed as early as the summer of 1942. He knew that the burning ruins were impossible to hide, excuse or explain away. Taking his cue from Winston Churchill's "blood, sweat and tears", which he believed to be a sound way to brace the public for further effort, he developed the theme of "terror attacks" on Germany and urged the press to make the most of them with a view to sharpening the German spirit. At a press conference in September 1942 he had said:

It will be impossible to state in one sentence that a city like Düsseldorf lies in ruins. Special sections of press correspondents will be formed, whose duty it will be to glorify the events of night bombing in the style of battlefield reports and present them in a mystical light.[23]

This illustrated his new policy of 'Strength through Fear', the harbinger of the total war campaign.

In Berlin he had ordered the evacuation of as many old people, women and children as could be spared in anticipation of the mass air-raids that he knew must come and did indeed eventually take place during August 1943 and in succeeding months. In contrast to Hitler and Göring, Goebbels moved here, there and everywhere in public, dispensing the comforts of his presence in the bombed areas and responding warmly to his actual or imagined popularity with the people. He visited the Ruhr and other industrial areas devastated by the ceaseless bombardment, and he was meticulous in fulfilling his duties as Nazi Gauleiter of Berlin, where his official residence was eventually to be destroyed, his Ministry damaged, the *Gau* office badly burned, and the Kaiserhof Hotel, so sacred to Nazi memories, completely gutted. "It is always wise to be at hand," he writes, for he knew he owed it to himself to be present to cope with the endless difficulties. There is always a certain poetic licence in Goebbels' accounts of any of his activities which he knows are to his credit, but, even allowing for this, there is no question that he never spared himself when it came to the exercise of his authority or the expenditure of his time and nervous energy in public appearances of every kind. He was even to some extent exhilarated by the endless difficulties that faced him.

I got up at an ungodly hour with my head throbbing worse than ever before. All day long headaches pursue me. What of it? I simply must go to work. I drive straight to the office to wash and shave. I am very much hampered in my work. All telephone lines are down; I can reach the outside world only with the help of messengers. Most of the Reich ministries have been bombed out. Ministers and departmental heads can be found only with difficulty. That makes my work more difficult in some respects, but easier in others.[24]

A typical decision he had to make on the spur of the moment was whether to save the Charlottenburg Opera House (which was under his personal patronage as distinct from the State Opera patronised by Göring) or an armaments factory. He unhesitatingly directed his over-strained fire-fighting resources to the factory.

Although about this time he claimed to von Oven that he was not afraid to make himself unpopular if need be, judging from the diary he took pleasure in seeking the applause of the public.

The Berliners gather around my car. I was amazed at their excellent spirit. Nobody cries, nobody complains. People slapped me on the back familiarly, gave me good advice, prevented me from continuing because, as they put it, nothing must happen to me since I am still very much needed. . . .

Sometimes I have the impression that the Berliners are almost in a religious trance. Women come up to me and lay their hands on me in blessing, imploring God to preserve me. . . . Show these people small favours, and you can wrap them around your finger. . . .

At the Gartenplatz I took part in feeding the public. The men and women workers received me with an enthusiasm as unbelievable as it was indescribable. . . . I had to eat with the people and was lifted on to a box to talk to them. I delivered a very earthy and slangy speech which won the hearts of the workers. Everybody accosted me with '*du*' and called me by my first name. . . . Women embraced me. I had to give my autograph. . . . There were deeply touching scenes. One woman had given birth to a child during an air-raid two or three days ago; nevertheless she insisted on getting up when she heard I had come, dressed, and hurried to the Platz. We can never lose this war because of defective morale.[25]

However that may be, throughout 1943 Goebbels had been pressing Hitler to consider what advantages there might be in negotiating a peace settlement with either Britain or Russia, preferably with Britain.

The morale of the German people, he felt, was sinking, and the strain was telling even on himself.

Much criticism now appears in the letters reaching us. Morale among the masses is so low as to be rather serious. Even people of good will are now worried about the future. The man in the street no longer sees any way out of the military dilemma. As a result there is criticism of the leaders, in some cases even of the Führer himself.[26]

The whole day brought nothing but work and worry. Alarming news kept piling in. One must certainly keep one's mental balance and hold one's nerves in check so as not to become jittery under the impact. But there can be no question about this in my case. I know that war is a tough business; I also know that one must see it through; I realise clearly that it involves an exceptionally severe strain; but when one tackles the job courageously and survives the crisis, victory beckons in the end.[27]

With the Germans finally defeated in North Africa, however, he wrote: "I sometimes feel that we lack the necessary initiative for fighting the war."[28] In conference with Hitler the following September he raised, not for the first time, the vexed question of a peace settlement.

I asked the Führer whether he would be ready to negotiate with Churchill or whether he declined this on principle. The Führer replied that in politics principles simply do not exist when it comes to questions of personalities. He does not believe that negotiations with Churchill would lead to any result as he is too deeply wedded to his hostile views and, besides, is guided by hatred and not by reason. The Führer would prefer negotiations with Stalin, but he does not believe they would be successful, since Stalin cannot cede what Hitler demands in the East. . . .

It is doubtful, really, whether we are in a position to choose between Russia and England. If we actually had a choice it would naturally be much more agreeable to start talks with London than with Moscow. One can always make a better deal with a democratic State, and once peace has been concluded, such a State will not take up the sword for at least twenty years to come. Psychologically the English would not be in a position to make war; besides the English people are too tired of it and possibly too exhausted also. It is different with the Bolsheviks. Because of their close-knit system they are naturally in a position to embark upon war at any time.[29]

Goebbels' attitude to Britain seemed to have undergone some change. Whilst advocating an implacable, irrevocable hatred in his

237

propaganda, he records such thoughts as these in his official diary:

We Germans are not very well fitted for administering occupied territory, as we lack experience. The English, who have done nothing else in all their history, are superior to us in this respect.[30]

Anglo-Saxon physical science has completely eclipsed us, especially in research. As a result, the Anglo-Saxon powers are very superior to us in the practical application to warfare of the results of research in physics. That is noticeable both in aerial and submarine warfare.[31]

Goebbels' bitterness as he watched the home front deteriorate extended to everyone who hindered the war effort, especially the generals of the High Command. Two passages in particular that occur in the diary reflect the strength of this hatred:

The Führer's judgment of the moral qualities of the generals—and that applies to all arms of the service—is devastating. He doesn't believe any general *a priori*. They all cheat him, fawn upon him, furnish him with statistics which any child can contradict, and thereby insult the Führer's intelligence.[32]

The total lack of confidence between Hitler and his General Staff was an important factor in losing Germany the war, and it came to a head in the most formidable of the plots to assassinate Hitler, that organised by the Generals in 1944.

The fall of Mussolini and the subsequent capitulation of Italy was a further blow to German propaganda. When the news of Mussolini's dismissal came through, Goebbels was in Dresden visiting his wife, who was receiving treatment in a sanatorium. This political disaster was coupled with terrible reports from Hamburg of the destruction brought about by a mass air-raid. It was von Oven's duty to tell the Minister both these things.[33] It was Goebbels' habit when he received bad news to say nothing for a minute or so but sit staring at the bringer of tidings with his mouth open and the incredulous expression of a child on his face. But now he just sat shaking his head. Eventually he spoke. "*Dreckhammel!*" was all he said. Subsequently, when he had had discussions with Hitler he was to become rather more cheerful; after all, he had never thought much of Mussolini. He sat back in his favourite position, and crouching in his swivel-chair with his knee propped up against the edge of the desk he suddenly burst out in mockery: "Duce, Duce, Duce," like the Italian crowds greeting their Leader.

Although the liberation of Mussolini gave Goebbels the propaganda story he needed, it came only after several weeks' delay, and he was disgusted by Mussolini when eventually he saw the condition the Duce was in—"in the last analysis he is nothing but an Italian and can't get away from that heritage".

The last entry of Goebbels' diary at present available to us is that for 9th December 1943. Contact with his personal opinions and behaviour is then maintained by the records of those who worked for him—in particular the published diaries written by his aide, Rudolf Semmler, and his press secretary, Wilfred von Oven. Semmler's last entry is dated 17th April 1945, only two weeks before Goebbels' suicide. For the preceding two and a half years, 1943-45, we have the advantage of his observant accounts of what Goebbels said and did during the most critical period of his life. For an almost identical period von Oven supplements Semmler's notes with detailed descriptions of Goebbels' personal habits and methods of work.

Von Oven was much impressed by Goebbels' manner at the conferences where he presided in the Ministry.[34] A great Gobelin tapestry hung behind the Minister's tall leather-upholstered chair; strangely enough, it showed a faun as a piper playing the tune to which other fauns and nymphs danced. Goebbels' audiences, representing senior professional people in broadcasting, the press or films, waited for him, and when he arrived the echo of their voices was hushed. Goebbels would sit down with his knee, as usual, pushed up against the edge of the table in front of him, and leaf through a mass of papers. He was in the habit of taking off his wrist-watch before beginning to talk. He would start speaking in a low, slow voice in order to make his audience lean forward and strain their ears to catch what he was saying. He issued his instructions in this style, quickly and to the point before dismissing his audience back to their work. As against this easy, professional manner of holding a conference, von Oven was shocked at the flippancy displayed behind the scenes at the more senior, restricted meetings, where the latest anti-Hitler jokes were re-told with hilarity.

Von Oven was charmed by Magda Goebbels, to whom Naumann introduced him at one of the lakeside estates. But he suffered like the rest from the frugality of Goebbels' meals. He describes in detail the Minister's study in the official residence in Berlin—at one end a large fireplace, at the other a desk covered with red leather. The curtains and the carpet were alike red. Behind the desk with its swivel-chair was a larger than life-size portrait of Hitler covering the greater part of the wall; to the left of the desk was a picture of Frederick the Great, one of six different pictures or portrait busts of the King to be found in the town-house alone. There were others at the Ministry and out in the country.

A normal working day for Goebbels in the middle of 1943 was recorded by von Oven in some detail. His valet Emil entered the dressing-room adjoining Goebbels' bedroom exactly at 7.30 in the morning, pushing before him a trolley on which there was a cup of coffee, a saucer with three different vitamin tablets, two thin slices of wholemeal bread cut into quarters and a large brief-case of red leather labelled "Telegrams for the Herr Minister". The valet then knocked on the bedroom door until he got some sort of response from his master. Goebbels had never been at his best in the early morning.[35]

It was von Oven's responsibility to receive at 6 a.m. the messages that had to be sorted and selected before being put into the Minister's brief-case. They were labelled Confidential, Secret or Top Secret; and they were coloured differently according to the level of their eventual release to the press, to the Gauleiters or to other officials. Von Oven was responsible for bringing the more significant of these releases to Goebbels' attention, and also for preparing the daily papers for the Minister. One of the papers Goebbels never omitted to read was the local journal from Rheydt.

Goebbels took exactly forty-five minutes to prepare himself for the day. He shaved and dressed meticulously. Once a week his hair was dressed while a manicurist attended to his hands. Goebbels favoured neat clothes, cream silk shirts and eau-de-Cologne. Even in uniform he usually managed to look civilian, frequently wearing evening trousers decorated with silk braid and patent-leather shoes beneath the brown coat of the uniform. Rumour had it that Goebbels possessed enough suits never to wear the same twice throughout the year. Even after several weeks on duty von Oven marvelled that he had never seen the Minister in the same suit twice. All his clothes were beautifully cut, elegant and inconspicuous in both colour and pattern. However hot the day, Goebbels always took an overcoat, hat and gloves to the office. When he did not wear the overcoat it was usually taken to the car for him neatly folded over and carried like a tray.[36]

At 8.15 each morning von Oven and Goebbels' aide would be given a cup of coffee and thin slices of dry bread for their breakfast while they waited for the Minister in the reception hall. It was also their responsibility to telephone the Ministry for any special news or points connected with the day's schedule which Goebbels expected to be told while they were driven to work in the bullet-proof Mercedes. Then Goebbels appeared, followed by Emil with two brief-cases—the red official case and the case containing his personal papers. These brief-cases had to be placed on his office desk at an exact distance from the edge, just as his secretaries had to lay out his carefully sharpened pencils in a neat parade, ready for work.

Rach, Goebbels' driver, always gave the Hitler salute as he held open the doors of the car, which had to be handled carefully owing to their enormous weight. Goebbels preferred to sit in front beside him; von Oven and the aide on duty sat in the back. Goebbels listened carefully to his assistant's briefly worded account of what he had heard from the Ministry. Within a couple of minutes the great car covered its three-hundred-yard journey and drew up at the Ministry, and the servants sprang to their duty of saluting the Minister.[37] Goebbels' batman Ochs stepped forward to take his master's hat, coat and gloves, and the little retinue carrying Goebbels' outer clothes and the brief-cases marched silently over the thick red carpets to the suite of offices on the first floor. The great double doors were silently shut behind him, and he walked over to the massive desk which was the symbol of his power. In an ante-room two secretaries were at work; they were members of a team who worked in shifts day and night. As for Goebbels, he at once applied himself to the sets of papers prepared for his attention.

At ten o'clock Werner Naumann, Goebbels' Under-Secretary of State, who had his offices situated next to the Minister's own suite, would be announced for the regular morning conference. At eleven o'clock the conference of heads of departments and other officials was held. After this came private interviews of various kinds until lunch-time.

Von Oven describes how he and the aide would sit waiting with rumbling stomachs because Goebbels always preferred to talk rather than to eat. Eventually the message came that the Minister was ready, and the routine of the return journey home to the frugal meal was rapidly put into action. The main course might be a rissole the size of a duck's egg, or three or four potatoes and spinach—Goebbels' favourite vegetable. After lunch the Minister might talk over a cigarette before retiring to sleep in an arm-chair. For this he used the same posture as Frederick the Great is said to have done, his head back, a blanket placed over his knees. The nap lasted half an hour. Von Oven was then required to attend the Minister with his note-book ready while Goebbels took his coffee, his wafers of bread and his three pills.

Von Oven was often made responsible for the research work needed for Goebbels' special contributions to *Das Reich*. These cost Goebbels much time and thought, but he had arranged to be paid the handsome sum of four thousand marks for each of them. He wrote the first draft in long-hand. He then dictated the article for typing and lastly set to work revising it. Petty details of fact were constantly needed, and von Oven had to hasten to verify such points for the Minister. Goebbels fussed over the proofs and listened with great critical attention, which often became irritable, to the regular broadcast of his articles each week.

The early evening period was an unpleasant one for von Oven because anything might be asked of him. He might be required in the shortest possible time to find out the date Hannibal crossed the Alps, or any other odd fact needed for the *Das Reich* article. Or he might be sent on some small matter of liaison or petty service the Minister required. He was sustained during this time by more black coffee and more thin slices of bread. Sometimes he was given a dab of marmalade. The china, however, was excellent Dresden. All he could do was look

Goebbels' social and domestic life. *Above, left,* at the theatre with Prince August Wilhelm and Princess Bathilde of Schaumburg-Lippe; *right,* at the marriage of his sister Maria to Max Kimmich in 1938. *Below,* at the helm of his motorboat on the Wannsee.

Lida Baarova at the time of her association with Goebbels (*left*). *Right*, with Magda and Hanke (bearded).

The Family group, 1942.

forward to dinner at eight, and watch for the sign that the Minister was in a good mood. This would be revealed by his talkativeness and a habit of snapping his fingers. When he was ready, Goebbels would give him the red brief-case for preparation early the following morning.

After dinner the Minister and those present for the meal would very often see a programme of films which might, if the date were appropriate, include a preview of the current newsreel prior to its public release. Goebbels invariably became excited by films. He saw everything on which his agents could lay their hands. The Press attachés in the German embassies in Sweden, Switzerland and Portugal were under orders to get hold of prints of American films and have them illicitly copied for him. One evening in the summer of 1943 *Mrs. Miniver* was screened at Goebbels' house. He was enraptured by it, according to von Oven. "What wonderful propaganda for the Allied cause!" he exclaimed. "What a wave of sympathy for the British and hatred for the Germans comes out of this film! Surely this isn't merely a work of art; it is also excellent propaganda." A few nights later they saw a new German film, which Goebbels disliked intensely. "What idiots!" he shouted. "We Germans seem to be people without any subtlety at all. We just don't know anything about intimate effects. Can't they do anything but shout? It's enough to drive you to despair!"

Goebbels would talk on till midnight, using those with him as a sounding board for his monologues. Then he would shake everyone by the hand. Often he would take books and gramophone records up to bed with him in case he could not sleep.

During the intense bombing-raids on Berlin, Goebbels remained very cool. He exasperated his valet, Emil, because of the inordinate time he would take to dress before descending to the air-raid shelter, which was luxurious and fully equipped as an office—it had been built at a cost estimated at 350,000 marks in March 1943. He prepared himself for this enforced public appearance just as meticulously as he dressed each morning. In any case, he was always ready during the raids to drive to the Central Air-Raid Post in order to receive the latest news and supervise the work of fire-fighting and rescue. The Minister was, after all, also Gauleiter of Berlin.[38]

When Goebbels travelled, as he frequently did either to speak in one of the main cities, to visit the badly bombed areas or confer with Hitler at his military headquarters, he would go either by car or train. He would work in his office up to the last minute, the staff cars standing ready. The journey to the Anhalter Bahnhof took three minutes exactly; the Minister entered the Mercedes, therefore, five minutes before any train he was taking was due to depart. Together with his staff he would march along the platform towards his special Pullman coach, which had been attached to the train. With a minute to spare he was on board, acknowledging in transit the Hitler salutes with which the station officials stood ready to greet him. The moment he had taken his place on the train, official work was resumed where it had been left off. Ochs, his Ministry batman, was there in charge of his luggage; Otte, his chief secretary, supervised his dictation. The Pullman had sleeping accommodation and a kitchenette, and the main compartment was well appointed in mahogany, with standard lamps dispersed over the carpeted floors. On arrival at any main station the coach would be connected instantly with the local Post Office telephone network. Von Oven remembers one such journey as this to Dresden, where Goebbels was due to meet his wife at the station because she was in the city taking a cure at a sanatorium. While Goebbels was greeting his wife and presenting her with a bunch of roses accompanied by a kiss on her mouth, the Post Office officials were busily engaged connecting up the Pullman telephones. Magda had dressed all in white in readiness for this public presentation of white roses from her loving husband.

1943 was a year of disappointment for Goebbels in his political ambitions, as we have seen from the evidence of his diary. This is confirmed throughout by Semmler's independent testimony. On 4th January at a conference of the Ministry's departmental heads he lectured them on the need for a total mobilisation of the nation's resources and manpower in order to prevent Germany losing the war, particularly on the Eastern front. Germany, he said, was still not making her maximum effort. Two weeks later he received a bitter blow when Hitler appointed a Committee of Three consisting of Lammers, Bormann and Keitel to carry out what Goebbels claimed were his own plans to put Germany on a total war basis. Goebbels found himself relegated to the position of adviser only to this executive group, every member of which he despised and disliked; their debates, he said at home, were like a Punch-and-Judy show on the very eve of the fall of Stalingrad.[39]

Goebbels' only answer to this was to issue a total war challenge of his own in a great speech—one of the outstanding pieces of oratory in his career—that he made on 13th February in the Sportpalast. With Stalingrad fresh in his heart, Hitler had refused to speak. Goebbels decided to use a new technique of shouting challenging and rhetorical questions at his vast audience in order to rouse them to roar back at him the replies he needed to show Hitler their determination to wage a total war.

He prepared the speech in a state of nervous anxiety, working with his secretaries on draft after draft until four o'clock in the morning of 13th February. The speech was designed to work the audience of twenty thousand into such a state of mass enthusiasm that when the time came to put the questions there could be no answer but "*Ja!*" from the mass of faces below him. Goebbels rehearsed every phrase, every significant gesture. He used a mirror for these rehearsals. Once before his audience his self-assurance was complete; he marked this speech by a new style in his delivery, abandoning his usual elegance for a grim urgency of utterance. He built up the threat of Bolshevism. He made it plain that Germany alone could save the civilisation of the world. Illusion was a thing of the past. "Total war is the command of the hour." Gradually he worked his audience up until their shouting became a feature of the performance. Then, and only then, he reached the point of challenge. He asked them, as representing the whole of Germany, to give their answers, yes or no, whether they were ready to make the great sacrifices necessary to bring about a lasting victory. Any eyewitness to the effect of this challenge on the audience described the result as a turmoil of enthusiasm, and the shouting rose like a hurricane. Taking his time, Goebbels expounded his ten questions, and demanded an unflinching "*Ja*" or "*Nein*" from his audience. He challenged them to affirm their belief in the Führer and in victory, their desire to continue the war with "wild determination" and to work when necessary sixteen hours a day to supply the means to defeat Bolshevism. Then he demanded their approval that women should give their whole strength to the war and that death should be the penalty for shirkers and racketeers. The whole German people must declare their willingness to shoulder equally the burdens of war. As question followed question from the booming loud-speakers the concourse resounded with the echoing roars of "*Ja!*"

After his triumph Goebbels was carried shoulder-high from the hall. He weighed himself that night, as he always did after any major exertion in public speaking, and he claimed that he had lost seven pounds.[40] But all this effort availed him nothing. Hitler did not give him the control of the measures for total war that he coveted.

And so he turned to the substitute for power, publicity. He prepared the public to accept him as a leader, if Hitler would not. He worked hard at his articles for *Das Reich* and at his broadcasts, and he saw to it that his name was prominent in the daily news. He spoke frequently at public meetings in Berlin and elsewhere, taking full advantage of the silence of the other Nazi leaders. He also, as we have seen, popularised himself by his frequent visits to badly bombed areas, as Semmler describes:

Yesterday I was in Cologne with Goebbels. I saw a heavily bombed city for the first time. Goebbels was very shaken and wants Hitler to visit the city as soon as possible. It is surprising that Goebbels was everywhere cordially greeted in the streets. He talked to people in the Rhineland dialect. One sees even in Cologne that, at the moment, he is the most popular of the nation's leaders. These suffering men and women feel that at least one of them is interested in their fate.[41]

His aim, according to Semmler, was to build himself up in the public esteem as the second man in Germany after Hitler. This substitute for real executive power would, he felt, stand him in very good stead when he eventually was able to persuade Hitler to give him the controls he sought.

Nevertheless, in one of those rare revealing moments in which Goebbels was prepared to face openly the truth about himself in front of others, he admitted to Semmler that this new popularity of his had been by no means inevitable and had had to be re-made from nothing.

Nothing, added Goebbels, is harder than to recapture lost popularity. He himself had learnt a bitter lesson. Only after four years of the most strenuous work had he won back some of the confidence and respect he had forfeited in 1938. Now he felt convinced that his star was in the ascendant again.[42]

It was evident from the date that he must have been referring to the public scandal over his affair with Lida Baarova which had nearly cost him his career.

That he had not lost his amorous touch even in these adverse times is revealed by this charming story told by Semmler. It happened in June.

Last night there was a rather delicate incident at Lanke, the Minister's country residence. For the last two days Goebbels has been living in a little block-house in the middle of the forest, about half a mile from the main house. He wishes to rest alone and see no one. No one is allowed to disturb him. Only the telephone connects him to the outside world. A servant brings his meals in a car and returns immediately to the house. Frau Goebbels is staying at the White Hart in Dresden taking the cure, and the children are at home on Schwanenwerder.

Generally visitors are notified beforehand to the sentries so that they may pass the barrier without difficulty. Yesterday, about 11 o'clock in the evening, the sentry noticed a strange woman cyclist on one of the paths within the property. It was a young and beautiful girl. The sentry stopped her. She refused to give her name or her reason for being on Goebbels' property. The sentry, evidently a perfect ladies' man, therefore escorted her through the darkness of the forest. He intended to take her to the guard or to the adjutant.

After he had gone a few steps he noticed about twenty yards ahead, between the pine trees, another dark figure. The sentry, his automatic ready in his hand, challenged this suspicious figure and ordered him to halt. The next moment he was horrified to recognise, from the oaths and abuse which the strange figure flung at him, that it was none other than Goebbels himself. The case of the woman cyclist was cleared up at once. From the rather confused excuses which Goebbels offered to the young woman, the sentry realised that Goebbels himself had been waiting for her. The sentry was quickly dismissed and the couple made their way no less quickly towards the block-house close by.

Goebbels had made an evening rendezvous with the young film actress. To avoid all gossip, his scandal-loving household and even his confidential staff were supposed to know nothing of the visit. That was why she had not been brought by car but had come by a forest path, known only to trusted visitors, and the only one not barred by an iron gate.[43]

Parallel with Goebbels' campaign of personal popularisation were his constant feuds with the other leaders, in particular with Ribbentrop, whose inept handling of the Foreign Ministry appalled him, and Göring, with whom, as we have seen, he tried for a while to come to terms in order to use his influence to help defeat the clique led by Bormann which surrounded Hitler. On 31st March 1943, Heroes' Day, he was very angry about "his low place in the seats allotted to the members of the Government". By April his plans to form a radical group to defeat this clique were sufficiently advanced to be explained at a conference with Naumann, who passed the information on to the others in the Ministry, including Semmler. The scheme did not succeed, at least in the sense that it won no increase in power for Goebbels and eventually he found it necessary to come to terms with Bormann, the "primitive Ogpu type" as he called him.[44] By the end of the year, when Berlin was about to experience the full weight of the bombing, he had become deeply depressed, nervous, and even, according to Semmler, defeatist.

The last few weeks he has struck me as falling into a mood of real defeatism. How else can one explain what he said today in front of his wife: "If all our efforts, work and struggle should lead nowhere, then I would not find it hard to die. For in a world where there was no room for my ideals there would be no room for me either."[45]

On another occasion, when dining with his former Under-Secretary of State, Leopold Gutterer, he went so far as to admit that he considered it unlikely for the Reich to be maintained even within its pre-war frontiers.[46]

Again Semmler noticed Goebbels' need for perpetual activity.

This bundle of nerves cannot live without worries, excitement and a quickened pulse. The prospect of the next day's work with its deadly certainty of more disappointments and vexations does not worry him. On the contrary, he says how pleased he will be to have things happening round him again: conferences, telegrams, visitors, telephone conversations, papers, instructions, quick results, and then back to anxiety and worries.

Sometimes there seems to me something sinister about his perpetual restlessness.[47]

When the raids came, Goebbels behaved with exemplary courage. On the night of 21st November, when the first raid on Berlin took place, Goebbels was speaking in a suburb when the bombers arrived. In the height of the raid he and Semmler drove back to Berlin's Air-Raid Centre in the Wilhelmplatz. There Goebbels stood chain-smoking, watching the reports come in until "he nearly loses control of himself" at the magnitude of the damage.

Goebbels considered himself personally responsible for maintaining a high level of morale in Berlin during these terrible nights and days. The Luftwaffe did nothing to help him. By Christmas his nerves were in pieces. He quarrelled bitterly with Magda and the household staff at Lanke on Christmas Eve merely because a Christmas tree had been put up in front of the cinema-screen on which he wanted to have an American film projected. He lost all control of himself, ordered his car and withdrew to spend Christmas entirely alone reading Schopen-hauer at Schwanenwerder. Magda was left to explain his absence to the children as best she could. He was working, of course. By January Goebbels was fuming again because the authorities of the devastated city of Berlin had come to him for advice about what they ought to give Göring for his birthday; the previous year he had extorted from them a quarter of a million marks for a Van Dyck. Goebbels did not recover from this all day!

Semmler also provides a gloss on certain events in which Goebbels was involved, in particular his part in frustrating the July Plot. For example, he reveals that Bormann attempted to prevent Hitler from receiving a forty-page memorandum Goebbels had drawn up in April in which he urged that victory was no longer possible on both the Eastern and the Western Fronts, and that peace negotiations should be initiated with Stalin since it seemed impossible to expect any success in attempting to discuss peace with Churchill and Roosevelt. The memorandum went into considerable detail as to the kind of terms that might be achieved with Stalin, and then ended with a broad hint that, since Ribbentrop had failed so signally at the Foreign Office, he would himself be prepared to take over that Ministry and with it the burden of the negotiations. Bormann utterly opposed the plan, and left the memorandum on his desk without passing it to Hitler. It was almost three weeks before Goebbels, in an agony of suspense, found this out, and at the same time discovered afresh how strong was Bormann's influence with Hitler. The memorandum was filed without further mention by Hitler, and Goebbels had to wait until after 20th July to get from the Führer certain of the powers he sought. He continued to associate himself with men such as Speer, Funk and Ley, all of whom acknowledged his authority and accepted his radical plans to reform Germany's war policy under Hitler. They met regularly on Wednesday evenings at Goebbels' house for discussion. Goebbels' personal attitude to the Führer at this time is described as follows by Semmler:

Whenever Goebbels goes to headquarters he starts off full of distrust of the Führer's genius, full of irritation, criticism and hard words. Each time he is determined to tell Hitler just what he thinks. What happens in their talks I don't know, but every time that Goebbels returns from these visits he is full of admiration for the Führer and exudes an optimism which infects us all.[48]

On 5th June, the eve of D-Day, Semmler and Naumann were with Goebbels who had been summoned by Hitler to meet him in Berchtesgaden. Goebbels had had hopes that Hitler would want to discuss the memorandum on Russia, but they were in conference about other matters until the small hours of 6th June. It was Semmler who had to wake Goebbels with the news of the Allied landings in Normandy.

At five minutes past four I suddenly receive the first reports of Allied landing operations on the Channel coast. There is no doubt the invasion has begun. I at once ring Goebbels and tell him the sensational news in a few headlines. I can almost see him, through the telephone, jumping out of bed; then after a few seconds the voice comes over: "Thank God, at last. This is the final round."[49]

On the way back to Berlin Goebbels told Semmler that the Führer was still very optimistic about ultimate victory. Three nights later the Minister gave a party and seemed unusually excited. "Goebbels finds it very hard to keep a secret," writes Semmler. He told them that Hitler's secret weapon was about to be used against Britain, so fulfilling at long last Goebbels' propaganda promises to the German people. It was he who chose the term V-1 for this weapon of Vengeance (*Vergeltung*) because the numeral would suggest that there were other, more crushing weapons of this new kind in active preparation. The first flying-bomb was launched against London on 15th June. Goebbels was very angry that this was done quite arbitrarily by the military authorities without notifying him in advance so that he could have given this tremendous event the full propaganda treatment.

Five weeks later, on 20th July, Goebbels was in Berlin when Hitler held a staff conference in a wooden guest-house at Rastenburg, his headquarters in East Prussia.[50] The meeting would normally have been held in the concrete bunker, had it not been under repair. This simple change of place altered the history of the war, by permitting Hitler to survive and so prolong the fighting for a further nine months.

Count von Stauffenberg, a colonel and Chief of Staff in the Home Forces, flew from Berlin to join the conference and carried with him a time-bomb in a brief-case which he left carefully placed under the wooden conference table before excusing himself to put through an urgent phone call to Berlin. He waited for a minute or two at some distance from the guest-house and heard the explosion; in the panic that followed he managed to leave Rastenburg by plane for Berlin. Before he left, he put a priority call through to the War Office with the news of Hitler's death. This set into motion the network of conspiracy which had long been planned and organised by a number of dissident generals, whose aim was to assume government of Germany in the name of the Army. In Berlin it was at once assumed that another associate in the plot in Rastenburg, General Fellgiebel, would have carried out his assignment which was to destroy the means of communication at Hitler's headquarters. Accordingly, the conspirators gave the order for the next stage in their plan, the occupation of Berlin. As part of the fulfilment of this, Major Remer was ordered to bring in the Berlin Guards Battalion to occupy the area of the Government offices, including the Ministry of Propaganda. Among the instructions given to Major Remer was responsibility for the arrest of Goebbels.

But Hitler was not dead, nor were his means of communication with Berlin destroyed. He had staggered out from the shattered guest-house dazed, shocked and bruised, his trousers torn, his eardrums pierced, his right arm partially paralysed. He thought there had been an air-raid. He was calm, and momentarily worried about his trousers, which were new. But while Stauffenberg was carrying the news of his certain death to Berlin, Hitler, still suffering from shock, was excitedly explaining to Mussolini, who had arrived at Rastenburg on a visit, just what it was thought had happened. He did not hesitate to point out the miraculous nature of his escape. This he took to be one more sign from Providence that he was intended to succeed in his plan to control Europe. Mussolini agreed it was a sign from Heaven itself. They then retired to have tea; then Hitler's nerves gave way and he raged uncontrollably for half an hour, shouting for vengeance on all those who opposed him as a man of destiny protected by Providence. Meanwhile throughout the afternoon the undestroyed telephones at Rastenburg had been busily connected to Berlin countering all rumours of Hitler's death and cancelling any orders which were not authorised by either Keitel or Himmler, who was in charge of security on the home front. The conspirators learned too late that their plot was abortive.

Meanwhile Major Remer's men, among others, were taking up the positions allotted to them in Berlin. The story of what happened then has been told in some detail by Rudolf Semmler.

Semmler had noticed how abnormally pale and nervous Goebbels had been at lunch, which was served as usual at two o'clock in his official house in the Hermann Göring Strasse. At that time, as he revealed later, Goebbels had news only of the explosion, followed after an agonising period by the bare fact that Hitler had narrowly escaped death. With this on his mind, Goebbels waited anxiously at home for further details. Semmler had gone off duty after lunch, catching his train home without difficulty since he avoided by an hour or so the arrival of Major Remer and the Guards to seal off the Government area.

Lieutenant Hagen, a convinced National Socialist and a junior officer attached to the Berlin Guards Regiment, first heard the rumour of Hitler's death around four o'clock together with the fact that the Guards Regiment was to occupy the Government quarter. He was ultimately the man responsible for warning Goebbels that suspicious activities were taking place. Although a lieutenant in the Army, he was also a scholar and a music critic serving on Goebbels' own journal, *Das Reich*. He was on friendly terms with Goebbels and also with Major Remer, and he was a keen Nazi. At first he accepted the preparation of the conspirators at the Ministry of War in good faith. The code-word for the operation was Valkyrie, and as far as the junior officers were concerned its purpose was to mobilise against a threatened rebellion by the million foreign slave-workers stationed in the district of Berlin. Both Remer and Hagen found these preparations unaccountable because the slave-labour appeared quite docile. Their suspicions were finally roused when they saw, on the morning of 20th July, Field-Marshal von Brauchitsch, who was supposed to be living in retirement after being dismissed by Hitler, drive to the War Office in full uniform. Hagen now admits that he had *ein ungutes Gefühl*, a queer feeling, and when later in the day the order came through for Valkyrie to be put in operation, Remer ordered him to go to Goebbels and make official inquiries, since he was the only senior minister present in Berlin that afternoon as well as being

Gauleiter and Plenipotentiary for Total War. The order they had received indicated that an attempt had been made on Hitler's life, and the result of the attempt was still in doubt. The Army, the order went on, had to assume full powers, and the Wach Regiment was to occupy the Government district and immobilise everyone, including ministers and generals.

Hagen went to Goebbels' house forthwith; there he was detained for a few minutes by the officer on duty in Goebbels' ante-room, another friend of his, on account of there being a 'Führerblitz' on (that is, a top priority phone call to Hitler's headquarters). Finally he was taken straight in to the Minister. Goebbels seemed quite calm.

"Well, Dr. Hagen, what can I do for you?" he said.

Hagen explained the terms of the order for putting Valkyrie into operation.

Goebbels interrupted him at the point when the outcome of the attempt on Hitler's life was described as still uncertain.

"This is nonsense," he said. "The Führer is alive. I was speaking to him only two minutes ago. There has been an attempt on his life, but by a miracle he escaped. The orders make no sense at all."

Hagen looked out of the window and then turned back to Goebbels.

"Herr Minister," he said, "at this moment a section of my regiment is going into action. I suggest we send at once for my Commander."

Goebbels remained calm, and sat at his desk making notes of their conversation. He then put a priority call through to the Commander of the Leibstandarte Adolf Hitler, which was Hitler's own bodyguard stationed at Lichterfelde, a suburb a few miles from the Government district. In his capacity as Gauleiter he ordered the Commander to mobilise his men and stand by for orders coming only from himself personally. He invited Hagen to listen in to his conversation with the Commander through an extension to his telephone. When he had replaced the receiver, Goebbels turned to Hagen.

"As you have heard, I have mobilised the L.A.H.," he said, "but not called them out. I want to avoid as far as possible any danger of the Army and the S.S. facing one another in arms. Now go and ask your Commander to come and see me."

At the door he gripped Hagen by the arm.

"Is Remer a safe man?" he asked.

"Herr Minister, I could vouch for him with my life."

"Very well, then," continued Goebbels. "Go and fetch him and tell him if he is not here inside twenty minutes I'll put the L.A.H. into action, since I shall by then assume he is being held at the War Office by force."

For the moment Goebbels did not know what immediate action to take. He was told that an officer and three men had come with orders to arrest him from the Commandant of the Berlin Garrison. He opened the drawer of his desk, took out a revolver that he kept there, and ordered their admission. At the same time he saw to it that the door of his room leading to the office of his adjutant was left open so that whatever was said could be overheard.[51]

When the lieutenant arrived, he found Goebbels in a formidable mood. The Minister shouted at him that he was obeying the orders of traitors, and that the Führer was alive. The lieutenant, abashed at this news, withdrew. Hagen meanwhile had reported his conversation with Goebbels to Major Remer, who at once went himself to Goebbels' residence. He declared that he realised now his orders had come from traitors and that he unreservedly placed himself at Goebbels' disposal. He removed the cordon from the Government quarter and assembled his unit of five hundred men in the garden of Goebbels' house. Goebbels then went down and harangued them for ten minutes on the importance of loyalty at such a time as this until he was interrupted by a message that telephone communication had at last been restored with Rastenburg. Goebbels returned to the telephone, taking Remer with him. The Major then had the honour of speaking to the Führer in person. Hitler ordered him to take what action was necessary to maintain security, commended him for his loyalty and promoted him Colonel on the spot. Remer then left with his men to arrest the leaders of the conspiracy at the Ministry of War in the Bendlerstrasse and to secure the Radio Centre from their interference. Stauffenberg, incriminated initially by his priority phone call from Rastenburg to Berlin, was among those who were the first to be shot by the lights of an armoured car beamed across the Ministry courtyard.

Goebbels immediately took control. He turned his house into what

Semmler described as "a prison, headquarters and court rolled into one". He was joined about eight o'clock by Himmler, who was fresh from Rastenburg, and a commission of investigation was set up forthwith under the chairmanship of Goebbels. One by one, the generals and others (among them Fromm, Witzleben, Hase and the Berlin Police President, Count Helldorf) were cross-examined by Himmler and Goebbels throughout the night. As more was learnt, orders for further arrests were made and executed. It was apparent by now that the roots of the conspiracy were widespread throughout the country, involving men in both military and civilian life.

At about twenty minutes to one on the morning of 21st July Hitler broadcast to Germany. He did not take the advice of Goebbels before doing so, and the result was bad. He sounded shaken and nervous to the point of panic; his delivery was broken and ragged, his voice rough and frequently unclear. He fulminated against the traitors and demanded the loyalty of Germany. Once more he spoke of a high intervention. "I regard this," he said, "as a confirmation of the task imposed upon me by Providence."

Goebbels was alarmed. He felt such a speech by the Führer in such a manner at this time was disastrous. He himself did not broadcast until 26th July, when he gave a long and carefully contrived description of the plot and of the manner in which it had been quashed. He had spent the ensuing days at Rastenburg continuing his investigations and conferring with Hitler.

There, according to Semmler, who accompanied Goebbels to Rastenburg, he found Hitler "very unwell", although he believed the mental effects upon him were worse than the physical. The Führer had mental black-outs; his hearing was impaired and he seemed to find difficulty in following a conversation. He had only one thought in mind, vengeance on the men who had betrayed him and their dependents. It was the Night of the Long Knives over again. All those who had in the smallest degree revealed a seed of revolt in their hearts waited for the arrival of the armed men to take them away. The number of victims who were either executed, imprisoned or sent to concentration camps during the following weeks and months is unknown. A list of some five thousand names of men executed was eventually drawn up, but thousands of others disappeared into confinement. Later Hitler was broken-hearted to find that even his favourite Rommel was involved in the Paris branch of the conspiracy; but, as we have seen, he was persuaded to commit suicide so that a propaganda funeral might be conferred upon him with the correct form of oration.

The leading generals involved were put to death by a process of slow strangulation. Goebbels arranged for the trial and executions to be filmed in relentless detail so that Hitler might be able to follow the gruesome events night by night on the screen. The generals were clothed in ill-fitting civilian suits with their trousers unbraced so that they experienced the greatest humiliation possible during their appearance in court. The endless lengths of film were, under Hitler's orders, edited to make a record several hours in length which Goebbels was finally persuaded not to show in public because its exhibition would have revealed only too clearly the Führer's pathological desire for a prolonged revenge. The condemned men were hanged alive on butchers' hooks and slowly strangled to death.

Meanwhile, in Rastenburg two days after the attempt, Goebbels took every advantage of Hitler's weakened condition. Now was his chance to urge the needs of total war and increased power for himself. A new army of a million men was necessary. He was prepared to take responsibility for raising this army and tightening the belt of Germany as well. Hitler agreed, and Goebbels returned in triumph to Berlin.

In his lengthy broadcast to the German people on 26th July giving an official account of the plot and combining this with the announcement of the measures for total war, Goebbels said:

Yesterday the Führer issued an order, published in the press today, that the whole apparatus of the State, including the Reich Railways and the Reich Post, all public institutions, organisations and concerns, are to be examined with a view to freeing the largest number of men for the armament industry and the Armed Forces through an even more rational employment of those serving in the aforementioned concerns, by cutting out or decreasing tasks which are less important to the war effort and by a simplification of organisation and procedure. Also, according to this order, the whole of public life must be adapted in every respect to the requirements of total war. All public activities are to conform with the objects of total war and in particular must not take anybody from the Armed Forces and the armament industry; in a word, total war thus becomes a practical reality. The comprehensive tasks connected with this gigantic reorganisation will be put into the hands of a Reich Trustee for Total War, who, so that he can carry out his task, will be entrusted by the Führer with comprehensive powers. At the request of the Reich Marshal, the Führer has entrusted this task to me and has appointed me Reich Trustee for Total War.[52]

In the train returning from Rastenburg to Berlin Goebbels said to Semmler:

If I had received these powers when I wanted them so badly, victory would be in our pockets today, and the war would probably be over. But it takes a bomb under his arse to make Hitler see reason.[53]

CHAPTER EIGHT

The Last Months

AT THE BEGINNING of the winter of 1944 France was lost to Germany, and in the West the Allied armies were at the German frontiers. In the South the Allies were pressing up towards Germany in the valley of the Po, while in the East the Russians had reached the Vistula. There seemed now to be an ominous pause on all fronts while the forces took breath for the final onslaught. This breathing space lasted longer than most people on either side thought possible.

Total war meant total mobilisation, and of this Goebbels had announced the details on 24th August. Women up to fifty were conscripted for labour to release more men fit for the Army. A sixty-hour week was introduced for the war industries. All men without disabilities between the ages of sixteen and sixty were ordered to serve in the *Volkssturm* or Home Guard under Himmler and Bormann. Children of fourteen were used to man the anti-aircraft guns. The untiring energy of Goebbels on the human front and Speer on the industrial front seemed to be giving Germany a completely new lease of life as the winds of autumn blew the leaves from the trees and the last fearful winter of the war began.

The restrictions that Goebbels was now at liberty to impose by decree on Germany were drastic. Travelling was virtually forbidden, theatres were closed, periodicals suspended, newspapers merged and simplified. Every action possible was taken to prevent the spread of despondency—even the organised beating-up of malcontents. All Germany was poised and ready to win the war.

The pause on all principal war-fronts lasted until December. Only in the Balkan area was there spectacular activity, with Rumania capitulating in August, Bulgaria in September, Greece and Yugoslavia in October. Hungary managed to hold out till the following year. Hitler, who had been confined to his bed during the autumn in a serious state of collapse, had meanwhile recovered sufficiently to plan an offensive in the West, which was intended to be a surprise attack in the Ardennes with the occupation of Antwerp as the ultimate objective. On this Hitler staked many of his new divisions. Effective when it was first launched in December, by January it had proved to be a failure. With his forces spread round the huge circle of Europe from the Baltic States to the North-Western Front, there was little hope of victory for Germany except in the deluded mind of Hitler and the aggressive propaganda of Goebbels, which began in the last remaining months to celebrate the self-destruction of Germany in the face of her enemies.

Hitler gave up his military headquarters in Rastenburg, East Prussia, and moved back to his bomb-scarred Chancellery; it was here that the Bunker, the deep air-raid shelter below ground, which was to be Hitler's last place of residence, had been built in the garden. Several of those who attended on Hitler, from generals to secretaries, have testified to his state of mind and body at this time. His rages alternated with bouts of self-pity; he felt deserted and betrayed by the very men whose lives and welfare he had sacrificed on the battlefronts. He seemed half-paralysed and senile in his movements. His head quivered. His eyes, according to Gerhard Boldt, an officer who met him for the first time in February 1945, had "an indescribable flickering glow . . . creating a fearsome and wholly unnatural effect". Nevertheless he retained his "queerly penetrating look".[1] No plea to withdraw and re-group his forces availed; no appeal to preserve Germany for the future welfare of her citizens. To Speer he said six weeks before the end: "If the war is to be lost, the nation also will perish." He believed that Germany had failed and must go down before the invading hordes of Russia. He thought only of destruction—the scorching of the earth, the mining of factories, bridges and railways, the death of people too weak to deserve to live. He refused to hear the bad news from the battlefronts as his enemies closed in on Germany and the Russians drew nearer to Berlin. When Goebbels sent him an album of photographs showing air-raid damage, Bormann sent them back with a note saying "the Führer did not wish to be worried with such irrelevant matters".[2]

For Hitler, war had been an affair of maps and paper, away from the blood and turmoil. Rastenburg had been a setting of lawns, lakes and woods, a landscape, as Boldt puts it, that "had nothing in common with the horrors of the war". He saw neither photographs nor films from the front line; nothing must interfere with "the decisive power of his genius".[3]

Mad and mentally isolated, Hitler shut himself in the Chancellery and finally in his Bunker listening to the advice of no one, poring over his maps and issuing impossible orders, often to non-existent divisions of the German Army. Had Hitler ever possessed a spark of human greatness to match his genius for power this could have been a tragic spectacle. As it was he struck terror into those who still tried to serve him or who were unable to bring themselves to break their oaths of loyalty. Among all the leaders in Hitler's hierarchy, only Goebbels and Bormann, the bitter rivals for his favour, kept their loyalty unimpaired to the end. Ribbentrop, though still Foreign Minister, had become a nonentity. For the rest, Göring and Himmler each wavered until it was too late in a common uncertainty as to whether they should displace Hitler and sue for peace, while Speer had the great courage to flout his master's orders for the destruction of Germany's industrial resources and keep what he could intact for the moment when capitulation would at last bring peace. He even planned to introduce poison gas into the ventilation system of the Bunker, but it proved impossible. But while Hitler lived no one replaced him, and the war went on. In January the Russians crossed Poland and reached the Oder and Silesia; in February they threatened Berlin and Vienna; in March the British and Americans crossed the Rhine; in April the Elbe was reached by both the Americans and the Russians and the war was all but over. In the same month the Russians overran East Prussia and captured Vienna. Berlin lay open before them.

Hitler had by now lost all control of events and scarcely knew what was happening. Maddened by the collapse of his destiny, he point-blank refused at a conference held on 20th April, his fifty-sixth birthday, to follow the rest of the administration in its evacuation south. Instead he set up his last headquarters in the Bunker and stayed there below ground until his death. On 22nd April he was joined by Goebbels, his wife and their six small children.

It is difficult to judge how far Goebbels retained an absolute belief in Hitler to the end. The evidence in his war-time diaries and in the observations of Semmler is in favour of his final disbelief in Hitler's miracles. But if love may admit of calculation, there can be little doubt that Goebbels loved Hitler, even while he made use of him to build up the final Nazi legend. Semmler always testifies to Goebbels' single-minded devotion to the Führer, even though he was often openly critical of the decisions Hitler took under the influence, as he thought, of men Goebbels despised and hated. And affection seemed to be characteristic of Hitler's own attitude to Goebbels towards the end. During a party at Lanke on Goebbels' birthday, 28th October, Hitler took the trouble to telephone to give him his personal greetings and then asked if he might speak to his wife. Frau Goebbels came back from the conversation with tears in her eyes; Hitler had promised her a great military victory for Christmas. He was, of course, referring to the offensive he was planning on the Western front. Semmler observed that the whole party took heart from this as they were convinced that Hitler had some great surprise up his sleeve.[4] Goebbels even allowed his mother to come to Berlin shortly before Christmas, largely because his sister, Maria Kimmich, who was also living in Berlin at the time, was expecting a baby in the New Year.[5]

The last occasion on which Maria and her husband saw Goebbels was at Christmas, 1944. They remember it as a purely family gathering out at Lanke. Maria and Magda talked together a great deal. Magda told her sister-in-law that Joseph had seen certain new weapons so fantastic that they would certainly bring about the victory by miracle that Hitler had promised Germany through her husband's propaganda. Though Maria was never to see her brother again, she had further meetings with Magda after the birth of her child.

On the following 12th January a notable social event took place and was recorded as follows by Semmler:

Today Hitler was a guest in the Goebbels' house for the first time in five years. Frau Goebbels had invited him to tea. The children received him in the hall with bunches of flowers in their hands.

At 4.30 Hitler's car arrived. Goebbels stood to attention with his arm stretched out as far as it would go. The children made their little curtsies and Hitler said how surprised he was at the way they had grown. He presented Frau Goebbels with a modest bunch of lily-of-the-valley, and explained that it was the best that could be found, as Doctor Goebbels had closed all the flower shops in Berlin!

Then Goebbels introduced colleagues who happened to be there. For the first time I shook hands with Hitler. With the Führer were an adjutant, the servant, and six S.S. officers of the personal bodyguard.

The servant was carrying Hitler's brief-case, which bore a large white F on it. From the pocket of the case a thermos flask could be seen sticking out. I realised that Hitler had brought his own tea and cakes.

Tea lasted an hour and a half. We were not allowed to be present. Only the Goebbels family, Hitler, his adjutant and Dr. Naumann sat together in the central drawing-room. In the evening I heard from Frau Goebbels that Hitler had enjoyed the family atmosphere very much. He was glad to have left his monastic life for half an afternoon and promised to come again soon.

Half the conversation had been made by Hitler, who described his building plans for Berlin and memories of 1932.

At supper Goebbels and his wife were both very proud of the visit. "He wouldn't have gone to the Görings," said Frau Goebbels.[6]

Naumann remembers this occasion well. There was a bustle of excitement after the telephone call had come through from the Chancellery to announce that the Führer was coming to tea. The notice was short, just like it used to be in older, happier days. Once he had arrived, Hitler was more serious and taciturn than had been his habit in the past on such occasions. The conversation at one point turned to Gerhart Hauptmann who at the age of eighty had been forced to leave his home in Silesia before the invading armies.

Goebbels worked ceaselessly during the last winter of the war, though he was subject to occasional fits of acute depression, when he shut himself away at Lanke. There he read history—he himself mentioned, in an article called 'History as Teacher', returning yet again for comfort to the letters and essays of Frederick the Great and to the account of the second Punic War in Mommsen's Roman History. He raged at any of his staff whose attitude implied defeat, and he constantly visited the battlefront to give talks to officers and propaganda workers on morale and the great future that awaited a victorious Germany. Yet as early as October 1944 he drew Winckler aside after lunch at Lanke on his birthday and took him for a walk on the estate during which he discussed the problem of how he could make suitable financial arrangements for his children in the event of his death. In November Ministry documents were already being systematically pulped to prevent them falling into enemy hands, but it was not until February that Goebbels finally decided to instruct his brother Hans, who was ill in a sanatorium in the Rhineland, to destroy all the family papers, including many of the original manuscripts and diaries of his youth. This Hans failed to do.[7]

Goebbels revealed his moods of despair in remarks which, if they had been said in his presence by subordinates, would have led to the fiercest reprimands, as he reproved Semmler for reporting to him the bad morale of the people in South Germany: "The veins were swelling in his forehead and his nostrils were twitching."[8] At one staff conference he said: "Let's make this perfectly clear. We have nothing left. There are no miracle weapons."[9] On another occasion when he was receiving a report from an Army liaison officer on the Ardennes offensive, he suddenly said to him in front of members of his staff: "There you sit and prattle about all sorts of trifles while someone like myself is wondering whether the time has come to poison his wife and children."[10] But to Semmler and Fritzsche he continued to talk about his day-dream of retiring from politics after the war and becoming a professional writer. To Fritzsche he once said: "After the war I'll go to America. There at least they will appreciate a propaganda genius, and will pay him accordingly!"[11] Up to the very last he was working on the proofs of a book in which some of his more recent articles were collected.[12]

Goebbels arranged for his official diaries to be microfilmed in case the original typescripts were destroyed, as indeed they almost entirely were. These microfilm records, which took many weeks to complete, both day and night shifts of technicians ceaselessly photographing the endless pages of script and type, were eventually stored by Naumann in a safe which he has every reason to believe came into the possession of the Russians. This means that there is some possibility that the millions of words written and dictated by Goebbels during the greater part of his career are in fact preserved.[13]

A hypochondriac, he feared he had cancer, when all that was wrong with him were his duodenal ulcers. He was also the victim of nervous superstition. "Goebbels is very superstitious," wrote Semmler. "The more obscure the situation and the gloomier the future, the more this is apparent." He claimed to Semmler that his mother once had second sight, until a Jesuit father had "freed her of the obsession". Semmler continues:

Goebbels too had had similar experiences. When he was a student at Würzburg his grandmother had appeared to him a week after her death. Another time he had seen his brother in the room, although at the time he was a prisoner in a French camp.[14]

Semmler himself witnessed Goebbels' fears when he accidentally knocked Hitler's autographed portrait from the Minister's desk. A piece of the broken glass transfixed the image of the Führer's left eye. "The whole evening Goebbels remained upset by this occurrence." In 1944 he even went so far as to try to trace a fortune-teller who had in 1923 successfully foretold Hitler's rise to power, so that she might prophesy the outcome of the war, but his agents failed to find her after twenty years had passed.

Goebbels by now was poverty-stricken as a propagandist, whatever he might be as a man of action. He became the prophet of doom, calling on the German people to resist to the death and to destroy everything they possessed that could be of use to the advancing enemy. His attempt at using atrocity propaganda backed by photographs of women and children tortured by the Russians only led to a refugee problem. The roads were blocked by Germans preferring to be over-taken by the Allies in the West rather than the East. A strange new facet to Goebbels' deep-rooted radicalism emerged from the final tumult of press and radio. Death was the leveller through the agency of the bombs:

Together with the monuments of culture there assemble also the last obstacles to the fulfilment of our revolutionary task. Now that every-thing is in ruins, we are forced to rebuild Europe. In the past, private possessions led us to a bourgeois restraint. Now the bombs, instead of killing all Europeans, have only smashed the prison walls which held them captive. . . . In trying to destroy Europe's future, the enemy has only succeeded in smashing its past; and with that, everything old and outworn has gone.[15]

For Goebbels all this destruction of the symbols of the past was turned into a symbol of some vague future in which the phoenix of a new Germany would emerge from the ashes and the rubble to flout the greedy capitalists of the West and the Communist barbarians of the East. Leave nothing for them to take. he urged. Scorch the earth, raze the factories and mine the transport. He did not care about the fate of the people. He was concerned now quite simply with the foundation of the great legend of Hitler and the Nazi movement. In the end he thought only of posterity, as Fritzsche who knew him so well has pointed out: "He furtively looked with both eyes toward posterity. If you want to understand what he wrote towards the end, you have to bear this in mind."[16] To one of his officers he said: "Only after my death will people really believe me."[17]

With more than one member of his staff Goebbels argued the case for adopting poetic licence in the handling of news. All along he had never hesitated to treat news as a stimulant to the German war effort rather than as a presentation of fact for fact's sake. Now during the last months of the war he introduced what Semmler, writing in November 1944, called a new reference in the vocabulary of propaganda, intended only for internal use in the Ministry. This was 'poetic truth' as distinct from 'concrete truth'. In order to help the public, Goebbels claimed that it had become necessary to create imaginary news where the facts themselves were incomplete—hence the flow of atrocity stories when news of any real atrocities which may have occurred were an insufficient stimulant, and his fictitious accounts of action by the armed forces or the virtually non-existent German resistance in order to inspire a higher level of heroism in the German civilian morosely waiting for his town or village to be occupied.

The German resistance movement—entitled the Werewolves and technically always in readiness for operation under Himmler to assist the German Army behind the lines of the Allied forces when they had entered Germany—was in fact operational only on the radio, for Goebbels saw the value of the idea from the point of view of poetic truth before there was any evidence of concrete truth becoming available. News from Radio Werewolf began on 1st April; the German people were told that they, too, had a resistance movement, and so a long-kept secret was revealed without any authority from Himmler. Goebbels by this time did not care that he had no contact with the inefficient Werewolf organisation; its headquarters were at Flensburg on the Danish border, near the final centre for the German High Command, and an admirable place from which to organise a capitulation when Hitler was finally cut off in Berlin. Goebbels poured out his last verbal stimulants in the name of resistance, adding for better measure that victory was certain because as soon as the Americans and the British came finally face to face with the Russians, war would be declared between them and Germany would no longer be the target for destruction.

He never ceased to goad the German people into final self-immolation. On 30th January Hitler had appointed him Defender of Berlin. Goebbels, a civilian, became in effect a leader of German armed resistance, and his appointment revealed, to the horror of the people of Berlin, that Hitler intended the city to become a battle area. He assumed an officer's cap, but wore no insignia of rank, and added military conferences to his established duties at the Ministry. It was evident that he intended to go down working. While other ministries were evacuating south or preparing to evacuate, Goebbels kept his staff labouring at full stretch. On 4th February and again on 23rd February the Ministry building was seriously damaged in the air-raids. Goebbels put his staff into the basements and turned his private residence into an annexe for the Ministry to house his senior officials.

In his nihilistic mood Goebbels conceived in February the infamous idea of repudiating the Geneva Convention. This so roused the humane Dr. Semmler that he himself decided to take action. No doubt he remembered what Magda Goebbels had told him the previous November:

Frau Goebbels knows better than I do that her husband is a genius who now and then turns into a very Satan. We were talking about this yesterday over a cup of tea, and she several times asked me to do what I could to modify decisions, taken in angry and reckless moods, which showed the devil in his nature. She told me she had often asked other members of his staff to do the same.[18]

Goebbels was maddened by the appalling destruction of Dresden during a single air-raid in mid-February, when four-fifths of the city was destroyed and thirty thousand people were estimated to have been killed. Semmler wrote:

For the first time I saw Goebbels lose control of himself when two days ago he was given the stark reports of the disaster in Dresden. The tears came into his eyes with grief and rage and shock. Twenty minutes later I saw him again. He was still crying and looked a broken man. But then there came a passionate outburst of rage; his veins swelled and he became red as a lobster.[19]

It was as a consequence of this anger that Goebbels thought of proposing to Hitler that the Geneva Convention be repudiated to stop the heavy air-raids. He argued that the Allied air-crews held in captivity should be shot as a reprisal. Semmler did what he could to oppose the idea. When he heard that Hitler had approved it, he took the only action open to him and dropped a hint of what might happen to a foreign journalist who was in a position to see that news was passed on to London. Official British spokesmen then issued sharp warnings of retaliation if these rumours of a repudiation of the Convention were well founded, and this in turn led to the abandonment of the order by the Reich Chancellery. Goebbels was furious that the news had leaked out but never discovered that the source of the leakage was the man who ate at his own table.

Destruction: this was the last obsession of the inner circle drawing together round Hitler. Destruction of Germany and her resources, of the German people who had preferred their bourgeois comforts to the great social revolution offered them by the most powerful ruler the nation had known since Frederick the Great. Destruction finally of themselves as the little phials of poison were passed like precious stones from hand to hand. Hitler knew and approved of this, and himself possessed supplies of poison to give out to those whom he regarded as loyal and devoted followers, the blessing of death conferred by the Leader. Magda Goebbels was one of the first to get her ration from Professor Morell, Hitler's obnoxious and unqualified medical adviser who had materially helped to reduce Hitler to a pathological wreck with his experimental drugs, but who was nevertheless trusted by the Führer's inner circle and frequently consulted by Goebbels. Morell gave her what she wanted, a dose large enough for herself and her six young children, something that would work quickly. Afraid of upsetting her husband, she had to turn to Semmler and his colleagues for comfort.[20]

In the evening nowadays she often comes into our room and opens her heart to us. I feel sorry for her. She sees her future quite clearly. She admits she is afraid of death, and she knows it is drawing closer every day. She does not like talking to her husband about these things. He has enough to do looking after his own sanity. Today she said that she had managed to attain some sort of composure about her end, but she still could not bear the thought of ending the lives of her children. "When I put my six children to bed in the evening, four-year-old Heide, five-year-old Hedda, seven-year-old Holly, nine-year-old Helmuth, ten-year-old Hilde and twelve-year-old Helga, and when I think that in a few weeks' time I may have to kill these innocent creatures, I go nearly crazy with grief and pain. I am always wondering how I actually will do it when the time comes. I cannot talk about it with my husband any more. He would never forgive me for weakening his resistance. As long as he can go on fighting, he thinks all is not lost."

A few days before that her husband had suggested she should move westward with the children—anywhere where they might meet the British. "They would do nothing to you," he said. Magda Goebbels rejected this idea without hesitation; "I do not leave without you," she declared.[21]

This was towards the end of February. Earlier in the month, on 10th February, she had written what comfort she could to her elder son, Harald Quandt, who was a prisoner of war in England:[22]

My darling son,

It is nearly four weeks since I wrote to you last, but I have been thinking of you all the time more than ever, and I was afraid you might be worried about us, the news, of course, being far from rosy. I want to reassure you, though, and tell you about the latest events as well as possible.

First of all, we are well and in good health and in good spirits, and since in such grave times the family should be together, we have all moved to Berlin and have shut the house at Lanke.

In spite of the air-raids, our house here is still standing up, and we all of us, including grandmother and other members of the family, are well provided for. The children are full of fun and merely concerned with the boon of being excused school. Thank goodness they don't realise the gravity of these times yet.

As for Papa and myself, we are full of confidence and we do our duty to the best of our ability.

I have had no proper news of you since November, but Father tells me that you are better. Do please write to me soon about the exact nature of your wounds. I want to know exactly which teeth you have lost and whether the shot in your hips will make you unable to walk.

I embrace you with all my love and my thoughts are with you all the time.

Your Mother.

On one of the last occasions Magda was to see her sister-in-law Maria, she seemed no longer to entertain any hope of survival, neither for herself nor the children. Maria implored her at least to spare her youngest daughter and let her live together with her own family. But Magda was adamant. "I will certainly not leave Joseph now," she said. "I must die with him and the Führer. And when I die the children will have to die too, all of them. I couldn't bear to leave even one of them alive, not even with you."[23]

Naumann has revealed that he was among those who tried to persuade Magda to save herself and the children. With their house in Berlin turned into the headquarters of the Ministry, Goebbels had sent her with the family to Schwanenwerder. There Naumann had arranged for one of the freight barges in common use on the lakes and canals near Berlin to be stocked with provisions and moored near the house. His plan was that she should hide with the children in one of the lakeside shelters till the worst weeks of the occupation of Germany were over and then give herself up to the authorities. Goebbels also wanted her to do this. But she refused. Her devotion to Hitler was absolute. She had only to dwell on the indignities she imagined the invaders would heap upon her to know what she must do. Early in April she returned to Berlin and took her place alongside her husband and her Führer.

Meanwhile Goebbels himself, as Gauleiter and Defender of Berlin, ordered the city to prepare itself for a fight to the finish. While the ministries, including the Reich Chancellery, Hitler's own staff, were packing the bare essentials for continued administration into lorries in preparation for the long haul south, Goebbels watched the evacuation with a scorn born of his fanaticism. He realised all that mattered now was an heroic finish, that death should be proud to take him and his Leader. But the witnesses to this noble end were vanishing—in trains and cars and lorries. He would not release his own staff. They must work till there were no desks or typewriters or telephones to work with, and then, like the rest of the Berliners, it was their duty to man the barricades against the Russian armies. Whilst the younger members of his staff were planning among themselves to escape—most of them to the West to meet the Americans and the British—Hitler and

Goebbels were planning the defence of the city, in which strong-points and shelters were being hastily constructed. Goebbels heard with contempt of the white flags with which the Germans were greeting the Allies in the West. "If a single white flag is hoisted in a Berlin street I shall not hesitate to have the whole street and all its inhabitants blown up," he threatened on 5th April. "This has the full authority of the Führer."[24] The Ministry staff were organised into a special *Volkssturm* unit of their own under Werner Naumann and called the Wilhelmplatz Battalion.

During April the inner circle debated and argued what was best for the Führer to do. According to Naumann, Goebbels advocated that Hitler should move south; Semmler, however, records that he persuaded the Führer to stay in Berlin and remain faithful to the oath he had taken on 30th January 1933 when he had sworn he would never leave the Reich Chancellery, and that no power on earth could force him to abandon his position. If a legend were to be established as Goebbels' last fulfilment of his duty, the Leader must die within the precincts of the building which was the symbol of his authority. Hitler apparently agreed that he should accept his fate and resisted the strongest pressure that was put upon him to move south, though not without misgivings. At the birthday conference on 20th April in Berlin he still left it in doubt whether he might not move south to Berchtesgaden and the Bavarian Alps and take command of this sector from Kesselring. At this meeting he appointed Grand-Admiral Doenitz to the Northern Command, with headquarters at Ploen in Schleswig-Holstein.

At the birthday conference the six remaining leaders of the Nazi movement had gathered round the table with their Service Chiefs for the last time. There can hardly have been in all history a group of men who so hated and distrusted each other; yet they were somehow still kept in association together by the aura of power that emanated from their deranged Leader. Goebbels and Bormann, who were to stay with Hitler to the end, sat side by side with Speer, Himmler and Göring, who were to betray him, and Ribbentrop, who deserted him. Among them only Goebbels firmly believed that Hitler should uncompromisingly sacrifice himself in the tradition of a god. The rest, except possibly Bormann, to judge from their actions during the following days, wished only for some compromise that would bring this hopeless war to a speedy end and salvage what was left of the broken body of Germany.

Goebbels never forgot his ambition for office. Göring and Ribbentrop he had long since come to disregard; they lacked power and were irritants without the status any longer of enemies. So useless had Göring become that Boldt describes him as quite ostentatious in his boredom at one of Hitler's midnight conferences in the Bunker; "he put his elbows on the table and sank his huge head into the folds of the soft leather of his attaché case" and obscured the Führer's map.[25] Speer had no ambition for power and Goebbels tolerated him because of his executive efficiency. But of Bormann and Himmler he had learned to be wary. Both had power; Bormann because he became Hitler's closest companion and guardian, Himmler because, as head of the S.S., he was second only to Hitler in his control of force, and had become Minister of the Interior, a post Goebbels had badly wanted when Frick had been retired from that office in 1943. With both these men Goebbels had come to some sort of terms. In February he had achieved a private interview with Himmler in the sanatorium of Hohenlychen some twenty-five miles north of Berlin; it seems likely he had put proposals that they should combine to persuade Hitler to remake his Cabinet along lines which Goebbels had spoken of to his wife in Semmler's presence, with himself as Reich Chancellor, Himmler in charge of the Armed Forces and Bormann as Minister for the Party. Since nothing more was to be heard of this particular plan, it is to be assumed Himmler preferred to bide his time. Indecision was to characterise every move Himmler made, or did not make, during his last days of power. Semmler's comment is again revealing:

Goebbels obviously dislikes Himmler, although in their work they get along together. Goebbels, who is at bottom a man of fine feeling, cannot stand 'unæsthetic men'. He puts Himmler in this category. The Asiatic cut of his eyes, his short fat fingers, his dirty nails, all revolt Goebbels. But Himmler's extreme radical point of view and his use of brutal methods to get his own way make him attractive to Goebbels.[26]

Later, according to Schwerin von Krosigk, he was intriguing to replace Ribbentrop as Foreign Minister, though what powers this could bring him at such a time is hard to determine.

With Hitler Goebbels became as close a companion as he could, restoring at moments something of the intimacy of the happy days of friendship when the Führer had been a constant visitor to Magda's flat in the year following her marriage. Count Schwerin von Krosigk, one of the minor figures associated with the last period of Hitler's life, but one who kept a useful diary, records how Goebbels told him that he had been comforting the Führer by reading aloud to him from Carlyle's *Frederick the Great*.[27] He referred to the passage he had been reading, in which that revered figure in German history, whom both Hitler and Goebbels took for their personal symbol, sat like Job while messengers of tribulation followed each other to bring their news of disaster. Like Hitler he had had his little phial of poison. Yet Frederick in the midst of the misfortunes of the Seven Years' War in which not the least was the hostility of Russia, wrote to Count d'Argenson in words of such eloquence and noble courage that Goebbels' practised voice must have made them resound in Hitler's ears:

The school of patience I am at is hard, long-continued, cruel, nay barbarous. I have not been able to escape my lot: all that human foresight could suggest, has been employed, and nothing has succeeded. . . . But for my Books, I think hypochondria would have had me in bedlam before now. In fine, dear Marquis, we live in troublous times and in desperate situations—I have all the properties of a Stage-Hero; always in danger, always on the point of perishing. One must hope the conclusion will come; and if the end of the piece be lucky, we will forget the rest.

As if Providence itself had responded to the great King in his need, the Russian Czarina had suddenly died and her successor, Peter, who favoured Frederick, came at once to the throne. Goebbels told how he roused Hitler's spirits with Carlyle's comment, and the tears welled up in the Führer's eyes:

We promised Friedrich a wonderful star-of-day; and this is it—though it is long before he dare quite regard it as such. Peter, the Successor, he knows to be secretly his friend and admirer; if only, in the new Czarish capacity and its chaotic environments and conditions, Peter dare and can assert these feelings? What a hope to Friedrich, from this time onward! Russia may be counted as the bigger half of all he had to strive with; the bigger, or at least the far uglier, more ruinous and incendiary; and if this were at once taken away, think what a daybreak when the night was at the blackest!

After the reading, horoscopes were at once called for—for the Führer and for the Republic. They were kept by Himmler in a special research department. Both foretold a victory in the second half of April, after terrible reverses. The excitement was intense.

The daylight and sunrise came to Goebbels, if not to Hitler, on 12th April. That afternoon he had been visiting the headquarters of the Ninth Army at Küstrin where, in the course of an address to the officers of the Army staff, he had once more referred to the story of Frederick's deliverance only to be asked afterwards by one of the officers with a taste for irony what Czarina would die this time to save Germany. In the midst of an air-raid on Berlin that night the news came through of Roosevelt's death, and Semmler, together with other members of Goebbels' staff, met him on the steps of the Ministry and told him the glad news the moment he got out of his car. Semmler noticed Goebbels turn pale; the news must have seemed quite incredible. He ordered champagne to be served in his study. He rang Hitler at once at the Chancellery, speaking in a tense, excited voice, words that were later remembered by some of those present.

"My Führer," he said. "I congratulate you. Roosevelt is dead. Fate has laid low your greatest enemy. God has not abandoned us. A miracle has happened. This is like the death of the Empress Elizabeth in the Seven Years' War. It is written in the stars that the second half of April will be the turning point for us. This is Friday 13th April. It is the turning point."[28]

Then these self-deluding men began to speculate on Roosevelt's successor. Would it be Truman? If so, he would be much more moderate. When Goebbels had finished talking to Hitler, he rang up the Ninth Army to tell them about the death of this American Czarina. No straw was too slender for clutching in April 1945, no historical parallel too remote for those who believed in Providence. Both Hitler and Goebbels were in a high state of excitement which did not wear off until the following day. The Allies did not cease hostilities, and the war went on without Roosevelt. By the evening Goebbels was downcast. "Perhaps fate has again been cruel and made fools of us," he said.

A few days later, on 17th April, Goebbels referred to a new colour film, *Kolberg*, which had been recently released. It is one of the anomalies of Goebbels' attitude to total war that the production of such lavish films as this seemed to be maintained in spite of the desperate situation in which Germany was now placed.

"Gentlemen," said Goebbels, "in a hundred years' time they will be showing another fine colour film describing the terrible days we are living through. Don't you want to play a part in this film, to be brought back to life in a hundred years' time? Everybody now has the chance to choose the part which he will play in the film a hundred years hence. I can assure you it will be a fine and elevating picture. And for the sake of this prospect it is worth standing fast. Hold out now, so that a hundred years hence the audience does not hoot and whistle when you appear on the screen."[29]

This was the last occasion on which Semmler was present at a Ministry conference to record what Goebbels said. He noted how the Minister left the meeting of some fifty men with a pale face and burning eyes, and that those present did not know whether to laugh or to swear. Semmler himself sent his wife with their child south in an official lorry, and gave her the diary to take with her.

Meanwhile another family exodus also took place. Goebbels' mother was still staying with her daughter Maria and her son-in-law at their flat in Berlin. They put off their departure to the very last moment, and then found that there was no transport. The old woman of seventy-five walked alongside her daughter out of the burning city; Maria had put her three-month-old child in a wheelbarrow and pushed her to safety. Her husband's hands were badly burned, and one of his arms was in a sling. They ended their flight in Icking, a village near Munich.[30]

On 19th April, the eve of Hitler's birthday, Goebbels delivered his last important broadcast. He tried to give it the ring of hope, to pin his faith to a lucky star, but the words have a valedictory sound, as if he could not prevent some revelation of his purpose to die beside the Führer:

I may have spoken in a happier or perhaps a less happy hour, but never before have matters been on the razor's edge as they are today. Never before has the German people had to defend its bare life under such enormous dangers and, by a last all-out effort, make sure that the Reich does not break apart.

This is not the time to celebrate the Führer's birthday with the usual words or to express our traditional good wishes to him. I have shared joy and sorrow with the Führer, the unparalleled victories and the terrible setbacks of the crowded years from 1939 to today, and I still stand at his side and am convinced that fate will after the last hard test award the laurel wreath to him and his people. I can only say that these times, with all their sombre and painful majesty, have found their only worthy representative in the Führer. To him alone are thanks due that Germany today still lives, and that the West, with its culture and civilisation, has not been completely engulfed in the dark abyss which yawns before us. . . .

Wherever our enemies appear they bring poverty and sorrow, chaos and devastation, unemployment and hunger with them. What remains of the loudly proclaimed 'freedom' is something that would not be considered worthy of mankind in the darkest parts of Africa. We, on the other hand, have a clear programme of restoration which has proved its worth in our own country and in all other European countries where it had a chance. Europe had the chance to choose between these two sides. She has chosen the side of anarchy and has to pay for it today.

By 20th April, the date of the birthday conference which Goebbels attended with Hitler's remaining ministers, it was clear that the Russians would soon encircle Berlin and that any who wished to move south must do so at once before the surface routes were closed. Hitler faced these anxious men in the confined quarters of his Bunker after the birthday ceremonies and speeches were all over; he gave no indication at the conference whether he would leave for the south or not. One by one ministers, generals and staff officers said good-bye. Göring, the failure, found no warmth in these last words with Hitler; he left the Bunker after a cold and formal leave-taking and made his way south to Obersalzberg. Himmler left for the northern sanatorium of Hohenlychen and Ribbentrop also disappeared to the north. Hitler would see none of them again.

Goebbels kept aloof from this luxury of departures. For him and his staff—though there were desertions among the juniors—work was as normal though Berlin now echoed to the sound of guns as well as bombs. Speer had managed to persuade Goebbels to let the *Volkssturm* make their stand outside the city and so spare the central areas from becoming a battlefield. Goebbels also gave way to Speer over the destruction of Berlin's bridges, which he had intended to blow up and which would have paralysed transport vital to the life of the population. Speer's mission now, as he saw it, was the preservation of Germany's resources against Hitler's and Goebbels' orders when this was necessary, a mission which he shared with Kaufmann, the Gauleiter of Hamburg, with whom he had an agreement to the same effect in that important area. Between them these two men, the Minister and the Gauleiter, saved Germany from a considerable measure of destruction which, coupled with the bombing, could only have led to the death of large numbers of the population from starvation and privation, the end ordained for them by their Führer.

The following day, 21st April, Hitler ordered an attack on the Russians which never took place, and by the afternoon of 22nd April he was beside himself at the lack of any news that his orders had been carried out and the attack launched. The Government district was now a shambles, and what staff remained was working in the innumerable basements and bunkers beneath the ministries and their gardens. Standing alone with Naumann at a window in the Propaganda Ministry, Goebbels on one of his last days above ground had said to his deputy:

"Mark my word, Naumann, what you are seeing happen here is an historical drama of such magnitude that there has been nothing to compare with it this century nor indeed in any century unless you go back to Golgotha."[31] The guns echoed their resonant, Wagnerian accompaniment to this pronouncement in which Calvary and the *Götterdämmerung* were strangely mixed in Goebbels' haunted imagination.

Hitler, however, was less than a god at his last major staff conference on 22nd April. He gave way to utter anger in a volume of denunciation which lasted hour upon hour until those with him were left stricken and helpless, while others listened breathless outside the narrow conference chamber of the Bunker. He raged at the villainy of the world, the wickedness and cowardice of men, the treachery of those who had deserted him and left him to die in the ruins of Berlin. The last vestiges of his monstrous energy were poured out in words which seemed as if they would never stop. Eventually, after three hours of the storm, a calm came over him and he recovered. The outburst was undoubtedly Hitler's admission to himself of defeat, the uproar of the stricken giant. Goebbels was spared the horror and indignity of this scene; all he knew was the outcome of it, an announcement which Hitler ordered to be broadcast that Berlin would be defended to the end and that in Berlin the Führer would stay no matter what might come.

When Hitler calmed he spoke more hopefully to Keitel, before he too left, about the possibility of the relief of Berlin by General Wenck's Twelfth Army, which was fighting on the Elbe. This army, which never reached Berlin or had hope of doing so, was to become Hitler's final obsession as he shut himself away from the noise outside in the deep recesses of the Bunker. Then in the evening he agreed that Goebbels and his family should join him in the narrow cells of his concrete castle beneath the shaking earth.

CHAPTER NINE

The Bunker

GOEBBELS, Magda and the children left their house for the shelter of the Bunker shortly after five o'clock in the evening of 22nd April. It was a Sunday. They travelled in two cars driven by Rach, Goebbels' chauffeur, and Günther Schwaegermann, his adjutant. Semmler was there to say good-bye before leaving to join his unit. Goebbels thanked him and told him to do his duty as a soldier. Semmler watched the cars pull away. Goebbels remained calm and formal, but Magda and the children were weeping bitterly.[1]

All through the day that had seen the terrible outburst of Hitler's despair Goebbels had worked calmly, conferring, dictating his diary, recording a speech for broadcasting in which he declared Berlin to be a military objective. During the recording the sound of shelling went on, and there was one explosion so near the house that the recording was momentarily stopped. When the speech was played back Goebbels remarked favourably on the realistic sound effects.[2] He saw his old friend Dr. Winckler and thanked him for all he had done. "We shan't meet again," he said.[3] He was less revealing to his tireless stenographer, Otte. He merely told him that he was going into the Führerbunker for a week or so and that as soon as Wenck broke through to Berlin he would come out again. Meanwhile Otte was to take care of himself and keep away from the fighting. Goebbels had work for him to do in the future.[4] Goebbels in fact, according to Naumann, still believed that some sort of political victory might be achieved once the Western Allies found themselves face to face with the Russians. Then, thought Goebbels, Churchill and Truman will see the light and invite Hitler to become their ally to oppose the Bolshevist invasion of Europe.

After lunch he slept as usual in spite of the shelling, which made

Magda and the Ministry staff uneasy. Later in the afternoon Goebbels made an astonishing admission to Fritzsche, which he remembered and included in his testimony at Nuremberg. "In the final analysis this is what the German people wanted," said Goebbels. "The great majority of the Germans voted in favour of our leaving the League of Nations, in other words against a policy of appeasement and for a policy of courage and honour. It was the German people who chose war." Fritzsche protested that the Party line then was that Germany wanted peace, but Goebbels refused to listen.[5]

The shell-fire was by now incessant and the house unsafe. Goebbels' declared intention was to remain in Berlin with Hitler, and as the normal means of communication gradually broke down it was only natural that the inner circle—reduced now to Hitler, Bormann and Goebbels—should make their last stand together in the Führerbunker. But the decision that Goebbels and his family should retire to the Bunker was taken suddenly following the break-through achieved by the Russians.[6] As soon as they had gone the staff of the Ministry and of Goebbels' household disintegrated like the crew of a vessel whose captain has left them before shipwreck. Most of them had had their bags packed for some time ready to move off to safety at a moment's notice. They were thankful for their release and worried that it had come too late. Only the members of the *Volkssturm* were under orders to remain on duty. Meanwhile in the Bunker Goebbels declared to Hitler his readiness to die with him, if need be, and Magda, in spite of Hitler's protests, swore that she would do the same after taking her children's lives.

The Bunker has been the subject of detailed description. Briefly, it consisted of two connected groups of rooms built on two levels below ground. The first group of twelve minute rooms (four of which were the kitchen suite) flanked a central passage or hallway where meals were normally taken. At the further end of the passage a spiral staircase led down to Hitler's own quarters, a group of eighteen rooms scarcely greater in size and disposed on either side of a similar central passage divided into two sections, the further of which was used for conferences. Boldt describes this conference-passage as "only seventeen feet square; its walls are painted grey and without pictures. The furniture consists of a brown bench along the wall, a huge table for maps and a desk chair."[7] Apart from the passageways, the living-rooms were like cells very little bigger than the compartments of a rail-coach. Of these six were set aside for Hitler and Eva Braun, while five others housed the lavatories, the power-house and the telephone exchanges. There were three entrances to the Bunker—the first through the butler's pantry of the New Chancellery, the second from the garden of the Foreign Office, while the third, which was situated at the further end of the lower section, led from the Chancellery garden. This last was intended to be an exit for use only in emergency, and it was through this that the bodies of Adolf and Eva Hitler were carried to their funeral pyre on the afternoon of 30th April.

Hitler, Eva Braun, Goebbels, his wife and their six children were the principal inhabitants of this double bunker. Magda and her young family were given four cells in the first section of the structure, and Goebbels himself had a room in the principal section facing Hitler's suite on the opposite side of the passageway used for conferences. The other senior residents were Dr. Ludwig Stumpfegger, Hitler's surgeon, who had taken charge of the Führer's health after the dismissal of Professor Morell on 22nd April, and Günther Schwaegermann, Goebbels' adjutant. The rest were Hitler's adjutant, his valet, his two secretaries and his vegetarian cook. Bormann was accommodated in an entirely separate bunker a short distance away.

Boldt was told by one of the officers guarding the Bunker area that the diminutive suite of rooms used by Goebbels was "very luxuriously furnished", though Naumann denies this; Boldt also added that in all between six and seven hundred S.S. men, guards, orderlies, clerks, servants and kitchen personnel were on duty in the area of the Führerbunker.[8] Boldt himself, who paid several visits to the Bunker, comments on the relief of getting outside again where the air was clean and cool. He found the atmosphere inside stifling. He comments further on the curious fact that until Hitler's marriage to Eva Braun he "had known nothing whatever about the existence of this woman, let alone seen her; and yet she had been with us in the Führer's shelter the whole time".[9]

The Bunker was, of course, the scene of constant arrivals and departures. The conventional hours of day and night meant little in the artificial light below ground. For Hitler sleeping was confined to the earlier part of the morning. By midday he was up and he worked and talked while the rest of the day and night passed outside. As the Russians gradually encircled the city the street fighting began during this last week of April and communications with the outside world became increasingly hazardous. Light aircraft landing on the East-West Axis roadway, which was relatively near the Chancellery, brought the last visitors from a distance, such as Ritter von Greim and Speer.

Goebbels during these last days became Hitler's shadow. The men and women who came and went were not concerned with him, but with the Führer. Even Naumann, his Deputy, reported to Hitler now, since his presence was required in his other capacity as Major in charge of the battalion guarding the Bunker. Naumann, however, kept in touch with Goebbels and with Magda as time and opportunity permitted. Only Goebbels' adjutant, Günther Schwaegermann, remained in the Bunker solely to look after him.

Naumann has revealed something of the atmosphere in which Goebbels and his family now lived. While Hitler maintained the urgency of the war surrounding him, Goebbels was relieved of almost all his duties. His Ministry was all but gone and the active defence of Berlin, such as it could be, was now under the direction, though not the control, of Hitler himself. Goebbels spent a great deal of time with his children, playing with them, reading to them and comforting them in this difficult and unnatural life. Magda was busy keeping their clothes washed and in order, because in the hurry of their departure for the Bunker she had brought an inadequate supply of clothes. She had thought they would be incarcerated underground for a short while only. They were to survive there for nine days.

Boldt pays tribute to Magda's courage. "Frau Goebbels," he wrote, "showed little sign of being afraid of death up to the very end. Lively and elegant, she pranced up the staircase, always taking two steps at once, while we descended. Always friendly, she smiled at the people she met. . . . She displayed an admirable strength of mind, doubtless inspired by her fanatical religious belief in Hitler. We cannot be sure how much of it at that moment was still sincere; but it is certain that she was not only moved by very strong political and social ambition, but had given herself over to a blind worship of the Führer."[10]

Goebbels watched the coming and going of the men on more active service than himself. Naumann says that he read a great deal and continued to maintain his diary. He took part in the conferences which Hitler summoned, and he shared to some extent what was left of the Führer's private life. Boldt describes Goebbels in conference with Hitler in the following terms: "This little thin man has . . . shrunk and looks very pale and hollow-cheeked. Only seldom does he ask a question; mostly he is silent and follows closely the report on the map; the play of his features and his normally fanatical eyes reveal torturing worries."[11] Naumann, however, maintains that Goebbels spoke his mind whenever he wanted to.

Hope, on the night of 22nd April, was still centred on General Wenck's Twelfth Army, which was south-west of Berlin on the Elbe; Hitler sent Keitel over-night to Wenck's headquarters with orders for him to proceed at once to the relief of Berlin. He still refused to move south himself, repeating this to Himmler who had telephoned him earlier the same day from Hohenlychen. It was this refusal, together with his permission to everyone to go if they wished, that determined the departure of so many of Hitler's outer circle of generals, adjutants and secretaries.

The following day, Monday 23rd April, saw dramatic developments. In the south Göring, inspired by the news brought by his representative in Berlin, General Koller, planned to take over the leadership of the Reich and sent a telegram to that effect to Hitler. In the north Himmler, wavering in his sense of duty, had his first interview with the Swedish Count Bernadotte with a view to arranging the capitulation of Germany in that area to the Western Allies. In Berlin itself Speer paid his last visit to Hitler and confessed what was so much on his conscience, that he had not carried out the Führer's orders to destroy the resources of Germany. Hitler, unusually calm, forgave him. He explained once more that he was determined to shoot himself in the Bunker when the time came and to have his body burned so that it might not become a showpiece for the conquerors. Goebbels continued to support him in this decision, and Speer also agreed that it was right. Bormann alone went on trying in vain to get the Führer to change his mind even at this eleventh hour. He was not looking for a martyr's death and by now the only escape from Berlin was by air over the Russian tanks and guns; there were Russian troops fighting all round Berlin and to leave by land meant dodging through the Russian lines.

But if Hitler was calm with Speer he was beside himself with anger over Göring's telegram. Urged on by Bormann and Goebbels, he dismissed Göring from all his offices and ordered the S.S. in Obersalzberg to arrest him for high treason. Boldt says that Goebbels "was boiling with fury, and expressed his feelings in a theatrical burst of words. His exaggerated remonstrances about honour, faith, duty, blood, and so forth, failed altogether to conceal his envy and personal jealousy of Göring who, so it seemed, was about to slip his neck out of the noose."[12] Be that as it may, for Goebbels was surely committed to share Hitler's fate by his own wish, Göring, Hitler's Deputy and his former friend, was now irrevocably lost.

On this tragic day Hitler saw also the last of Ribbentrop, who quietly slipped away to northern Germany, and of his faithful generals, Jodl and Keitel, whom he had sent on their various missions. Speer, too, left in the early hours of Tuesday 24th April, a day on which little of note seems to have happened in the Bunker. During the night of 25th and 26th April Ritter von Greim and Hanna Reitsch, the test pilot who was one of the more hysterical women Nazis, made their hazardous tree-top flight into Berlin to fulfil an order from Hitler, who had decided to make von Greim Göring's successor at the head of the Luftwaffe. Greim was wounded in the foot during the flight and was confined in the Bunker along with Hanna Reitsch until the early hours of the morning of 29th April. The presence of this sick man and the expostulatory woman obsessed with Nazi heroics only served to increase the already neurotic atmosphere which grew daily among the strange and unnatural collection of incarcerated adults and children.

On Friday 27th April, Hitler was able to find himself a victim. Hermann Fegelein, Himmler's representative attached to Hitler's staff and the brother-in-law of Eva Braun, was found to be missing. He had quite simply gone home to plan his escape south. Hitler had him dragged back across the wreckage of Berlin and placed under guard. That night, under heavy and ceaseless shell-fire above ground, Hanna Reitsch claims that Hitler called his loyal followers together and shared with them a grim discussion of the details of the deaths that everyone present felt in honour bound to pledge to their Führer the moment the Russians stood on the threshold of the Bunker. Yet Hitler persisted in his belief that Wenck's army, which was in fact a defeated remnant on the Elbe, was still moving to the relief of Berlin. 28th April was spent sending out excited telegrams demanding answers to impossible questions concerning these relieving forces which never came and did not even report their movements.

28th April, which was Saturday, brought further baiting of the tethered Leader. On this day Hitler discovered the treachery of Himmler whose half-hearted negotiations with Count Bernadotte were being conducted on the assumption that he would undoubtedly be Hitler's chosen successor. Unfortunately news of these discussions had leaked into the international press. The report was laid before Hitler, who at the sight of it collapsed once more into another of his soul-destroying rages which revealed the madness inherent in his nature and reduced his face and body to a bloodshot, trembling monstrosity. Such paroxysms of human ferocity are in any situation terrifying to watch; they reveal too openly the primeval forces that lie at the base of human nature. But in the straitened circumstances of the Bunker, where no one could escape from the savage onslaught of such erupting anger, there was nothing to be done but to stand, pale and exposed, until the screaming and the raving had spent themselves and calm was somehow restored. Then Hitler shut himself away with Goebbels and Bormann, and in this secret session, of which no note survives, they doubtless determined the actions which were put into force during the next forty-eight hours.

Fegelein, the unfortunate representative of Himmler, was questioned and afterwards taken into the garden and shot; he had admitted knowledge of Himmler's tentative discussions with Bernadotte. Then, against all expectations, with Russian tanks as near as the Potsdamer

Platz, a sergeant-pilot of the Luftwaffe managed to get a training plane from Rechlin by flying in at 13,000 feet and dropping down to the East-West Axis. He had come to take the new Commander of the Luftwaffe, Ritter von Greim, back to his headquarters. Though both von Greim (who was seriously ill and had been under the care of Stumpfegger ever since his arrival in the Bunker) and his strange companion Hanna Reitsch wanted to die with Hitler, he managed to persuade them to take their slender opportunity of retreat and to carry with them certain written instructions and private letters from the besieged inhabitants of the Bunker. Among them was Magda's last letter to her elder son, Harald Quandt, who was a prisoner-of-war. It has been preserved. It is dated 28th April, and is headed "Written in the Führerbunker":[13]

My darling son,

It is six days by now that we have been in the Führerbunker, all of us, Papa, your small brother, your five little sisters and I, so as to give our National Socialist life the only possible and honourable end.

I don't know whether this letter will ever reach you, but perhaps there is a human soul after all, enabling me to send you these, my last greetings. I want you to know that it was against Papa's will that I have decided to stay with him, and that even last Sunday the Führer still wished to help us to get out of here. But you know your mother, we have the same blood, and for me there was no other choice. Our glorious ideas are coming to an end, and with them everything beautiful and admirable and noble and good I have known in my life. The world to come after the Führer and after National Socialism will not be worth living in, and that is why I have taken the children along with me. They are too good for the sort of life to come after us, and a merciful God will understand my reasons for sparing them that sort of life. . . .

The children are wonderful. Without anyone to help them they look after themselves in these more than primitive circumstances. Whether or not they have to sleep on the floor, whether or not they can wash themselves, or have something to eat—there is never a word of complaint from them and they never cry. Artillery bombardment shakes the Bunker, and whenever that happens the bigger children look after the smaller ones; and incidentally their presence here is a blessing if only for the fact that from time to time they make the Führer smile.

Last night, the Führer took his own Party badge and pinned it on me. It made me very proud and happy. May God give me the strength for my last and most difficult duty. There is only one thing we want now, to be true to death to the Führer and to finish our lives with him. And in a way, this is a blessing of fate we never dared to hope for. . . .

My darling son, live for Germany!

Your Mother.

Naumann spoke to Magda shortly after Hitler had presented her with his own Party badge, which was made of gold. She was quite overcome with happiness; her mind for the moment was freed from the clouds of sorrow which the approach of death was massing over her.

Goebbels also wrote a last, very characteristic letter to his step-son:

My dear Harald,

We are shut away in the Führerbunker next to the Reich Chancellery, fighting for our lives and our honour. God alone knows how this struggle will end, but I do know that, alive or dead, we shall not leave the Bunker unless we can leave it honourably. I do not think we shall see each other again, and these are probably the last words you will ever receive from me. If you survive this war, I expect you at all times to do honour to your mother and your father. It is not necessary for us to remain alive in order to influence our people's future. The probability is that you will be the only survivor to continue the tradition of our family. Do it in such a way that we would never have been ashamed of you. Germany will survive this terrible war, but only if there are examples to guide its resurrection. Such an example of loyalty we are about to set here in the Bunker.

You can be proud of your mother. Yesterday the Führer gave her the golden Party badge that he has worn for so many years. No one deserves the gift more than she.

In future you should recognise one duty only: to be worthy of the great sacrifice that we are determined to make. I know you will be worthy, but do not be led astray by the unrest which will spread now all over the world. One day the untruths will collapse under their own weight, and truth will once more rise supreme. The time will come again when Germany will face the world unsullied, as spotless as our own faith and purpose have always been.

Good-bye, my son Harald. It is in God's hands whether we are ever to meet again. If this will never be, you can be proud of belonging to a family which, in these dark days, stood by the Führer and remained loyal to him with its last breath, and faithful to his great and sacred cause.

My best wishes to you from the bottom of my heart,
Your Father.

Von Greim and Reitsch left the Bunker some time after midnight, and in the early hours of the morning looked down on the furnace of Berlin as their plane climbed to heights for which it was never intended. But they reached Rechlin in safety, and then went on to Doenitz's headquarters at Ploen.

In the Bunker the first act of Sunday 29th April was the marriage of Hitler to Eva Braun. This seems to have taken place soon after the departure of Ritter von Greim. It was a civil wedding of the simplest, most austere type, and was conducted by a complete stranger, Walter Wagner, who was the nearest to a representative of the local city authority that could be found; he was one of Goebbels' *Gau* Inspectors and arrived wearing a Party uniform. Huddled together in one of the diminutive rooms in Hitler's private suite, the Führer and Eva Braun were hastily married with the fewest possible words. Nevertheless they both declared they were of pure Aryan descent. The only witnesses were Goebbels and Bormann, both of whom signed the marriage certificate. In the passageway outside a small party had been formed to congratulate the bride and groom, and when the hand-shaking and hand-kissing were over, Goebbels and his wife were invited to join a more select group in the private suite to drink champagne and attempt to banish for a while the sense of doom with gossip of old and happy times when Hitler had been a witness to the marriage of Joseph and Magda. But for Hitler such talk soon became impossible, and he reverted once more to the bitterness of his betrayal and his intention of killing himself. Then he left the party to dictate his last will and testament, in which he had little to say but what had been said countless times in the past—the innocence of Germany, the villainy of international Jewry, and the need for high standards of devotion in the fighting services, more particularly in the High Command. He then formally expelled Göring and Himmler from their offices of state and from the Party, and proceeded to appoint a new Head of State and Cabinet. Grand-Admiral Doenitz was made Reich President and Supreme Commander of the Armed Forces, but even so he was not to be permitted to make up a Cabinet for himself. Hitler did it for him. Among the senior appointments Goebbels was created Reich Chancellor and Bormann Party Chancellor. Goebbels' ambition was at last to be realised, but at the eleventh hour, under a new President. Ribbentrop, in disgrace by reason of his ineffectual position and absence during the last days, disappears completely from this distribution of power on paper.

Hitler's testament is an interesting solution to the wholly theoretical balance of power in Germany. There in the Bunker beneath the fires of Berlin and with the Russian tanks gradually nosing their way nearer and nearer through the streets, Hitler, Bormann and Goebbels, the surviving hierarchy of Nazi Germany, must in their secret conference have worked out this plan in order to preserve a form of status appropriate to their vanity. With the war about to end, Doenitz's Supreme Command was valueless and as President he would be no more than a figurehead in the tradition of Hindenburg's last year of office. The real power would be in the hands of the two Chancellors—the Chancellor of the Reich and the Chancellor of the Party. It was a neat and simple compromise, if only the body of Germany had contained no enemies. But the American and the Russian forces had already met on the Elbe.

A second document, Hitler's personal will, paid a brief but warm tribute to his wife and his staff, disposed of his property, appointed Bormann his executor, and referred to the suicide he and his wife were about to commit.

When these documents had been typed by Hitler's secretary, Frau Junge—the testament is dated 29th April and timed 4 a.m.—Goebbels and Bormann were invited to be the principal witnesses to the Führer's signatures.

While Hitler retired to rest, the need to add some words of his own took possession of Goebbels, who knew now that his great historical studies would never be written and all that mattered was to leave behind the right directives for the survival of the Nazi myth. He went apart and wrote what he called an Appendix to the Führer's Political Testament. It was a brief, clear and pointed address to the German nation in which he proclaimed the reasons for his suicide:

The Führer has ordered me, should the defence of the Reich capital collapse, to leave Berlin and to take part as a leading member in a government appointed by him.

For the first time in my life I must categorically refuse to obey an order of the Führer. My wife and children join me in this refusal. Otherwise—quite apart from the fact that feelings of humanity and loyalty forbid us to abandon the Führer in his hour of greatest need—I should appear for the rest of my life as a dishonourable traitor and common scoundrel, and should lose my own self-respect together with the respect of my fellow citizens; a respect I should need in any further attempt to shape the future of the German nation and State.

In the delirium of treachery which surrounds the Führer in these most critical days of the war, there must be someone at least who will stay with him unconditionally until death, even if this conflicts with the formal and (in a material sense) entirely justifiable order which he has given in his political testament.

In doing this, I believe that I am doing the best service I can to the future of the German people. In the hard times to come, examples will be more important than men. Men will always be found to lead the nation forward into freedom; but a reconstruction of our national life would be impossible unless developed on the basis of clear and obvious examples.

For this reason, together with my wife, and on behalf of my children, who are too young to speak for themselves, but who would unreservedly agree with this decision if they were old enough, I express an unalterable resolution not to leave the Reich capital, even if it falls, but rather, at the side of the Führer, to end a life which will have no further value to me if I cannot spend it in the service of the Führer, and by his side.[14]

Goebbels signed this statement at 5.30 in the morning. It is a document that takes a literary pleasure in the acceptance of death, and quite consciously and deliberately fulfils the grand gesture of tradition that the greatest thing a man can do is lay down his life for his friend. That his wife should offer to die with him is understandable, for, whether she loved her husband or not, she was always anxious to prove that she was not less devoted to Hitler than he. She became a willing victim in the vortex of violent emotion that was concentrated in the Bunker. What is less understandable is that with so many relatives surviving (among them Goebbels' mother and married sister and Magda's mother) they chose to include in their suicide their six children.

When it was morning outside, arrangements were made for the despatch of three copies that had been made of Hitler's testaments. Three special messengers were briefed to penetrate the Russian lines and carry the documents to safety. They were Major Johannmeier, one of Hitler's adjutants, Wilhelm Zander, a member of Bormann's staff, and Heinz Lorenz, an official from Goebbels' Ministry. Johannmeier was instructed to take Hitler's testament to Field-Marshal Schörner, the new Commander-in-Chief of the Army; Zander was to report to Doenitz with his set of documents, which included also Hitler's certificate of marriage; while Lorenz was told that he was also responsible for carrying the papers to Doenitz's headquarters, but that subsequently they should be sent to Munich, as the birthplace of Nazism, for preservation as documents of history. It was natural that Goebbels should attach his own personal addition to the Führer's testament to this third package. His statement had been made for history. Carrying their precious despatches, the three men left the Bunker together and picked their way west through the occupied city until they reached the northern part of the Havel which was still being defended by a detachment of the Hitler Youth. From here they were able to proceed south by water, passing on the way near to Goebbels' luxurious lakeside mansion of Schwanenwerder, deserted now and awaiting the arrival of the occupying forces.

In the Bunker Hitler spent his last day on earth in a succession of conferences during the course of which it was revealed that the Russians were likely to reach the Bunker in forty-eight hours at most. Goebbels took part in these discussions. In the middle of the night a last messenger, Colonel von Bülow, was sent out with a further statement—a farewell to the Armed Forces who had been let down by their Commanders. In the afternoon Hitler had his dog poisoned. Sunday had also brought the timely news of the death of Mussolini and his mistress and the savage treatment of their bodies by the crowds in Milan. Providence, which had so often shown its care for Hitler, gave him this particular message as his last report from the world beyond the ever-narrowing perimeter that his dying soldiers were holding round the hallowed Bunker. Goebbels' remark to Naumann was: "Proof, if any proof were needed, that one must not in any circumstances fall into their hands alive! If we had happened to capture Stalin or Churchill, the Führer had decided to give them honourable detention in some castle or other. Aren't we 'barbarians' actually the better people after all?"

Late that night, during the general meal in the upper passageway which was attended by a much depleted number of senior officers from the other bunkers, a message was received that Hitler would want at some time during the night to meet the women who were left in this strange community to say his formal farewell. Outside in the canteen of the Chancellery there was a dance in progress, but even this sad news of the Führer's wishes could not stop the hilarious noise made by the men and women who did not know whether they would be alive or dead in twenty-four hours. There were those who said their spirits rose when they heard what they knew was a prelude to Hitler's suicide. The dance went on even after the silent members of Hitler's intimate staff stood ranked in the Bunker at half-past two in the morning while the Führer solemnly moved along and, without audible words, stopped before each woman and shook her hand. The noise of the dance outside went on long after the ceremony, and the messages which had been sent to get it silenced were disregarded.

Day came outside, and the reports that arrived by noon showed that the narrow circle of German-held territory surrounding the Bunker had shrunk yet further. The Russians were less than a mile away to the north and west. Hitler ordered everyone away from the Bunkers and the Chancellery except for the chosen participants in the rites of his death. After lunch had been eaten, another ceremony of hand-shaking was held in which Eva Hitler also took part. Goebbels held his Leader's hand in his for the last time. His wife was not there; she had already said good-bye during the night and was shut away with her children. She had begun to realise how soon she would have to part from them, and the thought of accomplishing their death began to become a reality to her now that the task of killing drew appreciably nearer. Even so she undoubtedly heard the shot at half-past three in the afternoon when Hitler put a bullet through his mouth. He lay dead on a sofa beside Eva, who had poisoned herself. It was reserved for Goebbels and Bormann to be the chief mourners while men of the S.S. and Hitler's household carried the bodies through the further exit from the Bunker up into the garden where the ceremony of the burning was to be completed. The Russian guns sounded in mocking salute and the petrol-soaked bodies were slowly, methodically and with some difficulty consumed by fire. As the flames roared up Goebbels and the others raised their arms in the salute to which the dead man had given his name. Then those not concerned with maintaining the fire turned back silently to the Bunker. The bodies were kept burning for over two hours, and were eventually buried at night in the vicinity of the garden.

With the passing of Hitler life in the Bunker entered an entirely new phase. The all-powerful personality of the Führer was there no more. Bormann, whose personal ascendancy had depended solely on Hitler, at once lost his authority in the face of Goebbels, the new Reich Chancellor. Goebbels saw that everyone now, including Bormann, was intent on escape.[15] Bormann telegraphed Doenitz to tell him he was to be Hitler's successor but did not reveal the Führer's death; Doenitz addressed his reply to Hitler, pledging his unconditional loyalty.

On the night of 30th April Goebbels and Bormann called a conference at which it was decided that, by virtue of the offices to which they had been appointed by Hitler, they should communicate with Marshal Zhukov to arrange for a truce. After that, they considered, it would be for Doenitz to take over the negotiations. When it was clear that the Russians were prepared to receive an intermediary, General Krebs, who had been present at the conference, was sent to arrange the armistice. Zhukov's answer came back at noon and was disappointing; it admitted of no privilege such as Bormann had hoped for himself and Goebbels; only the unconditional surrender of all persons trapped in the Bunker. A further conference was held at once. None of those present was prepared to accept such terms.

Zhukov's ultimatum determined the last actions of Goebbels. While the rest were planning how their escape must be accomplished, Goebbels thrust aside the prevarications of Bormann's telegrams to Doenitz and sent the new President (who had still not yet received a copy of Hitler's testament) a wholly explicit telegram:

GRAND-ADMIRAL DOENITZ—
Most secret—urgent—officer only.
The Führer died yesterday at 15.30 hours. Testament of 29th April appoints you as Reich President, Reich Minister Dr. Goebbels as Reich Chancellor, Reichsleiter Bormann as Party Minister, Reich Minister Seyss-Inquart as Foreign Minister. By order of the Führer, the testament has been sent out of Berlin to you, to Field-Marshal Schörner, and for preservation and publication. Reichsleiter Bormann intends to go to you today and to inform you of the situation. Time and form of announcement to the press and to the troops is left to you. Confirm receipt.—GOEBBELS.[16]

This message was sent at a quarter-past three in the afternoon. It was Goebbels' last official act. He then joined his wife and children to prepare them for the end.

Five hours were to elapse before Goebbels and Magda climbed the steps up to the garden where they faced their death. During that time they were to say good-bye to a number of people, among them Naumann and Schwaegermann. Naumann in fact stayed some part of the time with them. But in the confines of the Bunker they remained like ghosts while the besieged remnants of Hitler's staff and bodyguard prepared themselves for the mass break-out at night when the darkness would hide them as they crept their way through the Russian-occupied streets to what seemed to be the comparative safety of the south and the west. They took no more notice of the man and the woman with their six children who were to share the ceremony of death with the Führer.

No one now can reconstruct their thoughts as they shut themselves away from those preparing to leave them. Schwaegermann told them that the break-out was planned to take place in groups that would leave the Bunker at various intervals once darkness had fallen. Naumann's group had in fact arranged to leave at ten-thirty. General Weidling, the Commandant of Berlin, had given them until midnight to make their escape; at that hour he proposed to surrender the capital to the Russians. Goebbels then gave Schwaegermann his final instructions. After he and Magda were dead their bodies, like Hitler's and Eva's, must be burned with the aid of petrol. Goebbels looked round for something to give Schwaegermann as a parting present. He had nothing but Hitler's signed photograph. He gave him that. Schwaegermann left and sent Rach, the chauffeur, to gather what petrol he could find.

Goebbels spent the rest of the time left to him in writing his diary with the pride of a man who imagined his words were history. He gave the half-dozen pages to Naumann, who read them carefully. But after Goebbels' death he decided to burn them. Reich Chancellor Goebbels had written nothing new: he lamented that total war had begun too late and that the Western World was behaving with incredible folly because it had not drawn together at this last moment in order to prevent the enslavement of Europe by the Bolshevists. This, he said, would now happen because Churchill and Roosevelt had sabotaged the only nation capable of destroying the Communist menace—Germany under National Socialism.

Goebbels and Magda postponed their suicide to the last possible moment. But before they set about killing themselves while there were still men left to cremate them, they had to achieve the deaths of their children. Magda gave them a sleeping draught with their evening meal and put them to bed. When they had at last fallen asleep she gave them one by one their poison with a spoon. Only when they were safely dead could their parents leave the tender bodies to turn cold and make their own departure.[17]

It was about half-past eight that Naumann, Schwaegermann and Rach—the civil servant, the adjutant and the chauffeur—became the principal witnesses to what followed. Goebbels and Magda came out of their room arm in arm. Magda was deathly pale and hung upon her husband. Goebbels was calm. He said a few words of thanks to Naumann for his friendship and loyalty and his speech was clear and articulate. He even tried to make light of the moment by saying that they were climbing the steps together to save their friends the trouble of carrying the bodies up the steep flight of stairs leading to the garden. Magda could say nothing. But she held out her hand to Naumann who kissed it in silence. Goebbels said no more but shook hands; after this he put on his gloves most carefully, easing his fingers into place. Then he and Magda turned away very slowly and arm in arm went up the stairs out of sight.

Naumann never saw them again. He stood with the others transfixed by the emotions of the moment, waiting for the sound of the shots which would be the signal of death. In his pocket was the capsule of poison which Hitler had given him and which they all carried about them during the final days. He knew Magda intended to take the poison the instant before her husband shot her. And he knew that Goebbels would bite his own capsule at the same moment he shot himself.

After the time of waiting the shots came once, then twice. Naumann left immediately, for he must think now only of his escape. Schwaegermann went up to fulfil his promise to throw petrol on the bodies and see to their destruction. But time was short, and he too had his escape to keep in mind. As soon as the bodies were well alight with the blazing fluid he left them in the garden, the flames darting up into the night sky from their burning clothes.

It was between half-past eight and nine o'clock on the night of 1st May. The orders were that the Bunker was to be destroyed. An attempt was made to do so and it almost cost Schwaegermann his life because the force of the explosions jammed the doors. Then the partially demolished Bunker that had locked so much agony of mind in its cells beneath the ground was left silent and empty except for the stiffening bodies of the children lying shut away in their beds. While the last defenders of Hitler's power were dodging and creeping their way through the Russian lines, some like Naumann and Schwaegermann to reach safety and some like Bormann to be killed, the corpses of Goebbels and Magda lay side by side in the garden. The flames licked at them until the damps of nature and the spring night put out the fire, leaving the deserted bodies blackened but undestroyed.

The following day new visitors, with eyes alert and guns ready, moved warily from room to room on their first inspection of the Bunker. They found nothing there but death and débris. Then they went up the steps beyond and out into the garden. At their feet lay the body of Goebbels; one hand turned black and claw-like seemed to be reaching up at them. His blistered head lay back with the sightless sockets of its eyes fixed in greeting. The Russians left the bodies unburied until they had been identified, and Fritzsche, who had just been taken prisoner, was brought to the Bunker to perform the sickening duty of identification. But there was no doubt at all to whom these charred and gaping features had belonged in life. The last horrifying photograph was taken to complete the record of Goebbels' story.

So the corpses were disposed of, like the bodies of the children, by enemy hands. The man who strove to become master of our thoughts as he had become the master of the minds of millions of others was shovelled with his wife into the conquered earth of Berlin. No note was kept of the site. He was probably interred in the garden where he and Magda were found and where so many others were pushed with spades into their nameless graves. His broken remains like Hitler's have disappeared without honour or recall.

Notes

CHAPTER ONE

The sources for this Chapter are mainly the personal accounts given to Heinrich Fraenkel (referred to hereafter by the initials H.F.) by Goebbels' sister, Frau Maria Kimmich, and by the friends of his youth, Alma, Else (both of whom request that we use only their first names), Dr. Fritz Prang and his mother, Frau Prang. The documents quoted were kindly loaned for the purpose by them and by the Albertus Magnus Society. Most of the legends of Goebbels' childhood, adolescence and early career originated in the official biographies of the Nazi period, notably those written by Bade and Krause, and have been in many cases repeated by Riess, Ebermayer and others recording either the life of Goebbels or the history of the Nazi movement. The facts concerning Goebbels' introduction to the Nazi Party have been confirmed by Dr. Prang, Karl Kaufmann, Dr. Otto Strasser and Dr. Helmuth Elbrechter. The quotations from Goebbels' short novel *Michael* are translated from the original edition published by the Eher Verlag.

1. Maria Kimmich has stated to H.F. that her maternal grandmother was born on 18th April 1869 at Uebach over Worms, a Dutch township. (Worms has nothing to do with the German city on the Rhine; it is the name of a Dutch rivulet on which Uebach is situated.) The grandmother's maiden name was Coervers, which is Dutch, and her ancestry was entirely Dutch. In 1932 Goebbels saw fit to have certain allegations that his grandmother was Jewish refuted in a pamphlet published in Berlin, *Doktor Joseph Goebbels—wer ist das?* by Viator. In this pamphlet his grandmother's maiden name is given the German spelling of Coerdes, and her Dutch origin is concealed. Her husband, Goebbels' maternal grandfather Odenhausen, was a German who had emigrated to Holland.

2. Wilfred von Oven, *Mit Goebbels bis zum Ende* (Dürer-Verlag, Buenos Aires, 1950), Vol. I, p. 243.

3. Goebbels spells his first name Josef. In his maturer years he was to adopt the more normal spelling Joseph.

4. Goebbels after long delay attempted to settle this debt by sending the Society 10,000 deflated marks which were technically worth at the time only 1.09 gold marks. The Society generously credited him with two marks, and sent in the bailiffs! The case dragged on until 1931, when

Goebbels was a Reichstag deputy. He finally paid the debt plus legal expenses in three much-delayed instalments.

5. This letter was published in the *Kirchenzeitung für das Bistum Aachen*, 27th October 1946.
6. See Curt Riess, *Joseph Goebbels* (Hollis and Carter, London, 1949), p. 16.
7. See H. R. Trevor-Roper, *The Last Days of Hitler* (Macmillan, London, 1947), p. 18.
8. See Sir Nevile Henderson, *Failure of a Mission* (Hodder and Stoughton, London, 1940), p. 76.
9. Rudolf Ullstein once said jokingly in conversation with H.F. that it was a pity they had never accepted *Michael* and so perhaps diverted Goebbels' energies into literature instead of politics.
10. Later Rathenau was to be assassinated by the Nazis, and the murderers feted by Goebbels.
11. The script of this play is preserved among the private family papers at Bonn. At the time of the writing of this book it was inaccessible pending a lawsuit.
12. Dr. Klauck of the Albertus Magnus Society claims that Goebbels' love affair with Anka first began during the Sommer-Semester of 1919 at Freiburg.
13. A list of these documents is held by the Wiener Library in London.
14. A copy of this document is in the possession of Goebbels' sister, Frau Kimmich.
15. This story was told to H.F. by Joachim von Ostau.

CHAPTER TWO

The condition of Germany after the First World War and the story of the rise of the Nazi movement has been the subject of many books of varying authority culminating in Dr. Alan Bullock's *Hitler—A Study in Tyranny* (Odhams, 1952). Where original sources were no longer available and the published facts varied as between historians, we have normally preferred those given by Dr. Bullock and by W. M. Knight-Patterson in *Germany from Defeat to Conquest*, 1919–33 (Allen and Unwin, 1945). Goebbels' own hand-written diary from 3rd August 1925 to 16th October 1926 is preserved in the Hoover Institution at Stanford University, and was consulted in microfilm; it consists of some 200 pages written in a series of notebooks. The contents of this diary were checked with a number of the people mentioned in it, and in great detail with Else, Kaufmann and Otto Strasser. Others consulted were Helmuth Elbrechter and Salomon von Pfeffer. All of these were in constant touch with

Goebbels at this time. A photostat copy of this diary has now been deposited with the Institut für Zeitgeschichte in Munich.

1. The facts about these two conferences, so important in the history of the early Nazi movement, are published here correctly for the first time. The details are vouched for by Karl Kaufmann, Otto Strasser and Helmuth Elbrechter. All three were personally present at the Hanover conference. Though none of them was present at Bamberg, Kaufmann knew the details of what happened. Otto Strasser has recently confirmed that his early reports of Goebbels' 'treason' at Bamberg were exaggerated. When H.F. confronted Otto Strasser with Goebbels' day-by-day entries in the diary, he admitted that in his previously published statements (on which all historians have relied, including Dr. Bullock) he had contracted in time what was a gradually-deepening rift between Goebbels and the Strassers, and made it appear that this breach had become immediately apparent at Bamberg. Goebbels remained in touch with the Strassers for a considerable period subsequent to the Bamberg conference.

2. Stated by von Pfeffer in conversation with H.F. Von Pfeffer was soon to become Supreme Leader of the S.A., though he subsequently quarrelled with Hitler and fell into disgrace.

3. Dr. Elbrechter, now a physician and practising in Düsseldorf, has asserted in conversation with H.F. that he thought little enough of Goebbels at this time. He underrated him because he could not stand his supercilious manner.

CHAPTER THREE

Goebbels wrote his own highly biased account of his first year's work as Gauleiter of Berlin in *Kampf um Berlin* (Eher Verlag, Munich, 1934). The quotations that appear in this chapter taken from his book are translated from the ninth edition (1936). The facts have been checked with Otto Strasser, who was in frequent contact with Goebbels since he was resident in Berlin. Following are the page references in *Kampf um Berlin* corresponding to the numbered quotations that occur in our text:

1, p. 21; 6, p. 24; 7, p. 52; 8, p. 44; 9, p. 86; 10, p. 249; 12, p. 46; 13, p. 168; 14, p. 188; 15, p. 86.

The remaining notes are:

2. See *Hitler's Table Talk* (Weidenfeld and Nicolson), p. 532.

3. See *Mein Kampf* (translation published by Hurst and Blackett, 1939), pp. 158–63.

4. *Mein Kampf*, pp. 390–1.

5. *Mein Kampf*, p. 478.

11. Thonak was later to become Goebbels' chauffeur.
16. Quoted by Curt Riess in *Joseph Goebbels*, pp. 70-1.
17. Ibid., pp. 72-3.
18. Ibid., p. 74.
19. Berger, in conversation with H.F.
20. Magda's devotion to Hitler was universally known. Particular reference to the friendship between Hitler and Goebbels' wife is made by Otto Dietrich in *The Hitler I Knew*, by Rudolf Semmler in *Goebbels—the Man Next to Hitler*, by Wilfred von Oven in *Mit Goebbels bis zum Ende* and by Goebbels himself in *My Part in Germany's Fight*. That Magda had at one time been in love with Hitler is regarded as certain by both Dr. Naumann and von Wedel, who have said as much in conversation with H.F. Von Wedel was one of Goebbels' aides from 1934-38, and Dr. Naumann was to become his second-in-command at the Propaganda Ministry.

CHAPTER FOUR

Goebbels' own account of the final period of the Nazis' fight for power is given in his published diary *Vom Kaiserhof zur Reichskanzlei* (Eher, 1934). Quotations here and in Chapter Five are taken from the English translation of the diary published as *My Part in Germany's Fight* (Paternoster Library, 1938; original edition Hurst and Blackett, 1935). Following are the page references in the Paternoster Library edition for those numbered quotations in our text which have no other indication (such as dates) as to where they may be found in the diary:

2, p. 40; 3, pp. 20, 30, 130; 5, p. 51; 6, p. 165; 7, p. 182; 11, p. 220; 13, p. 201; 14, p. 214; 16, p. 267; 17, p. 106; 18, p. 97; 19, pp. 135 and 143; 20, p. 14; 21, p. 168; 22, p. 39; 23, p. 136; 24, p. 13; 25, p. 152; 26, p. 103; 27, p. 80; 28, p. 105; 29, p. 131; 30, p. 11; 31, p. 87; 32, p. 65; 33, p. 16; 34, p. 34; 35, p. 11; 36, p. 138; 37, p. 12; 38, p. 138; 39, p. 32; 40, p. 189; 41, p. 179; 42, p. 114; 43, p. 62; 44, p. 101; 45, p. 44; 46, p. 101; 47, p. 214; 48, p. 23; 49, p. 248; 50, p. 222; 54, p. 226.

The remaining notes are:

1. Joachim von Ostau has told H.F. how he became one of the three messengers sent by the leaders of the political Right to try to persuade both Hitler and Hindenburg to withdraw their candidature for the Presidency in favour of the Crown-Prince Wilhelm. Hindenburg had once before stated that he was prepared to withdraw if a Hohenzollern Prince should come forward as Head of State in any capacity. Von Ostau said that he found Hitler sympathetic to the idea, but that it was Goebbels who pressed him vehemently to refuse any such overtures to withdraw.

4. Dietrich, *The Hitler I Knew*, p. 204.

8. Von Papen claimed in conversation with H.F. that this attempt to oust Hitler from power could never have succeeded; Kaufmann, however, like many politicians of the period, believes it might have done.

9. Von Papen told H.F. that his meeting with Hitler at von Schroeder's house was undertaken at the request of his friend von Schleicher. There was in fact little secrecy about the meeting, since Hitler was accompanied by Hess and others. Von Papen on arrival was surprised to find himself being photographed. After the meeting he wrote a report in his room at the Excelsior Hotel in Cologne and posted it at once to von Schleicher. The following day, however, the press blazed the headlines about the secret meeting that had just taken place between von Papen and Hitler. The photographer was none other than Dr. Elbrechter, who has now admitted to H.F. that he had been asked to take the photograph by von Schleicher, with whom he was on terms of personal friendship.

10. For a full account of these intricate negotiations see Bullock's *Hitler*, pp. 220–6.

12. Serge Chakotin, *The Rape of the Masses* (Routledge, London, 1940), p. 30.

15. Quoted by Riess in *Joseph Goebbels*, p. 118.

51. See H. Hoffmann, *Hitler was my Friend* (Burke, London, 1955), pp. 71–2.

52. See Dietrich, *The Hitler I Knew*, p. 25.

53. At the Nuremberg Trials Gisevius, among other important witnesses, pointed to Goebbels as the principal instigator of the arson. Such evidence as was brought together at the legal enquiry held in London in 1933 revealed that Göring was at least equally implicated. There seems now to be little doubt that several of the Nazi leaders were actually involved.

55. Hitler insisted on this clumsy title against the advice of Goebbels, who objected to the introduction of the word Propaganda because, he thought, it would defeat its object. He would have much preferred the word '*Kultur*'.

CHAPTER FIVE

The first three months of power, February to April 1933, are commemorated by Goebbels in *My Part in Germany's Fight* (see advance note to Chapter Four). The most thorough account of the administrative machinery built up by Goebbels during the first ten years of his Ministry is contained in *The Goebbels Experiment* by Derrick Sington and Arthur Weidenfeld (John Murray, London, 1942) to which we are indebted for many facts. Other sources are indicated in the notes below.

1. *My Part in Germany's Fight*, p. 227.
2. Ibid., p. 231.

3. Ibid., p. 228.
4. Ibid., p. 216.
5. Ibid., p. 232.
6. Ibid., p. 235.
7. When Goebbels first came to her house as a Minister of State, Frau Prang remembers addressing him as Herr Reich Minister, although as her son's great friend since early youth she had always called him by his first name. Goebbels at once asked her to continue to call him Joseph and to use the intimate term 'Du'. While he acknowledged the applause of the crowds outside the house, he whispered to her: "Look at that rabble. A few months ago they hounded me out of the town."
8. *My Part in Germany's Fight*, p. 249.
9. Quoted by H. L. Childs in *Propaganda and Dictatorship* (Princeton University Press, 1936).
10. Quoted in *The Goebbels Experiment*, p. 139.
11. *My Part in Germany's Fight*, p. 237.
12. Ibid., p. 251.
13. That same night in the Artists' Club, Goebbels boasted to a circle of film directors about how he timed this use of the sun as a propaganda device! Both Georg C. Klaren and Helmuth Käutner were present and have told H.F. the story.
14. Quoted by Louis P. Lochner in his Introduction to *The Goebbels Diaries*, p. xxvi.
15. See Heinrich Hoffmann, *Hitler was my Friend*, p. 71.
16. For example, at one stage there were three departments dealing with Foreign Affairs, and there were never less than two separate Secret Services. Each poached on the others' preserves, and Goebbels tried to out-poach them all!
17. See Henderson, *Failure of a Mission*, p. 29. The point was made again in the film *Ohm Krüger*, which Goebbels in part scripted.
18. Otto Strasser has laid particular stress on the closeness of Goebbels and Röhm.
19. On the other hand, von Pfeffer has stated to H.F. that he does not think that Goebbels was in any way implicated in these assassinations. The proprietor and the head-waiter were apparently homosexuals and were killed automatically because of their association with Röhm.
20. Otto Dietrich, *The Hitler I Knew*, p. 29.
21. See H. B. Gisevius, *To the Bitter End* (Houghton Mifflin, 1947), p. 160.
22. Quoted by Bullock in *Hitler*, p. 280.
23. Lang confirmed these details personally to H.F. The words quoted can be found in Kracauer *From Caligari to Hitler*, together with the story of *The Testament of Dr. Mabuse*. See pp. 164 and 248–50.

24. These details were confirmed by Rudolf Ullstein in conversation with H.F.
25. These Divisions are listed in *Propaganda and Dictatorship*, p. 19.
26. See Lochner, *The Goebbels Diaries*, p. xxxi. According to Otto Dietrich in *The Hitler I Knew* (p. 143) criticism was forbidden by Goebbels at the express command of Hitler.
27. See *Propaganda and Dictatorship*, p. 23.
28. Quoted in *Propaganda and Dictatorship*, p. 20.
29. See Henderson, *Failure of a Mission*, p. 85.
30. See *Hitler was my Friend*, pp. 173 and 181.
31. For an elaboration of Goebbels' principles see *Cinema Quarterly* (Edinburgh) Summer 1935, Vol. III, No. 4, pp. 213-4.
32. Details told to H.F. by Frau Gussy Jannings and Dr. Max Winckler.
33. See Sington and Weidenfeld, *The Goebbels Experiment*, p. 80.
34. See Edgar Mowrer, *Germany Puts the Clock Back* (Penguin Books, London, 1937), p. 213.
35. See William L. Shirer, *Berlin Diary* (Knopf, New York, 1941), p. 104.
36. See Louis Lochner, *The Goebbels Diaries*, p. xxxii.
37. See Vernon McKenzie, *Here Lies Goebbels* (Michael Joseph, London, 1940), p. 31.
38. *The Von Hassell Diaries* (Doubleday and Co., New York, 1947), p. 26.
39. See *Ambassador Dodd's Diary* (Gollancz, London, 1941), p. 102.
40. See Henderson, *Failure of a Mission*, p. 76.
41. See Shirer, *Berlin Diary*, p. 29.
42. See Lochner, *The Goebbels Diaries*, p. xxix.
43. Ibid., p. xxv.
44. See McKenzie, *Here Lies Goebbels*, p. 96.
45. These figures given in Riess, *Joseph Goebbels*, p. 149.
46. See McKenzie, *Here Lies Goebbels*, p. 72.
47. See *Ambassador Dodd's Diary*, p. 142.
48. See Shirer, *Berlin Diary*, p. 44.
49. Quoted by Riess in *Joseph Goebbels*, p. 148.
50. These figures are given by McKenzie in *Here Lies Goebbels*. See p. 98, and also Chapters Seven and Eight.
51. See McKenzie *Here Lies Goebbels*, pp. 233 and 235.
52. The instruction to the Fichte League quoted in *The Goebbels Experiment*, p. 91.
53. See Riess, *Joseph Goebbels*, pp. 176-7.
54. See *Ambassador Dodd's Diary*, p. 287.
55. See *The Goebbels Experiment*, p. 80.
56. Dietrich, *The Hitler I Knew*, p. 116.
57. See *Here Lies Goebbels*, p. 95.

58. For saying this Boemer was sent to a concentration camp by Goebbels, and on release put in a suicide squad where he was killed. Semmler has vouched for this in conversations with H.F.

59. Dietrich in *The Hitler I Knew* (p. 41) claims that Hitler ordered Goebbels to organise the pogrom.

60. See Lochner, *The Goebbels Diaries*, p. xxv.

61. See Henderson, *Failure of a Mission*, p. 172.

62. Quoted by Riess in *Joseph Goebbels*, pp. 204–5.

63. Documentation for the Nuremberg Trials held in the Wiener Library, London. Alpers was the equivalent of Head of the Forestry Commission.

64. See Lochner, *The Goebbels Diaries*, p. ix.

65. Idem, p. xxviii.

66. Idem, p. x.

67. The story of the banknotes is told by von Oven. See *Mit Goebbels bis zum Ende*, Vol. I, p. 35.

68. Told by Dr. Winckler to H.F.

69. See Semmler, *Goebbels—the Man next to Hitler* (Westhouse, London, 1947), p. 21.

70. Dietrich, *The Hitler I Knew*, p. 240.

71. See *The Von Hassell Diaries*, p. 4. Dietrich also comments in *The Hitler I Knew* (pp. 237–8) that this was the only period Hitler was on bad terms with Goebbels. Sources for the details of Goebbels' love affair are only too easy to come by. The matter became legendary, and many of the extravagant stories associated with it are to be found in *Evil Genius*. Our main sources are the private revelations of Dr. Naumann, Dieter von Wedel, Semmler, Gustav Fröhlich and Lida Baarova herself.

72. *The Von Hassell Diaries*, p. 10.

73. Dr. Naumann has requested us to deny categorically that he himself had at any time intimate relations with Magda Goebbels. This has been claimed in certain books. The same accusation has been levelled against Hanke, but von Wedel as well as Naumann are of the opinion that no such relation was established, although Hanke undertook to help Magda get evidence for her divorce and was prepared to jeopardise his career in order to do so. Hanke was killed during the final days of the war. Naumann is convinced that he was not the type of man to have any appeal for Magda.

Additional Note:

It has frequently been alleged that Goebbels attempted to exacerbate the legal dispute over *A Nous la Liberté* and *Modern Times*, the films made by René Clair and Charles Chaplin. René Clair has made the following interesting statement for us:

"To the best of my knowledge there never was any intervention by Goebbels or the Nazi Government in the *A Nous la Liberté*–*Modern Times* affair. This story seems to me to have been entirely created by lawyers more concerned about their briefs than the truth.

"It was certain papers in New York that first remarked on the resemblances that struck them between the two films. This followed the first showing of Chaplin's film in 1935, some three years after the initial screening of *A Nous la Liberté* in the United States. The case between the two distributing companies started up immediately but was interrupted by the war. I always refused to become involved in it, but I never had the least reason to believe the case had any political flavour behind it. I should add that I was given to understand that the distribution of *A Nous la Liberté* in Germany had been forbidden the moment the Nazis came to power."

Goebbels' interest in this case was said to be his desire to injure Chaplin.

CHAPTER SIX

During the early and middle period of the war the more intimate sources for Goebbels' opinions and characters are the published sections of his diary edited by Lochner and starting in January 1942, and the personal diary of his aide Rudolf Semmler, starting in January 1941, and subsequently published in an English translation as *Goebbels—the Man next to Hitler* (Westhouse, London, 1947). Dr. Semmler (whose name should in fact be spelled Semler, and not as published in his book) has also given us much valuable information in conversation with H.F. *The Goebbels Experiment* (see introductory note to Chapter Five) gives a useful analysis of the organisation of Goebbels' Ministry at this time.

Following are the page references in Semmler's *Goebbels* for those numbered quotations in our text which have no other indication (such as dates) as to where they may be found:

22, pp. 13 and 15; 23, p. 17; 25, p. 18; 26, p. 29; 29, pp. 35–6; 30, pp. 40–1; 31, p. 20; 32, p. 49; 33, p. 31; 34, pp. 56–7; 35, p. 28; 36, p. 24.

Following are the page references in Lochner's *The Goebbels Diaries* (Hamish Hamilton, London, 1948) for those numbered quotations in our text which have no other indication (such as dates) as to where they may be found:

38, p. 90; 39, p. 91; 40, p. 115; 41, p. 84; 42, p. 27; 43, p. 87; 44, p. 93; 45, p. 94; 46, p. 148; 48, p. 31; 49, p. 22; 50, p. 50; 51, p. 86; 52, pp. 97–8; 53, p. 188; 54, p. 117; 55, p. 18; 56, p. 169; 57, p. 244; 58, p. 133; 59, p. 29; 60, p. 38; 61, p. 190; 62, p. 55; 63, p. 35; 64, p. 51; 65, p. 17; 66, p. 37; 67, p. 229; 68, p. 55; 69, p. 43; 72, p. 170; 73, p. 142; 74, p. 165; 75, p. 151; 76, p. 159; 77, p. 190 (see also Semmler, *Goebbels*, pp. 60–1).

The remaining notes are:

1. See Bullock's *Hitler*, pp. 520–1.
2. Idem, p. 543.
3. See Semmler, *Goebbels*, p. 27.
4. Bullock's *Hitler*, p. 617.
5. Quoted by Riess, *Joseph Goebbels*, p. 216.
6. Shirer, *Berlin Diary*, p. 182.
7. The form of this 'Service' is given in *The Goebbels Experiment*, p. 62.
8. Dietrich in *The Hitler I Knew* (p. 117) claims that his high-sounding title merely covered "publicity" and "keeping Hitler informed on press matters". He adds: "In the sphere of culture Goebbels and Rosenberg quarrelled incessantly; in art Göring and Goebbels were rivals; in the control of German writers Goebbels, Rosenberg and Bouhler tilted against one another." Divide and misrule!
9. See Shirer's *Berlin Diary*, p. 521.
10. See *The Goebbels Experiment*, p. 22.
11. Idem, p. 117.
12. Idem, p. 118.
13. See Riess, *Joseph Goebbels*, p. 222.
14. C. J. Rollo, *Radio Goes to War* (Faber and Faber, London, 1943), p. 51. See Chapter Five for an account of Germany's invasion by radio.
15. Von Oven in his diary (Vol. I, p. 230) claims that Goebbels thought the radio interval-signal sounded too lugubrious and after much trial and error himself composed a more cheerful series of notes—c, g, e, c.
16. See *The Goebbels Experiment*, p. 152.
17. Idem, p. 170.
18. Idem, p. 217.
19. Idem, p. 36.
20. Idem, p. 20.
21. See *Sight and Sound* (British Film Institute, London), Vol. 10, No. 37, p. 5.
24. Quoted by Riess, *Joseph Goebbels*, pp. 48–9.
27. In conversation with H.F., Semmler said of Goebbels: "He had no heart." This he felt lay at the root of Goebbels' failure as a man.
28. Fritzsche in conversation with H.F.
37. Frau Otte in conversation with H.F.
47. See Bullock, *Hitler*, pp. 617–18.
70. There is further information about Lord Haw-Haw in C. J. Rollo's *Radio Goes to War*, Shirer's *Berlin Diary*, and J. W. Hall's *Trial of William Joyce*.
71. Shirer, *Berlin Diary*, p. 524.

The principal sources for this chapter are Goebbels' own diary, together with Semmler and von Oven.

Following are the page references in Lochner's *The Goebbels Diaries* for those numbered quotations in our text which have no other indication (such as dates) as to where they may be found:

2, p. 216; 3, p. 219; 4, p. 266; 5, p. 257; 6, p. 385; 7, p. 221; 8, p. 314; 9, p. 370; 10, p. 293; 11, p. 217; 12, p. 227; 14, p. 296; 16, p. 349; 17, p. 281; 18, pp. 276, 332, 385; 19, p. 96; 20, p. 197; 21, p. 200; 22, pp. 235–6; 24, p. 430; 25, pp. 435, 436, 440–1; 26, p. 299; 27, p. 302; 28, p. 298; 29, pp. 386–7; 30, p. 298; 31, p. 300; 32, p. 214.

Following are the page references in Semmler's *Goebbels* for those numbered quotations in our text which have no other indication (such as dates) as to where they may be found:

39, p. 68; 41, p. 88; 42, p. 98; 43, pp. 87–8; 44, p. 107; 45, p. 104; 47, p. 103; 48, p. 128; 49, p. 127; 52, pp. 206–7; 53, pp. 146–7.

The remaining notes are:

1. See Bullock, *Hitler*, pp. 642–3.
13. See von Oven, Vol. I, p. 61.
15. Idem, Vol. II, p. 299.
23. Quoted by Riess, *Joseph Goebbels*, pp. 302–3.
33. See von Oven, Vol. I, p. 68.
34. See von Oven, Vol. I, p. 17. The daily routine of Goebbels' life is described in Vol. I, p. 43 et seq.
35. Goebbels was always liable to nervous irritation. Semmler told H.F. how this characteristic increased when, every six months, Goebbels' orthopædic surgeon and his shoe-maker paid their visits to attend him. Goebbels was quite prepared to lie about his handicap when he could bring himself to mention it; he would claim, for instance, that he had been run over as a child.
36. Told to H.F. by Frau Otte.
37. Semmler told H.F. of a revealing incident in connection with this routine journey. One morning Goebbels, who was always fiddling with something or other (he never kept his hands still, according to Semmler) accidentally released the catch on the door, which swung open as the car turned a corner. Goebbels fell out, and was dragged a few yards before Rach could stop. He suffered some bruises, but later was heard by Semmler boasting of his calm at the time of the accident.
38. Semmler in conversation with H.F. recollects how Goebbels would deliberately stand about in the open during raids to show off his courage.

40. This typical exaggeration was frequently quoted by Goebbels and his aides. Semmler told H.F. that he was present at this speech and went home afterwards with Goebbels, who was bathed in sweat. But his only interest, like an actor, was in how his speech had gone over. Semmler added that for all his big speeches there were flower decorations on the rostrum to hide his legs. He was abnormally sensitive about his handicap on these occasions.

46. Gutterer in conversation with H.F.

50. The main account of the July Plot is taken from Bullock and Semmler, but supplemented by many unpublished details supplied by Dr. Hagen. Hagen is relatively unknown, but in his double capacity as Remer's adjutant and Goebbels' friend he was in fact the one person really instrumental in saving the day for the Nazi régime on 20th July. He was a much-wounded man who combined great scholarship in music with utter devotion to militarism —the blend of scholar and soldier that traditionally appeals to the German imagination. When H.F. met him the question rose whether his vital part in the prolongation of the war and the consequent loss of life weighed on his conscience. He assured Fraenkel that he took his sacred oath of loyalty to Hitler as absolute. For him Hitler was, as he put it, the *Eidträger*, the sacred person to whom a soldier's obedience was due without doubt or question. But, he added, had Hitler been killed by Stauffenberg's bomb, his duty would then have been to obey the generals in the Bendlerstrasse. "I would have shot Goebbels, even though he was my friend," he said.

51. Naumann told H.F. that at this time he was addressing an important meeting in Hamburg at the request of Kaufmann, the city's Gauleiter. A telephone call from Goebbels of the utmost urgency forced him to break away from the meeting. Goebbels told him to get into a plane and return to Berlin at once. "There's been an attempt on the Führer's life," he said, "and we don't know whether we'll be alive or dead in five minutes." Naumann returned in the only plane immediately available—an old training machine in the charge of a young pilot who had never flown solo before!

CHAPTER EIGHT

The history of the final period of Hitler's life has been told in detail by Professor H. R. Trevor-Roper in *The Last Days of Hitler* (Macmillan, London, 1947). Other sources for this chapter include Semmler's diary, Gerhard Boldt's account of his experiences as a member of Hitler's staff in *In the Shelter with Hitler* (Citadel Press, London, 1948) and the private testimonies to H.F. of

Naumann, Semmler, Hans Meyer and Hitler's secretary, Frau Christian.

Following are the page references in Semmler's *Goebbels* for those numbered quotations in our text which have no other indication (such as dates) as to where they may be found:

2, p. 177; 4, p. 162; 6, pp. 174–5; 8, p. 159; 14, pp. 166–7; 18, p. 164; 19, p. 181; 21, p. 186; 24, p. 190; 26, p. 178; 29, p. 194.

The remaining notes are:

1. Boldt, *In the Shelter with Hitler*, p. 5.
3. Idem, p. 21.
5. Frau Kimmich in conversation with H.F.
7. Frau Kimmich in conversation with H.F.
9. Quoted by Riess, *Joseph Goebbels*, p. 385.
10. Quoted by Riess, p. 373.
11. Quoted by Riess, p. 373.
12. See Riess, idem, p. 398.
13. The story of the microfilm of Goebbels' diaries was told H.F. by Naumann.
15. Quoted by Trevor-Roper, *The Last Days of Hitler*, p. 56.
16. Quoted by Riess, p. 380.
17. Quoted by Riess, p. 384.
20. Semmler in conversation with H.F. affirmed that Magda was a very lonely woman, well aware that her husband "had no heart".
22. Documentation Wiener Library.
23. Told to H.F. by Maria Kimmich. Both Semmler and Naumann agree with this explanation of Magda's decision to die with her family. To Semmler she said: "Das kann ich meinem Mann nicht antun." ("I can't do that to my husband.")
25. See Boldt, *In the Shelter with Hitler*, p. 27.
27. See Trevor-Roper, *The Last Days of Hitler*, pp. 106–9.
28. See Semmler, *Goebbels*, p. 192 and Trevor-Roper, *The Last Days of Hitler*, p. 110.
30. Told to H.F. by Maria Kimmich.
31. Told to H.F. by Naumann.

CHAPTER NINE

The detailed record of what took place during the last days in the Bunker is given by Professor Trevor-Roper in *The Last Days of Hitler* (see introductory note to the previous chapter). The final events in the life of Goebbels and his family have been told us in detail by Naumann who was a constant visitor to the Bunker and was with Goebbels and Magda until their deaths. Schwaegermann, with whom we established contact, felt unable to say more than that these last moments in the Bunker were so painful in his memory that he will never speak of them to anyone again. Frau Christian, one of Hitler's two principal secretaries in the Bunker, has also added some information.

1. Semmler in statement to H.F.
2. This recording is mentioned by Riess, *Joseph Goebbels*, p. 422.
3. Dr. Winckler in a statement to H.F.
4. Otte in a statement to H.F.
5. Quoted by Riess, *Joseph Goebbels*, p. 423.
6. According to Naumann in conversation with H.F.
7. Boldt, *In the Shelter with Hitler*, p. 15.
8. Idem, p. 48.
9. Idem, p. 63.
10. Idem, p. 61.
11. Idem, p. 51.
12. Idem, p. 60.
13. These letters are given in von Oven, *Mit Goebbels bis zum Ende*, Vol. II, pp. 312-13.
14. Quoted by Trevor-Roper, *The Last Days of Hitler*, pp. 202-3.
15. Both Naumann and Frau Christian have emphatically denied the allegations that have frequently been made that as soon as Hitler was dead, the relief experienced by everyone in the Bunker led to drunkenness and other excesses. Naumann admits that the survivors in the Führerbunker lit cigarettes, but, he says, "almost with a sense of desecration". Any excesses that might have taken place, he adds, would have been confined to the "soldateske" bunkers some distance away.
16. This telegram is signed by Goebbels alone in the version quoted by Trevor-Roper, *The Last Days of Hitler*, p. 229. Grand-Admiral Doenitz in his recent Memoirs gives the telegram as signed by both Bormann and Goebbels.
17. The details of the children's deaths are those believed to be true by Naumann. The Goebbels family were alone when the poison was administered.

Chief Events in the
Life of Goebbels

1897. Joseph Goebbels born in Rheydt on 29th October.

c. 1901. Operated on for infantile paralysis.

c. 1906. Enters Gymnasium at Rheydt. At this school begins his friendship with Fritz Prang.

1914. Rejected for military service.

1917. Matriculates at Easter, and enters Bonn University. In September appeals to the Albertus Magnus Society for financial help to continue his studies.

1918. Attends Freiburg University and later Würzburg University. Friendship with Anka Stahlhern.

1919. Returns to Freiburg University; later moves to the University of Munich.

1920. Moves to his final University of Heidelberg, where he studies under the celebrated Jewish Professor Gundolf. Height of friendship with Richard Flisges. Writes his last will and testament bequeathing his "literary estate" to his brother Hans.

(Hitler becomes Head of the National Socialist Party.)

1921. Completes his Doctor's thesis at Heidelberg. Writes among other things his novel *Michael* which is rejected by every publisher to whom it is submitted.

1922. End of friendship with Anka and beginning of friendship with Else. Prang joins the Nazi Party.

1923. Employed as a clerk from January to September in the Cologne branch of the Dresdener Bank, and later at the Cologne Stock Exchange.

(Abortive putsch by Hitler and his associates in Munich on 9th November.)

1924. Applies unsuccessfully for work on the *Berliner Tageblatt* and in the theatre.

Becomes Secretary to Franz Wiegershaus, Reichstag Deputy of the

Völkische Freiheitspartei and writes for the Party Journal, the *Völkische Freiheit*. Approaches Karl Kaufmann, the Nazi Gauleiter for the Rhine-Ruhr district, and offers to work for him. Appointed to the staff of the Northern Party organisation.

(Hitler imprisoned at Landsberg Fortress, February to December.)

1925. Goebbels is based on Kaufmann's office in Elberfeld, and his influence as a Party speaker begins to grow. Helps to edit new journal, the *Nationalsozialistische Briefe* (first published in October). Formally introduced to Hitler by Kaufmann in Elberfeld late in the year. Begins to come under the spell of Hitler.

(First part of *Mein Kampf* published; Hitler presents Goebbels with a signed copy.)

1926. 25th January. Attends Hanover Conference convened by Gregor Strasser.

14th February. Attends Bamberg Conference convened by Hitler, but fails to speak. Beginning of break with the Strassers and adherence to Hitler's faction of the Nazi Party.

April. Begins to accept invitations to speak with or for Hitler in various parts of Germany, including Berlin.

June. His appointment as Gauleiter of Berlin first mooted. Speaks at annual Party Congress in Weimar.

July. With Hitler at Berchtesgaden.

November. Appointed Gauleiter of Berlin, and begins task of cleaning up the Party organisation.

1927. July. First issue of Goebbels' journal *Der Angriff*.

1928. May. After the Reichstag elections is chosen to become one of the twelve Nazi deputies.

November. Appointed by Hitler Head of Party Propaganda.

1929. *Michael* published by Eher Verlag, the Nazi publishing house.

1930. September. Storm-Troopers revolt in Berlin; Hitler comes to restore order. Nazi landslide in the Reichstag elections; Goebbels one of the Party's 107 deputies.

1931. February. Nazi deputies march out of the Reichstag; Goebbels loses his immunity from legal proceedings.

12th December. Goebbels marries Magda Quandt, divorced wife of Günther Quandt, an industrialist.

1932. February. Goebbels excluded from the Reichstag for causing an uproar and insulting the President.

April. Hitler unsuccessful in second successive election for President; Goebbels in charge of election campaigns, including State and Reichstag elections. Indicted for High Treason, but escapes by accepting the mandate of the Prussian Diet.

May. Takes part in a battle with the Communists in the Prussian Diet.

July. Nazis win 230 seats in Reichstag election.

1st September. Birth of daughter Helga.

November. Nazis lose 34 seats in second Reichstag election.

1933. 30th January. Hitler appointed Chancellor by President Hindenburg.

February. Suppression of 60 Communist and 71 Social Democrat newspapers.

27th February. The Reichstag Fire. Used to promote the further suppression of the Communists.

14th March. Goebbels appointed Minister for Propaganda and Public Enlightenment. Takes over German broadcasting for the Party.

1st April. Organised boycott of the Jews.

April. All but Nazi-controlled newspapers virtually abolished.

1st May. Annual Nazi Day of Celebration initiated by Goebbels.

2nd May. Suppression of the Trade Unions.

10th May. The Burning of the Books.

September. Reich Culture Chamber founded to control all participants in the arts.

October. The Journalists Law; all journalists become licensed civil servants.

1934. February. Reich Film Law sets up Censorship Committee to review films.

April. Hess sets up Examining Committee for the Protection of National Socialist Literature.

13th April. Birth of daughter Hilde.

29th June. The Röhm purge initiated by Hitler.

2nd August. Death of Hindenburg. Assumption of full powers by Hitler under the title of Führer and Reich Chancellor of Germany.

Goebbels acquires the Schwanenwerder estate on the Wannsee.

1935. January. Order forbidding anyone concerned with the arts to leave Germany to fulfil contracts abroad without prior sanction.

April. Chamber of Literature empowered to draw up a black list of prohibited books.

21st October. Birth of son Helmuth.

During this year Goebbels acquires a fine villa to act as a club for German artists in Berlin.

1936. During the autumn makes an official visit to Greece.

29th November. Forbids all criticism of the arts.

1937. Hitler institutes German National Prizes for Science, Art and Literature to replace German acceptance of any Nobel Prizes. Goebbels buys out UFA.

9th February. Birth of daughter Holde.

1938. February. Ribbentrop as Foreign Minister gets foreign propaganda out of Goebbels' hands.

5th May. Birth of daughter Hedda.

October. Munich Agreement. Goebbels initiates long-term anti-British propaganda campaign.

10th November. Jewish pogrom incited by Goebbels. During this year Goebbels falls into disfavour with Hitler owing to his love affair with Lida Baarova.

Hitler prevents Magda from suing for divorce.

1939. 10th April. William Joyce (Lord Haw-Haw) begins his broadcasts to Britain from Hamburg.

June. Goebbels makes two inflammatory speeches in Danzig.

August. Goebbels' anti-Polish campaign reaches its height. Non-aggression pact with Russia.

3rd September. Britain declares a state of war with Germany.

Acquires during this year the Lanke estate on the Bogensee.

1940. Birth of daughter Heide in October.

1941. 22nd June. Germany invades Russia. Later Goebbels' memorandum to Hitler on Russian policy set aside.

1942. February. Plans revision of German-language dictionaries for occupied territories.

February to March. Entries in Goebbels' diary show his awareness and approval of the mass destruction of Jews in Europe.

March. Goebbels makes his first approaches to Göring to form an alliance to regain influence over Hitler.

30th March. Hitler transfers care of bomb-damaged areas to Goebbels' Ministry. During this period Goebbels constantly pressing Hitler to give him increased power over the domestic affairs of Germany and to institute a campaign for total war.

26th April. Hitler prompted by Goebbels obtains from the Reichstag plenary powers to override all normal laws in the interest of the State in a campaign against bureaucracy.

1st May. Hitler approves Goebbels' broadcast on the tightening of conditions in Germany.

May. The R.A.F. makes the first of its thousand-bomber raids on Germany.

December. An attempt on Goebbels' life frustrated.

1943. January. Hitler appoints an Executive Committee of three to control Germany. This includes Bormann, but excludes Goebbels.

31st January. Goebbels puts all newspapers in mourning when the Germans surrender at Stalingrad.

13th February. Goebbels' great total war speech in the Berlin Sportpalast.

March. Goebbels makes a second attempt to form an alliance with Göring.

Constructs a private air-raid shelter in Berlin at a cost of 350,000 marks.

10th July. Allies land in Sicily; fall of Mussolini.

September. Goebbels advises Hitler to consider the advantages of negotiating a peace settlement with either Britain or Russia.

1944. 10th June. After Allied invasion of Normandy on 6th June, the first flying-bomb is launched against Britain. Christened by Goebbels the V-1.

July. Given increased internal powers in Germany by Hitler after the attempt on the Führer's life on 20th July. Appointed Reich Trustee for Total War.

24th August. Announces measures for total war and total mobilisation.

1945. 12th January. The Russians reach the Oder and Silesia. Hitler pays his first social visit to Goebbels' house for five years.

30th January. Goebbels appointed Defender of Berlin.

March. The British and Americans cross the Rhine.

22nd April. With his wife and family, Goebbels joins Hitler in the Führerbunker.

29th April. Acts as witness to the marriage of Hitler and Eva Braun, and to Hitler's last will and testament, to which he adds his own appendix.

30th April, about 3.30 p.m. Hitler and Eva Braun commit suicide. Goebbels becomes Reich Chancellor of Germany.

1st May, about 8.30 p.m. After failure to obtain special terms from the Russians, commits suicide with his wife and children.

Plan of the Führerbunker

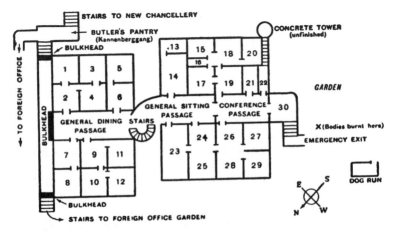

Reproduced from *The Last Days of Hitler* by kind permission of Hugh Trevor-Roper and the publishers, Messrs. Macmillan and Co.

The above sketch-plan was prepared to Professor Trevor-Roper's specifications before the Bunker was finally demolished by the Russians. It is not drawn to any particular scale. To judge from the memories of those who knew the Bunker, it seems that no room exceeded about 8 feet by 10 feet in size, though Boldt in his book *In the Shelter with Hitler* refers to two larger rooms, one 10 feet by 23 feet and the other 17 feet square. These were probably the passage areas used for meals and conferences. Boldt gives the depth of the Bunker as 30 feet; it was reached by a flight of 37 steps, the interconnecting flight between the sections being 12 steps. Rooms 15–20 made up Hitler's and Eva Braun's suite; rooms 9–12 the suite for Goebbels and his family. The rooms had beds and built-in cupboards. Goebbels also had room 26 allocated to him for his private use.

Bibliography

1. Publications in book or pamphlet form by Joseph Goebbels

Das Kleine ABC des Nationalsozialismus. Elberfeld, 1925.
Lenin Oder Hitler? Streiter Verlag Zwickau, 1926. Reprint of a speech delivered in the Königsberg Opera House on 19th February 1926. Violently anti-Communist. One of Goebbels' earliest big speeches.
Die Zweite Revolution. Zwickau, 1926. Collection of open letters, some to individuals such as von Reventlow and Scheidemann, some to types such as "narrow-minded intellectuals". The first letter is devoted to the "Führerfrage" and addressed to "sehr verehrter Herr Hitler".
Wege Ins Dritte Reich. Eher Verlag, Munich, 1927. Letters and articles for "contemporary people".
Das Buch Isidor. Eher, Munich, 1928. Violently anti-semitic articles largely reprinted from *Der Angriff* and illustrated by the paper's cartoonist, Mjoelnir.
Knorke. Eher, Munich, 1929. A sequel to the above.
Michael. Ein Deutsches Schicksal in Tagebuchblättern. Eher, 1929.
Die Verfluchten Hakenkreuzler. Etwas zum Nachdenken. Eher, 1929.
Signal zum Aufbruch. Eher, 1931. A speech given in Danzig in March 1931 and described as "the speech of a man who had been banned from speaking in Prussia". Attacks the Weimar Republic, Brüning and the Jews.
Vom Proletariat zum Volk. Flugschrift. Eher, 1932.
Preussen Muss Wieder Preussisch Werden. Eher, 1932.
Das Erwachende Berlin. Eher, 1933.
Wesen und Gestalt des Nationalsozialismus. Junker & Dünnhaupt, Berlin, 1933. A pamphlet designed to explain the Party ideology in terms suitable for middle-class intellectuals.
Goebbels Spricht. Gerhard Stalling, Oldenburg, 1933. A collection of speeches from the period 1929–33.
Rede Bei der Eröffnung der Reichskulturkammer. Frankfurt am Main, 1933.
Revolution der Deutschen. Gerhard Stalling Verlag, Oldenburg, 1933. A selection of Goebbels' speeches made between 1929–33 edited by Hein Schlecht.
Signale der Neuen Zeit. Eher, Munich, 1934. A selection of Goebbels' speeches made between 1927–33.

Nation im Aufbau. Eher, Munich. (Undated, but probably 1933-4.) This is clearly stated to be "for speakers only", and publication of its contents, particularly in the press, is strictly forbidden. The pamphlet contains all the principal Party slogans.

Der Faschismus und Seine Praktischen Ergebnisse. Junker & Dünnhaupt, Berlin, 1934. A pamphlet containing a speech delivered in the Deutsche Hochschule für Politik. A pointedly intellectual speech, largely in praise of Mussolini.

Vom Kaiserhof Zur Reichskanzlei. Eher, Munich, 1934. (Translated later by Kurt Fiedler with the title *My Part in Germany's Fight.* Hurst and Blackett, London, 1935.)

Rassenfrage und Weltpropaganda. Hermann Beyer Verlag, Langensalza, 1934. A pamphlet which attempts to deal in pseudo-scholarly terms with the Nazi racial theories.

Kampf um Berlin. Eher, 1934.

Student, Arbeiter und Volk. Frankfurt am Main, 1934.

Das Nationalsozialistische Deutschland Als Faktor des Europäischen Friedens. Berlin, 1934.

Kommunismus Ohne Maske. Eher, Munich, 1935. A speech attacking Communism delivered at the Nuremberg Party Rally in September 1935. English, French and Spanish translations were also published.

National-Sozialistischer Rundfunk. Eher, 1935. A pamphlet stressing the importance of broadcasting "in shaping the unity of the nation".

Richtlinien Für Die Gesamthaltung der Deutschen Presse. Berlin: Zentralverlag, ?1935

Goebbels Spricht Zur Welt. Berlin, 1935.

Der Angriff. Eher, 1935. Articles by Goebbels published in *Der Angriff* between 1927-30.

Der Bolschewismus in Theorie und Praxie. Eher, 1936. A speech by Goebbels against Communism delivered at the Nuremberg Party Rally of 1936. An English translation was also published.

Die Wahrheit Über Spanien. Mueller & Sohn, Berlin, 1937. A speech by Goebbels against "the Bolshevist rape" of Franco's Spain delivered at the Nuremberg Party Rally of 1937.

Wetterleuchten. Eher, Munich, 1938. A collection of articles, most of which had been published in *Der Angriff,* and belonging to the period 1928-33.

Die Zeit Ohne Beispiel. Eher, 1941. A comprehensive collection of articles and speeches amounting to some six hundred pages belonging to the period 1939-41.

Das Eherne Herz. Eher, 1943. A collection amounting to some 470 pages of articles and speeches belonging to the period 1941-2. "Das Eherne Herz", a speech of a violently anti-Semitic character delivered to the Deutsche Akademie in the University of Berlin, was also published separately.

Der Blick Nach Vorne. Eher, 1943. A short collection of articles written between 1941–3 issued as a special pamphlet for distribution to the German Army.

Der Geistige Arbeiter im Schicksalskampf des Reiches. Eher, 1943. The text of a speech delivered at Goebbels' own University of Heidelberg in July 1943. It is pretentiously intellectual, with many quotations from Nietzsche.

Der Steile Aufstieg. Eher, 1944. A collection of articles and speeches amounting to 474 pages and belonging to the period 1942–3.

The Goebbels Diaries. Translated and edited by Louis P. Lochner. Hamish Hamilton, London, 1948.

2. *Selected Book List with Special Reference to Joseph Goebbels*

Dr. Goebbels—Wer Ist Das? Viator. Hermann Seyring, Berlin, 1932.

Joseph Goebbels. Wilfrid Bade. Druck u. Verlag von Charles Coleman Lübeck, 1933.

Goebbels. Hans O. Seeler. Paul Schmidt, Berlin, ?1933

Reichsminister Dr. Goebbels. Willi Krause. Verlag Deutsche Kultur-Wacht, Berlin.

Dr. Joseph Goebbels. A. Knesebeck-Fischer. Paul Schmidt, Berlin.

Propaganda and Dictatorship. H. L. Childs. Princeton University Press, 1936.

Göbbels Erobert Die Welt. Jack Iwo. Editions du Phénix, Paris, 1936.

Germany Puts the Clock Back. Edgar Mowrer. Penguin Books, London, 1937.

Mein Kampf (English translation). Adolf Hitler. Hurst and Blackett, London, 1939.

Goebbels "Chef de Publicité" du IIIe Reich. Sorlot, Paris, 1939.

The Rape of the Masses. Serge Chakotin. Routledge, London, 1940.

Failure of a Mission. Sir Nevile Henderson. Hodder and Stoughton, London, 1940.

Ambassador Dodd's Diary. Gollancz, London, 1941.

Berlin Diary. William L. Shirer. Knopf, New York, 1941.

The Goebbels Experiment. Derrick Sington and Arthur Weidenfeld. Murray, London, 1942.

Radio Goes to War. Charles J. Rollo. Faber and Faber, London, 1943.

Der Führer. Konrad Heiden. Gollancz, London, 1944.

Germany From Defeat to Conquest. W. M. Knight-Patterson. Allen and Unwin, London, 1945.

Goebbels. Porte-Parole du Nazisme. Imre Gyomai. Les Editions Nagel, Paris, 1945.

Wie Konnte es Geschehen. Max Fechner (Editor). Dietz, Berlin, 1945–6.

The Von Hassell Diaries. Doubleday, New York, 1947.

BIBLIOGRAPHY

Goebbels—the Man Next to Hitler. Rudolf Semmler. Westhouse, London, 1947.

To the Bitter End. H. B. Gisevius. Houghton Mifflin, New York, 1947.

The Last Days of Hitler. H. R. Trevor-Roper. Macmillan, London, 1947.

Betrachtungen zu Goebbels' Tagebüchern. Hans Kriesi. Druck von Huber, Frauenfeld, 1948.

In the Shelter With Hitler. Gerhard Boldt. Citadel Press, London, 1948.

Joseph Goebbels. Curt Riess. Hollis and Carter, London, 1949.

Dr. Goebbels Nach Aufzeichnungen aus Seiner Umgebung. Boris von Borresholm (Editor). Verlag des 'Journal', Berlin, 1949.

Joseph Goebbels: Dämon Einer Diktatur. Werner Stephan. Union Deutsche Verlagges, Stuttgart, 1949.

Mit Goebbels bis zum Ende. Wilfred von Oven. Dürer-Verlag, Buenos Aires. Two volumes, 1949–50.

Goebbels' Principles of Propaganda. Leonard W. Doob. The Public Opinion Quarterly, Fall, 1950. Princeton.

Hitler—A Study in Tyranny. Alan Bullock. Odhams, London, 1952.

Gefährtin des Teufels. Leben und Tod der Magda Goebbels. Erich Ebermayer and Hans Roos. Hoffmann und Campe, 1952. English edition, *Evil Genius*, Allan Wingate, 1953.

Hitler's Table Talk. Weidenfeld and Nicolson, London, 1953.

Hitler Was My Friend. Heinrich Hoffmann, Burke, London, 1955.

The Hitler I Knew. Otto Dietrich. Methuen, 1955.

Index

323